T0121164

Praise for Nina Munk's *The Idealist*

"Writing accessibly about development economics is a high-wire act, but Munk accomplishes it brilliantly. She shadows Sachs as he cajoles world leaders to fund his Millennium projects, and also visits those places to tell the whole story. The final chapter, in which Munk interviews a chastened Sachs (usually an oxymoron), is particularly devastating."
—Foreign Policy

"A fascinating portrait of an innovative thinker as well as a fair-minded examination of his methods. It's also a testament to the enduring value of old-fashioned, shoe-leather reporting—it should be read not just in policy circles but also at J-schools."
—Vanity Fair

"Munk tracks a messianic economist's quixotic attempts to show that he can end African poverty. In one village his team gets farmers to grow maize instead of traditional *matoke*; there are no buyers for the bumper crop, and rats end up eating much of it. Munk describes a growing gulf between good intentions and hard reality with nuance and sensitivity."
—Forbes

"A fascinating and essential exploration of what goes wrong when unchecked audacity and clinical precision encounter the frailties, ambiguities, and unpredictabilities of human beings, societies and histories."
—The Plain Dealer

"[Munk is] a fine writer with a gift for deploying spare, vivid detail. . . . A lively and, at times, quite funny book."
—Fortune

"[Munk] not only reminds us that there are good, solid reasons why certain areas of the world remain desperately poor, she raises troubling questions about the credibility of an economist embraced by rock singers and film stars." —*The Spectator* (London)

"Munk is a sly, relentless reporter with a gift for wedding her observations to a fluent, even graceful, writing style." —*The Globe and Mail* (Toronto)

"This book is stark proof that [trying to impose Western thinking on Africa] just does not work. . . . The world needs to pay attention to these lessons and stop wasting resources." —*Bloomberg*

"A deep and important book. . . . *The Idealist* tells the stories behind the numbers, and its evidence is as compelling and as important as anything in the data." —Angus Deaton, *The Lancet*

"*The Idealist*, Nina Munk's brilliant book on Sachs's antipoverty efforts, chronicles how his dream fell far short of reality." —*Reason*

"A devastating portrait of hubris and its consequences." —Howard W. French, *Pacific Standard*

"Munk's book is a readable and fast-paced chronicle of the real-world consequences of elite intellectual arrogance. . . . Munk's authoritative telling of Sachs's story is most valuable as an exhortation to intellectual humility, and a compulsively readable portrait of a man without any." —*Commentary*

"Not only an important book, but a truly enjoyable read. She does not boast, but the reader cannot avoid the impression that her intrepid years in Sachsland have demanded all the inner steel of the most hardened explorer or war correspondent." —*The Weekly Standard*

"Nina Munk has written a fascinating book about a fascinating man—and even more important, about a set of ideas that are intriguing and important."
        —Fareed Zakaria, editor-at-large of *Time* and author
    of *New York Times* bestseller *The Post-American World*

"A powerful exposé of hubris run amok, drawing on touching accounts of real-life heroes fighting poverty on the front line."   —Robert Calderisi,
                    author of *The Trouble with Africa*

Nina Munk

The Idealist

Nina Munk, a contributing editor at *Vanity Fair*, is a journalist and the author of *Fools Rush In: Steve Case, Jerry Levin, and the Unmaking of AOL Time Warner*. She was previously a senior writer at *Fortune*, and before that a senior editor at *Forbes*. Her work has appeared in *Vanity Fair, The New York Times Magazine, The New Yorker, Fortune*, and *The New York Times*. She lives in New York.

www.ninamunk.com

The Idealist

The
IDEALIST

Jeffrey Sachs and the Quest

to End Poverty

Nina Munk

Anchor Books
A Division of Random House LLC
New York

FIRST ANCHOR BOOKS EDITION, OCTOBER 2014

This book is based on a July 2007 article that appeared in *Vanity Fair.*

All photographs are from the author's personal collection except those taken by Guillaume Bonn.

The Library of Congress has cataloged the Doubleday edition as follows:
Munk, Nina.
The idealist : Jeffrey Sachs and the quest to end poverty / Nina Munk.—1st ed.
p. cm.
Includes bibliographical references.
1. Sachs, Jeffrey. 2 Millennium Villages (Project). 3. Poverty—Africa. 4. Economic development projects—Africa.
5. Poverty—International cooperation.
6. Community development—Africa. I. Title.
HV438.M86 2013   362.5526—dc23   2012047128

Anchor Books Trade Paperback ISBN: 978-0-7679-2942-4
eBook ISBN: 978-0-385-53774-2

Book design by Michael J. Collica
Author photograph © Mark Schäfer

www.anchorbooks.com

This book is dedicated to the memory of Linda Munk (1937–2013). As she often said, quoting Henry James: "Live all you can; it's a mistake not to."

Contents

The Idealist

Jeffrey Sachs pointed to the cup of Starbucks coffee in my hand. Before I had a chance to introduce myself, he said, "You know, I've done a formal breakdown of what it would cost to fully fund the global prevention of malaria, and it's two-fifty a year for every American. Two dollars and fifty cents! That's a single cup of Starbucks coffee."

It was September 2006. A year earlier Sachs's book *The End of Poverty* had been excerpted on the cover of *Time* magazine. It also made the *New York Times* best-seller list. By the time I met Sachs, *The End of Poverty* had been translated into eighteen languages. I'd come across his name while reporting for *Vanity Fair* on Bono's involvement in Africa. Time and again I'd hear references to "Bono's Guru." "My name is Bono and I am the rock star student," to quote Bono's foreword to *The End of Poverty*. "The man with me is Jeffrey D. Sachs, the great economist, and for a few years now my professor."

Sachs, born in 1954, was fifty-one years old when I first met him, the Quetelet Professor of Sustainable Development at Columbia University and special adviser to the secretary-general of the United Nations. During the 1980s and 1990s he was nicknamed "Dr. Shock," the brilliant, controversial macro-economist from Harvard who'd prescribed radical fiscal and monetary discipline, so-called shock therapy, to countries emerging from Communism. He'd also had a distinguished academic career, but with the publication of *The End of Poverty*, he had become a celebrity. More than 200,000 copies were sold in the United States, an extraordinary feat for a book that can be, truthfully, a slog, with a few charts and graphs for company. He'd also starred in MTV's documentary *The Diary of Angelina Jolie and Dr. Jeffrey Sachs in Africa*. In the movie, Jolie calls him "one of the smartest people in the world."

Sachs is very smart. He's one of those people who can (and does) go on about, say, the shortcomings of covariance matrices, the etymology of Nilo-Saharan languages, the difference between two species of mosquito, *Anopheles gambiae* and *Aedes aegypti,* and the effect of "the adiabatic process" on temperatures in the highlands of Kenya. He has an insatiable, unself-conscious fascination with the world in all its complexity. Once, when we were driving past the equator in Uganda, Sachs asked us to stop the car so he could phone his son, Adam, at that time a Harvard undergraduate majoring in earth and planetary science. The purpose of the call? To discuss whether the Coriolis effect influences the direction that water swirls down a drain. (It doesn't, apparently.)

What struck me after I'd spent some time with Sachs was his genius for reducing huge and complex issues to their essence. Above all, it's his ability to synthesize, to turn ideas into bullet points, that has allowed him to move the issue of global poverty into the mainstream. He has convinced the developed world to consider his utopian thesis: that with enough focus, enough determination, and enough money, we can "end the suffering of those still trapped by poverty." In fact, from Sachs's point of view, the problem can be solved by 2025, and it can be solved "easily."

In his mind, the most stubborn problem becomes as easy to grasp as a $2.50 cup of Starbucks coffee. With the right approach, anything is possible; he's sure of that. Malaria can be prevented with the widespread use of insecticide-treated mosquito nets. The problem of hunger can be solved with subsidized fertilizers and high-yield seeds. Universal education can be achieved by eliminating primary school fees. "We have enough on the planet to make sure, easily, that people aren't dying of their poverty," he assured me. "That's the basic truth."

In his speeches, Sachs presents his audience with an ethical choice that is no choice: "Either you decide to leave people to die or you decide to do something about it." Who can resist Sachs's call to action? After all, two billion people on the planet are scraping by, barely, on less than a dollar or two a day. Industrialization has passed them by. They have not been lifted out of poverty by what proponents of free markets like to call "the rising tide" (the tide that lifts some boats but not all of them). Trapped by disease, hunger, physical isolation, dysfunctional governments, environmental degradation, and, as Sachs argues, poverty itself, their life expectancy hovers around fifty.

In most of sub-Saharan Africa, per capita income is so low it looks like a misprint. In Malawi, for example, per capita income, adjusted for purchasing power, is $870 a year. In Tanzania, $1,510 a year. "The countries at the bottom coexist with the twenty-first century, but their reality is the fourteenth century: civil war, plague, ignorance," to quote the economist Paul Collier in *The Bottom Billion*.

The bare truth is, for all the hundreds of billions of dollars spent on foreign aid in the past decades, no one has come close to ending poverty in Africa. Development experts keep publishing books and articles promoting one theory after another, but so far there's been no workable solution. If Jeffrey Sachs, one of the greatest macroeconomists of his generation, believed he had the answer to poverty, I was eager to hear him out.

But the more time I spent with Sachs, the more questions I had. Are we really at a defining moment in history, as he imagines? Can extreme poverty—one of the great unsolved problems of our time, a condition as old as human society itself—be eradicated? In remote African villages, where there are no roads or power or running water, and where most people are illiterate, how does sustainable economic development take hold? Can people be lifted out of poverty, as Sachs puts it, or do they have to lift themselves? To embrace his view of the world requires courage and conviction. Call it idealism, if you'd like, or faith.

"Have you seen children dying?" Sachs challenged his audience, using rhetorical shock therapy. I'd followed him to Montreal to attend an all-day conference on poverty. He was wearing a blue oxford-cloth shirt and khakis. His head seemed too large for his slight frame, and characteristically, he was badly shaven. His deep midwestern voice was resonant, compelling; he spoke for almost an hour without notes. Projected onto a giant screen just above his head was a photograph he'd taken a few months earlier in Malawi, at Zomba Central Hospital. Covered by thin sarongs, small children in malaria comas were lying on the bare floor, row after row, their yellow eyes rolled back.

"I never thought in the twenty-first century, growing up in the twentieth century, I'd ever see that," Sachs exclaimed, outraged by the shortsightedness implicit in the photograph. "Lack of a bed net. Lack of a dollar medicine. Lack of an oral rehydration solution in time to save a child dehydrated from a diarrheal infection. Lack of antibiotics to cure a child of acute lower respiratory infection contracted from living in a hut where dung is burned to cook the meals in a smoke-filled chamber."

He went on: "Lack of a five-cent immunization, so that you have hundreds of thousands of children dying of vaccine-preventable diseases. Half a million mothers dying in childbirth because there's no obstetrician or even emergency care to stop the hemorrhaging, to deliver a child in breech, to do a C-section. *The most straightforward things that we've known how to do for centuries.*"

To dismiss Africa as a lost cause offers an easy excuse for doing nothing—about malaria, preventable diseases, mothers dying in childbirth, infant mortality, hunger, and smoke-filled huts. For Jeffrey Sachs, the solutions to such injustices are obvious. His one question is, How long will it take the rest of us to come around?

Part One

Maybe it's having had the good experience of hearing, as I have many, many times, "Impossible, impossible, impossible, impossible, impossible—obvious." If you've gone through that over a period of twenty-five years, it helps you to filter out a lot of what you're told. Everything seems impossible until it becomes inevitable.

—Jeffrey Sachs

Chapter 1

Shock Therapy

As a young child growing up in Oak Park, Michigan ("The City with a Future"), Jeffrey David Sachs displayed a preternaturally brilliant mind. At twelve or thirteen years of age, in middle school, he won a mathematics contest for gifted children, with the result that he spent the summer taking college-level math courses at Oakland University in Rochester, Michigan. As a teenager, he was single-minded, ambitious, and from all reports, unusually self-disciplined. He played in adult tournaments at the local bridge club. Once, not uncharacteristically, when a high school teacher assigned a five-page essay, Sachs handed in forty pages. "He never had a rebellious day in his life," according to his sister, Andrea Sachs.

At Oak Park High School, Jeffrey Sachs was elected president of the student council. In his senior year, he got near-perfect scores on his SATs. Unsurprisingly, he was named class valedictorian when he graduated in 1972. Nothing less was expected of him. "His father was extremely bright and was top of his class," said his mother, Joan. "We just assumed our children would be the same."

Sachs's father, Theodore, was a legend in Detroit. A labor and constitutional lawyer who successfully argued several cases before the U.S. Supreme Court, Ted Sachs was said to have one of his generation's finest legal minds. He was stunning in the courtroom and was admired for his commitment to social justice. While arguing his most important case before the Supreme Court, *Scholle v. Hare,* Ted Sachs helped establish the principle of "one man, one vote" for legislative apportionment. "Sachs not only fought against precedent but against legal inertia," according to a 1962 *Detroit News* article about his victory in the case: "Sachs seems to have anticipated history, sensed impending change in the attitude of the courts, and to have worked industriously for a cause that more experienced lawyers long ago had abandoned."

It was taken for granted that Jeffrey Sachs would attend his father's alma mater, the University of Michigan, and that he too would become a lawyer. In the worst case, his family imagined, he'd become a medical doctor. Instead, when he was seventeen years old, he left Oak Park to study economics at Harvard University.

Martin Feldstein, the well-known economist and a longtime professor at Harvard, remembers meeting Sachs for the first time. "I was teaching the graduate macroeconomics course," he recalled. "And he came along—remember, he's a second-year undergraduate, so he's about nineteen years old—and he says 'Well, I'd like to take your course.'" Warning Sachs that he was an unforgiving and demanding teacher, Feldstein discouraged him and advised the young man to stay away from trouble. "I'll take my chances," replied Sachs.

Sachs received an A in Feldstein's class. "He was one of the very best performers in a course where he was competing with the best graduate students in the country," said Feldstein. "It was clear from that point that this was a very unusually talented young man."

On earning his undergraduate degree, summa cum laude, from Harvard in 1976, Sachs was ranked third in his class of 1,650 students. During his graduate studies at Harvard, which he completed in record time, he was elected a Harvard Junior Fellow, an honor reserved for "persons of exceptional ability, originality, and resourcefulness, and . . . the highest calibre of intellectual achievement." A scant three years after being awarded his Ph.D. in economics, with a focus on international macroeconomics, Sachs was granted tenure and made a full professor at Harvard. It was 1983, and he was twenty-eight years old.

It was at Harvard, at a screening of *The Sorrow and the Pity,* Marcel Ophüls's four-hour documentary about life in France during the Nazi occupation, that he met his future wife, Sonia Ehrlich. "In the beginning, Jeff would say, 'Wait until I finish my undergrad thesis,'" Ehrlich said, describing her husband's single-mindedness. "Then it was 'Wait until I get my Ph.D. thesis' and 'Wait until I get tenured.' Then it was 'Wait until I finish my first book.' Then Bolivia came up."

In July 1985, when he was thirty years old, Jeffrey Sachs was invited to the Andean mountains of La Paz, Bolivia, to act as an adviser to the country's president, Victor Paz. Desperately poor and chaotic, Bolivia, with its annualized inflation rate of 25,000 percent, was spiraling out of control. Among other problems, the country was spending far more than it could afford. To finance such runaway spending, the government kept printing more and more pesos; the more pesos it printed, the more worthless its currency became. Bolivia was a textbook case of hyperinflation, the likes of which no one had seen since the early 1920s, in Germany's Weimar republic.

Sachs had never worked outside academe. Nevertheless, as Gonzalo Sánchez de Lozada, who was then Bolivia's president of the Senate and the nation's official economic adviser, explained, Sachs had a rare skill for translating theory into practice, a talent for explaining and selling his ideas to people who knew nothing about economics. "I was twenty-five years older than he was, and our president was eighty years old," recalled Sánchez de Lozada, "but Jeff always seemed to be an equal because he was very forceful, and very convincing, and he just made a lot of sense."

Consulting studies of hyperinflation and drawing on his academic training, Sachs designed a radical austerity plan to jump-start Bolivia. It called for huge cuts in government spending, massive layoffs of state employees, the end of fixed gasoline prices, a complete overhaul of the tax system, and above all, an abrupt shift to a free-market-based economy. With the country in disarray, the government of Bolivia agreed to follow Sachs's advice. It had few other options. "We couldn't get any support from the International Monetary Fund, or the World Bank, or the U.S. government, or anybody, because we'd been written off as a basket case," said Sánchez de Lozada. "We were in the hands of Jeff Sachs."

Sachs's plan for Bolivia was pragmatic and impersonal—hundreds of thousands of people lost their jobs, their pensions, their dignity—and yet the plan worked, at least in the short term: strict fiscal and monetary discipline managed to lower the country's annual inflation rate to about 15 percent. "Shock therapy," as the approach was later called, was to become Sachs's trademark.

From Bolivia, Sachs went on to Poland. It was 1989, and the Berlin Wall had just come down. With the abrupt collapse of Communist rule, Eastern Europe was in chaos. In Poland, where the new Solidarity government had taken over, the economy included black markets, soaring prices, an extreme shortage of goods, and a worthless currency.

George Soros, whose foundations promoted the transition to democratic market economies in Central and Eastern Europe, arranged for Sachs and his former student David Lipton to meet Jacek Kuroń, the Polish intellectual known as "the brains behind Solidarity." Sachs's description of that meeting is one of the more remarkable passages in *The End of Poverty*. No one doubted Sachs's intelligence; what became obvious in Poland, however, was his supreme self-confidence.

> Kuroń sat at a crowded desk in a room filled with books piled high on the table and everywhere else. He took out the first of many packs of cigarettes that he would smoke that evening, and a bottle of alcohol. . . . He smiled and said, "Okay, so why are you here?"
>
> "Well, I was asked to see you to talk about how Poland can get out of this mess."
>
> "Okay, then," he replied . . . , "what do you say?"
>
> I started weaving a story about what economic reforms in Poland might really mean. I said that Poland needed to become a "normal" country again with a "normal" economy. . . . I continued to improvise, sketching out an economic strategy for Poland's return to Europe, drawing a bit on my experience in Bolivia, since that country had "returned" to the world economy after decades of self-imposed protectionism. I also compared Poland's situation with that of Spain's and Portugal's in the 1970s, after their long periods of military rule under Franco and Salazar, respectively. . . .
>
> Every couple of minutes Kuroń would hit the table and say, *Tak, rozumiem! Tak, rozumiem!*—"Yes, I understand! Yes, I understand!" Smoke was filling the room, and the bottle kept pouring. I talked and talked, probably for another three or four hours. I was drenched in sweat. I do not know how many packs of cigarettes he smoked that night, each stub being crushed into an ever filling ashtray. At the end of the evening, he said, "Okay, I understand this. We'll do it. Write a plan."

I thought to myself, "This is exciting. He liked the ideas." I said, "Mr. Kuroń, we will go home and fax you something within a week or two about these ideas." He hit the table. "No! We need the plan now." I said, "What do you mean?" "I need this tomorrow morning."

It was midnight when Sachs left Kuroń's apartment. Borrowing an old computer at the offices of *Gazeta Wyborcza,* the Solidarity newspaper, Sachs and Lipton worked until dawn. They wrote a fifteen-page, single-spaced memo ("Summary of the Proposed Economic Program of Solidarity") advising the new government how to jolt Poland out of socialism and into a market economy. "This strategy can be called a 'shock' approach to Poland's economic crisis, in contrast to the [current] muddling-along approach of the Coalition Government," begins the memo.

Page after page, Sachs and Lipton outlined "the nuts and bolts of stabilization." Their plan was straightforward—an updated version of the model Sachs had developed for Bolivia: a convertible hard currency, a stock exchange, a commercial banking sector, the privatization of state enterprise, the end of state subsidies and central planning, a brand-new tax code, the free exchange of goods, the recognition of private property, a balanced state budget . . .

"One of the most spectacular and spectacularly risky macro-economic experiments ever undertaken," is how the so-called Sachs Plan was described by Lawrence Weschler, a staff writer for *The New Yorker* and an expert on Poland's Solidarity movement. Many informed Poles agreed with Weschler's assessment. "Polish shock therapy has been described as a dive off a high tower without knowing if there was any water in the pool," said Maciej Kozlowski, a Polish diplomat and historian. "Jeff Sachs was the one assuring us that there was water in the pool."

While acknowledging that the "shock program will cause

disruptions in the short run and no doubt pain for some in the society," Sachs and Lipton argued that the country had no choice. For Poland to follow a path of moderate, gradual change would be a "pure, unmitigated disaster," predicted Sachs. "In any event," concluded his and Lipton's memo, "there is no viable alternative. Unless Poland jumps to a market economy, the current misery and chaos will surely continue."

In an interview with Weschler, Sachs compared himself to a trauma doctor who arrives in the nick of time to resuscitate the patient. "Look, when a guy comes into the emergency room and his heart's stopped," he said, "you just rip open the sternum and don't worry about the scars that you leave. The idea is to get the guy's heart beating again. And you make a bloody mess. But you don't have any choice."

When the Sachs Plan was finally implemented in Poland, it followed the authors' road map and timetable almost to the letter. Sachs, now thirty-five, had become an international star in policy circles—a "wunderkind," the media liked to call him. Widely considered one of the most promising economists of his generation, he was presented with the 1991 Frank E. Seidman Distinguished Award in Political Economy. Some people considered him the most influential economist since John Maynard Keynes. He was a "virtuoso," according to *The New York Times:* along with two other young and ambitious Harvard-trained economists, Paul Krugman and Lawrence ("Larry") Summers, Jeffrey Sachs was one of the "three whiz kid economists of the 90's." *The New York Times Magazine* went even further, referring to Sachs as "probably the most important economist in the world."

Not everyone agreed. Increasingly, in academic circles, at least, Sachs was being written off as an exhibitionist, a show-off. "He was clearly capable of doing pretty important work, but I don't think he did it," the influential Harvard economist Robert Barro told a reporter in 1991. More recently, when I interviewed him, Barro elaborated: "I mean, Jeff had some good articles, but he didn't have stuff that was of real permanence and brilliance. Nothing that matches the potential he had when he was, say, twenty-eight."

Throughout the 1990s, Sachs was still a professor at Harvard, lecturing to students and writing papers and books at an astonishing pace, but academia was starting to bore him. It was parochial, inbred. Whereas advising world leaders, shaping a nation's economic policy, changing the course of history—that was intoxicating. "My colleagues, they'd say, 'Well, it's great what you're doing, but you should focus on your work.' And I said, 'But this *is* my work,'" Sachs recalled. "I would have been perfectly comfortable as an academic at Harvard if I hadn't seen what was actually happening in the world."

In the early 1990s, at the invitation of Boris Yeltsin, Sachs intended to straighten out Russia's economy. He found himself at the Kremlin on the very day that Yeltsin announced the end of the Soviet Union. "I said, 'Gee, you know, this is once in a century,'" Sachs recalled. "'This is the most incredible thing you can imagine; this is a true liberation; let's help these people.'"

Together with a dozen colleagues from the Harvard Institute for International Development, he settled into an office at Moscow's Ministry of Finance and got to work. Characteristically, his approach to Russia's economy was defined by a combination of optimism and impatience. "If Poland can do it, so can Russia," he declared.

Broadly speaking, Sachs's plan for Russia mirrored his plan for Poland: it was shock therapy writ large. "As a broad measure," he explained at the time, "the Soviet republics should also follow the three pillars of privatization, liberalization, and stabilization. The ruble, like the Polish zloty, could become a convertible currency within months. Almost no Russian economist believes that, but they're wrong. It was not believed in Poland either. They can create a working monetary system, they can create the normalcy of markets, free prices and supply and demand. The basic strategy can work."

In hindsight, Sachs was naïve. For one thing, he'd underestimated the extent of the problem. He'd misread it. Presuming that his program of economic reform could be imposed on Russia as easily as it had been imposed on Bolivia and Poland, he was defeated by a massively bloated and corrupt economy. In one decade, between 1989 and 1999, Russia's GDP dropped by half. State assets were systematically looted, and anything of value—raw materials, for instance—wound up in the hands of a few clever men.

In a scathing 1999 speech, delivered when he was chief economist for the World Bank, Joseph Stiglitz argued that the failure of reform in Russia was due to "a misunderstanding of the very foundations of a market economy"; "a failure to grasp the fundamentals of reform processes"; and "an excessive reliance on textbook models of economics." Sachs wasn't mentioned by name, but he didn't have to be. "Not surprisingly," said Stiglitz, "those who advocated shock therapy and rapid privatization argue that the problem was . . . that there was too little shock. The reforms were not pursued aggressively enough. The medicine was right; it was only that the patient failed to follow the doctor's orders!"

In fact, concluded Stiglitz, alluding to Sachs obliquely, "Those advocating shock therapy, with its focus on privatization, failed because they failed to understand modern capitalism; they were overly influenced by the excessively simplistic textbook models of the market economy."

Years after the fact, when I questioned Sachs about his failure to reform the Russian economy, he became defensive, prickly, like a hedgehog. "Do I consider Russia a failure of the West? Yes, definitely. Do I consider it a personal failure? No! I find that absolutely preposterous!" he insisted. He'd been blindsided, I inferred, or else his timing was off, or he'd been undermined. "I don't understand why somebody doesn't ask Robert Rubin, or ask Dick Cheney, or ask Larry Summers, or ask anybody who actually had power at the time about it." He was fed up with my questions about Russia: "It's preposterous by now, and tired. And it's tiresome, and it's a tired question, and it's absolutely absurd." With that, he stood up and walked out of the room.

Later, in a long e-mail, he took the same tack: "I took a ridiculous amount of criticism for Russia, even though I was not the adviser, not empowered, and my ideas were not adopted. The true actors in this case—the Bush Sr. Administration (especially Cheney), the Clinton Administration (Rubin, Summers, others), the IMF, and others—got a free walk. Ridiculous. I constantly warned that we should be doing more and [doing it] differently. Nobody wanted to hear it." His failure to resuscitate Russia was due, he explained, to "the triumph of politics over economics." In other words, no one followed his advice.

Jeffrey Sachs's crusade to eradicate extreme poverty began in 1995, when, for the first time, he traveled to sub-Saharan Africa. "I was asked to visit Zambia," he said, "and that was the first place I really saw AIDS, and the first place where I really saw malaria, and the first place where I really started asking myself, 'What the hell is going on here?' I hadn't realized that we were leaving so many millions of people to die every year. I had no idea."

Africa was being ravaged by fast-moving epidemics of AIDS, tuberculosis, and malaria. Everywhere on the continent, health care systems—exhausted, chronically underfunded—had collapsed. There were severe shortages of doctors and nurses, of medicines, even of such basic supplies as surgical gloves and IV fluids. Sachs was outraged. "I really had this sense that things were spinning out of control," he continued. "I'd say, 'What do you mean he just died last week? Did he go to the doctor?' And they'd say, 'No, no, no, people don't go to the doctor here.' What do you mean? What about the medicine? And they'd say, 'No, no, no, there's no medicine here.' What?!"

What Sachs saw in Africa defied logic and offended his sense of human decency. Since the industrial revolution, the West's per capita income had increased twentyfold, whereas in Africa, over the same period, per capita income had increased not even fourfold. Why, at the most prosperous time in human history, was so much of our planet impoverished? Why were millions of human beings dying every year from diseases that we learned to prevent and treat a generation ago?

Earlier in his career, when he was thinking about ways to improve people's lives, Sachs had been convinced of the power of open markets, free trade, deregulation, privatization, and fiscal discipline. After his first trip to sub-Saharan Africa, however, he started looking at the world with new eyes. You might call it a spiritual conversion, a change of heart.

"Economists say, 'Reform the value-added tax. Get the budget deficit down. Open the borders,'" Sachs told a reporter in 2000, distancing himself from other economists. "That's great stuff if you happen to be Poland. But it's not the answer if you happen to be Tanzania, where you're suffering holoendemic malaria, schistosomiasis, and everything else you can imagine."

Chapter 2

Ahmed Maalim Mohamed

According to his Kenyan passport, Ahmed Maalim Mohamed was born in 1965. In fact, Ahmed doesn't know when or where he was born. Like many Somalis in the Horn of Africa, his father was a nomadic pastoralist who, along with his three wives, twenty-one children, and large herds of cattle and camels, kept moving from place to place in the vast semidesert region where Somalia, southern Ethiopia, and Kenya's North Eastern Province meet.

Ahmed is certain of this: he was born sometime during the Shifta War of 1963–68, a war between ethnic Somalis and the Kenyan government for control of North Eastern Province, then known as the Northern Frontier District. Ethnically speaking, North Eastern Province was, and still is, Somali; nonetheless, when the colonial powers carved up Africa, they ignored ethnic and tribal boundaries, with the result that borders sometimes bisected kingdoms, clans, lakes, and even villages. Nor did the mapmakers take into account patterns of nomadic migration. In short, colonial frontiers were no more than lines on a map—lines drawn by Europeans who, in many cases, had never been to the interior of Africa.

The 682-kilometer border between Somalia and Kenya was drawn up during secret backroom negotiations in London, as part of a treaty between Britain and Italy during the First World War. Like so many other colonial borders in Africa, it was arbitrary, disconnected from the lives of people actually living there—yet, even after the collapse of European colonialism, the border remained in place. Thus when Kenya gained independence from Britain in 1963, North Eastern Province—a parcel of land that should have been part of Somalia—was instead controlled by Kenya. The result was the Shifta War. Armed with AK-47s, hand grenades, and machetes, Somalis in North Eastern Province conducted hit-and-run raids on Kenyan police posts and took cover from aircraft fire by hiding in camel caravans. Enraged, the Kenyans declared martial law throughout the entire district, and Somali insurgents (and suspected insurgents) were detained without trial.

Kenyans regarded the Shifta War as guerrilla warfare. (*Shifta* means "bandit" in Somali.) "Hooligans" was how Jomo Kenyatta, Kenya's first president after independence, described the Somali secessionists. In a 1964 speech to Kenya's parliament, Kenyatta made his position clear—the entire population of North Eastern Province was guilty of treason: "To the people who live in the Northeastern region, I have this much to say: We know that many of you are herdsmen during the day and *shifta* at night; others conceal *shifta* and refuse to give information about their movement."

By local standards, Ahmed's father, Maalim Mohamed Maalim, was prosperous. Having three wives testified to that. Still, for the most part, a Somali's worth is measured by his camels, not by his wives: the more camels he has, the greater his wealth and status in the community. The great Somali oral poets reserve their praises for she-camels, not for women. "O you who make such a sound of beauty with your bellow / O you who so blithely give voice to your bubbling growl / It is you I call!" was how the nineteenth-century pastoral poet Raage Ugaas addressed his she-camel. "O soft-footed soundless stalker / It is you I call!"

Camels are expensive, but that's not the whole story. Somalis revere camels because they represent heroic values: self-reliance, fearlessness, intelligence, and the ability to thrive in a harsh and unforgiving environment. For months at a time (as many as six, it's said), a Somali nomad can subsist on nothing but camel milk. The Prophet Muhammad is believed to have extolled the medicinal properties of camel urine; according to many Somalis, drinking a she-camel's urine can prevent or cure cancer, liver disease, digestive disorders, and HIV/AIDS, among other maladies.

Maalim—whose full name, like that of all Somalis, comprises three first names: his own (Maalim), his father's (Mohamed), and his grandfather's (Maalim)—earned money by breeding long-horned Ankole cattle and selling the heifers. He then purchased camels. By the time his eldest son, Ahmed, was born, Maalim had a herd of approximately one hundred camels. In Western terms, his camels were a store of wealth, like a mutual fund or a savings account. Just as some Western children receive silver spoons or cups at birth, so Maalim gave his firstborn son a she-camel. As soon as Ahmed's umbilical cord was cut, it was tied to the tail of his she-camel—a Somali talisman meant to ensure the she-camel's fertility. Her offspring and her offspring's offspring, and so on, would provide Ahmed with enough capital to underwrite his future.

Ahmed can't recall being hungry as a young child. Like that of most Somali nomads, his family's diet consisted mainly of camel's milk supplemented with *nyiri nyiri* (dried camel meat preserved in fat). For the most part, Somalis do not farm the land—farming is menial work, and farmers rank far below nomadic herders on the social scale. From time to time Ahmed's father traded a heifer at the market for sacks of sorghum or other grains. On special occasions—to celebrate the end of Ramadan, for example—he'd return home with bags of sweets, Somali halvah, or a sugared bread known as *kac kac*. Ahmed's happiest childhood memories are of his father returning from market with grains and sweets.

Maalim's three wives took pride in maintaining the family's homestead, erecting tall fences of brambles to protect it from lions and other beasts. They were responsible for constructing the family's compound of Somali *aqals*, small dome-shaped huts. Using soft, sturdy twigs bound with braided-leather rope, they'd first erect a domed scaffolding in the sand. Next, slung over the scaffolding, came the roof and walls, made of heavy grass matting and cowhides to keep out sand and dust and rain.

Every morning at dawn, Ahmed and his siblings headed out with their donkeys to gather firewood and fetch water from nearby streams or wells. Afternoons, the children herded the camels and cattle, roaming barefoot through the bush in search of grazing land. When the seasons changed and the soil began to crack and the wadis ran dry, Ahmed's father and his wives would dismantle their *aqals*, pack up their few belongings, and with their livestock and children, begin the long walk upland to greener pastures.

For a long time, the Shifta War seemed far away, remote. Ahmed's father had never paid much attention to politics, until it became impossible to ignore what was going on. All around him Somali civilians were being rounded up and detained by the Kenyan police. Their livestock was confiscated or slaughtered, and the Somalis were herded into overcrowded, filthy compounds surrounded by barbed wire. Inside these camps, Maalim had heard, populations were being decimated by cholera and measles. No one was permitted to move in or out without official papers. Years later, in *Famine Crimes,* the British scholar Alex de Waal would describe the Shifta War as "a military onslaught on the entire pastoral way of life."

At the time, Maalim knew that he had to save his family. Along with thousands of other displaced Somali-Kenyans, he, his three wives, and his children took refuge in southern Somalia. Hemmed in by war, unable to migrate with the seasons, they found it increasingly difficult to find pastureland for their animals. For the first time, Ahmed became aware of tribal conflict: regularly now his family's clan battled other Somali clans and subclans for water and grazing rights.

Eventually, once the Shifta War was over, Ahmed's family returned to their traditional grazing lands in North Eastern Province. Then, just as they were getting their bearings, the long droughts started.

The world was full of dangers; Ahmed knew that. When he was five or six, his eldest sister died in childbirth. Another sister was devoured by a crocodile while gathering water from the muddy banks of the Dawa River, where Ethiopia meets North Eastern Province. Once, when a fight between two clans broke out at a water well, Ahmed witnessed an uncle being stabbed to death. But it was not until the great drought of the early 1970s that Ahmed knew what it meant to die of hunger. News reports from the great drought (known as *lafaad,* or "white bones") describe a wasteland littered with bleached carcasses. "The hyenas now don't even eat all the dead cattle," an Italian priest living in northern Kenya told *The New York Times* in 1971. "They have had more than they can eat."

First Maalim's cattle died. Then, one by one, the family's camels died. Ahmed was stronger than most children his age. He could go all day on little more than camel's milk. But as famine spread across the parched Sahel and through the Horn of Africa, Ahmed too began to show signs of wasting. When Ahmed's youngest sister died of malnutrition, Maalim, defeated, finally moved his family into town. There, instead of herding livestock, Ahmed and his siblings spent their days lining up for humanitarian food aid.

"My father was once rich," Ahmed recalled. "He had about one hundred cattle and camels. Life was so good. Then the rains

stopped. Soon my father had only two animals remaining—
from one hundred to two. How can he manage life now? He
cannot. For a nomad, resilient and proud, to be reduced to a
beggar of food aid! My father almost became crazy. He was
finished. His motivation, his morale—gone. That is what a
drought is."

Even after the Somalis of North Eastern Province gave up
their battle for independence, the region remained under a
state of emergency, marginalized, and cut off from the rest of
Kenya for another twenty years. North Eastern Province was
never connected to the national electric grid. Roads were left
unpaved. The number of schools and health clinics remained
sharply inadequate.

To humiliate and control the restless Somalis, Kenya's military police continued to detain and abuse them. In the infamous Wajir Massacre of 1984, the Kenyan army rounded up
thousands of Somalis, set fire to their homesteads, and forced
them to strip naked. Those who resisted were tortured, burned
alive, or beaten to death. The official death count at the time
was 57. Eventually, however, the Kenyan government revised
that figure to 380. In truth, according to witnesses and human
rights organizations, the actual number of people killed in the
Wajir Massacre was probably more than 1,000.

In one generation, as the nomadic pastoralists of North
Eastern Province fell into acute poverty, more and more Somalis abandoned their traditional way of life. Proud and prosperous herders became beggars, con men, prostitutes, and petty
thieves; dependence on relief aid became the norm, an accepted
part of life.

Apart from attending a *dugsi* or madrassa, where boys mem-
orized, recited, and wrote out the Koran on wooden tablets

known as *loh*, few Somalis in North Eastern Province attended school. Ahmed's parents were illiterate and innumerate; they'd never gone to school. After all, what could formal schooling offer a nomadic Somali herder? Besides, the languages of instruction in Kenyan schools were Swahili and English. (Somali wasn't a written language until the 1970s. Even today the Somali language is not taught in Kenyan schools.) "We were not sent to government schools for fear of being converted to Christianity," Ahmed said.

Ahmed was lucky: "When the drought came my father was told, 'You will only get water if you put your son in school.' That is how my father was forced to send me to school."

Every day Ahmed walked two hours to get to school in Rhamu, on the Ethiopian border. He'd leave his family's homestead before dawn, cut a path through the scrubland, and move as fast as he could to avoid lions and pythons. Ahmed's school was rudimentary; the few available textbooks were leftovers from the colonial era, and there was one teacher for every fifty students. Nevertheless, Ahmed thrived at school. When the rains came and his father moved on to better pastures, Ahmed, encouraged by his teachers, refused to drop out. His father abandoned him. "Livestock was his number one priority, not education," said Ahmed. It was 1974; Ahmed was around ten years old.

Supporting himself by doing odd jobs—fetching water, digging and hoeing, selling camel's milk and mangoes—Ahmed managed to complete primary school. When he graduated, he was offered a job as a clerical worker at a refugee camp. It was assumed he'd take the job. If he was careful with the money he earned, he'd have enough each month to help support his mother and his siblings. But Ahmed hesitated. He had bigger ambitions than clerical work. If he could find a way to pay for secondary school, he might one day get a civil servant's job—there was no better job in postcolonial Africa. He'd seen

men with fine government jobs: they wore European suits and
drove black Mercedes sedans; they lived in permanent houses
with tin roofs and servants. That was the life!

Eventually, after sitting outside the office of the deputy
district commissioner for days, Ahmed convinced the man to
recommend him for a government scholarship. "Either I succeed or I don't leave the office," Ahmed recalled. "I told him, 'I
need your help.' He told me, 'We are sorry, but we have no support to give you.' I said, 'Look, I have gone to the chief, to the
assistant chief, to the counselor, to the member of parliament,
and now I come to you as the last resort.' He was an old man.
He removed his eyeglasses. I said, 'Mr. Deputy District Commissioner, you are a Big Man and I need your help. If you don't
help me, I don't know where I am headed to. I want to be like
you. Please tell me how you made it so I can one day become
like you. I have nothing.' The man was moved. He started
shedding tears. He took my hand. Then he wrote a letter that
changed my whole life."

At first Ahmed lagged behind the other secondary school
students. But in a short time he became an outstanding student. From being ranked twenty-eighth in his first year, he
moved to twelfth rank and finally to third rank. In 1984 he
gained entrance to Egerton Agricultural College in Njoro,
earning a three-year diploma "with distinction." From there
he was accepted at Kenya's Moi University in Eldoret, where
in 1991 he earned a B.Sc. degree in forestry. A few years later,
while working on a Kenyan agroforestry project funded by the
Belgian government, he won a scholarship to Gembloux Agricultural University in Belgium.

Everything about Belgium was a shock to Ahmed. He knew
Europeans were rich, but he'd never imagined how rich they
really were. He spent hours in supermarkets staring at shelves
stocked with food. His dorm room was the most comfortable
room he'd ever seen. Sometimes he amused himself by fiddling

with his sink, marveling at how water—clean water!—rushed from the taps. In the letters he wrote home, he found it hard to describe his life in Europe; he knew it would be unimaginable to a nomad in North Eastern Province.

In Ahmed's last year at Gembloux, when he was still months away from completing his Ph.D. thesis (on the management of natural resources in dry lands), his scholarship money ran out. Right away one of his professors intervened, personally paying for Ahmed's room and board through the end of the school year. To Ahmed, this act of kindness was a sign from God. He was not especially religious—nonetheless, as Ahmed explained, he had discovered his calling, his vocation: he would use his education to help his people, the Somalis of North Eastern Province.

Chapter 3

The End of Poverty

What was the solution to global poverty? After his first trip to sub-Saharan Africa in 1995, Jeffrey Sachs started reading everything he could find on global health, disease, epidemiology, and development. He sat in on lectures at Harvard's School of Public Health and visited dozens of poor countries. In the central plateau of Haiti, in the village of Cange, he studied the work of Dr. Paul Farmer, whose charity, Partners in Health, cares for people in some of the most poverty-stricken, godforsaken places on earth. According to many experts in the field of international health, Farmer's efforts to treat AIDS and tuberculosis among the poorest people on the globe were all very well, very noble, but highly impractical—too ambitious, too expensive, too complicated, unsustainable. In Sachs's opinion, however, Farmer wasn't being ambitious enough.

"I remember when [Sachs] came to Haiti," Farmer said. "He went to visit patients in their homes, and to meet community health workers, and I remember what he said to me: 'This is doable, but you guys'—meaning, you people in medicine and public health—'you have to stop using the M-word and start using the B-word.' In other words, you don't need millions of dollars to fix this, you need billions of dollars."

"We had everyone saying, 'It's not doable,'" Farmer continued. "Then Jeff got involved and said, 'Buck up, stop whining, and start getting work done.'"

What came next was one of Sachs's most significant contributions to the cause of ending world poverty: a gigantic seven-volume report, published by the World Health Organization in 2001, *Macroeconomics and Health: Investing in Health for Economic Development.* Sachs spent two years directing the report—supervising a commission of seventeen economists and policy makers, six separate task forces, and more than one hundred experts in fields related to the project.

The WHO report laid out the facts in stark terms. Every year eight million people die of poverty on the planet. Many of those eight million people, children especially, are killed by diarrhea, measles, malaria, and respiratory infections like pneumonia that can easily be prevented or treated. Others die from AIDS and tuberculosis. Others starve to death.

Spending money on health care in the world's poorest countries is more than a humanitarian imperative, Sachs's report argued; it is at the same time the key to driving economic growth. Taking over the rhetoric of corporate America, cunningly, Sachs's report managed to transform a health catastrophe into a business proposition: saving lives can offer huge returns to investors. With an annual investment of $66 billion, we can save eight million lives a year *and* generate economic benefits worth $360 billion a year.

In the language of Jeffrey Sachs, macroeconomist, inconceivable numbers sound reasonable, even modest. "He's not embarrassed by large numbers. And he's not apologetic for large numbers," said Richard Feachem, who served on the commission for Sachs's report and was the first executive director of the Global Fund to Fight AIDS, Tuberculosis and Malaria. "What he's saying is, 'If it needs billions for health and development, don't be ashamed to ask for it.' And by the way, to anyone who says, 'Oh, that's a lot of money,' say, 'Well, by whose standards?' because by the standards of military expenditure it's not a lot of money."

"Jeff really changed the way we think about the problem of

health," said Paul Farmer. "What we were always saying is, 'Do this because it's the right thing to do,' but Jeff said, Yeah, it's the right thing to do—and it also is going to open the door to real development. *Because you can't have development if everybody is sick all the time.*"

By the early 2000s, Sachs's life was devoted to one cause: ending extreme poverty. The stumbling block, he concluded, was a "poverty trap": an overwhelming, interconnected burden of disease, illiteracy, high fertility rates, dismal agricultural productivity, lack of capital, weak or nonexistent infrastructure, debt, hunger, drought, malnutrition. . . . Tackling one problem at a time, piecemeal, was pointless, he concluded. The way out of extreme poverty depended on a "big push" in foreign aid— a massive, coordinated investment designed to lift countries up and out of poverty, once and for all.

"It is often said that past aid to Africa has little to show for it," Sachs wrote in a hundred-page paper, "Ending Africa's Poverty Trap," published by the Brookings Institution in 2004. "In fact, there has been too little aid to make a difference."

Consider Sachs's provocative claim: "there has been too little aid to make a difference." Since the end of the colonial era—since the 1960s, that is—more than $700 billion in foreign aid has been poured into sub-Saharan Africa—yet for all that, sub-Saharan Africa is poorer than ever. "Money down a rat hole" was how the late Jesse Helms, former chairman of the Senate Foreign Relations Committee, famously dismissed foreign aid. Sachs's counterargument is simple: if foreign aid has failed to produce obvious and long-lasting results, *it is because we haven't spent enough money to get those results.*

In one of his favorite analogies, Sachs compares the crisis in sub-Saharan Africa to a forest fire. If you try to put out the fire with one hose and the fire keeps raging, do you conclude that fighting fires is hopeless? From his point of view, the only logical conclusion to draw from a fire that's out of control is simple: you don't have enough firefighters.

In that case, how many firefighters do we need? How much money would it take to eradicate extreme poverty? Sachs's estimate is somewhere in the range of $250 billion a year, a figure that's twice what the developed world spends annually on foreign aid. Yet from Sachs's perspective, $250 billion a year is a bargain: at that rate, he claims, extreme poverty could be eradicated by 2025. The cost of ending extreme poverty is less than 1 percent of the total income of the "rich world," according to Sachs: "It's much cheaper than having wars. And it's much cheaper than having mass migration."

Not long after I met him, Sachs invited me to hear him address the General Assembly of the United Nations. His message was clear: "Millions of people die every year for the stupid reason they are too poor to stay alive. . . . That is a plight we can end." Afterwards, over lunch in the crowded UN cafeteria overlooking New York's East River, he continued. "The basic truth is that for less than a percent of the income of the rich world, nobody has to die of poverty on the planet," he said, eating his Cobb salad. "That's really a powerful truth."

Day after day, without pausing for air, it seemed, Sachs was making one speech after another, as many as three in one day. At the same time he lobbied heads of state, testified before Congress, held press conferences, attended symposiums, advised government officials and legislators, participated in panel discussions, gave interviews, published papers in academic journals, wrote opinion pieces for newspapers and magazines, and sought out anyone, anyone at all, who might help him spread the word. The only time he seemed to slow down was when he was sleeping, never more than four or five hours a night. "I'm a happily married single parent," said his wife, Sonia, a pediatrician and the mother of his three children.

"It feels like we're running a campaign—all the time," remarked one exhausted member of his staff. In a way, Sachs was running a campaign. In 2002 he'd been made "special adviser" to the United Nations secretary-general. And in a triumph for Columbia University, he'd left Harvard that year to become Columbia's Quetelet Professor of Sustainable Development; professor of health policy and management; and director of the university's Earth Institute. For all his titles, Sachs's true vocation is to draw our attention to the scandal of global poverty and to force us to do something about it. In his words, his job is to be "a pest."

"He's an irritant," confirms his friend Bono, not without respect. "He's the squeaky wheel that roars." Mark Malloch Brown, who was deputy secretary-general of the United Nations under Kofi Annan, describes Sachs as "this magnificent battering ram," adding: "He's a bully; for the record, he's a bully."

One of Sachs's idiosyncrasies is list making—he keeps a precise tally of the countries he has visited in his role as global economic adviser. The number jumps every few months: 103; 118; 124; 130—like Leporello's catalog of Don Giovanni's conquests. A week after he addressed the UN, Sachs scheduled three overnight flights in five days. First, after a full day of teaching at Columbia, he flew from New York to Rio de Janeiro, São Paulo, and Brasília for two days of meetings with President Luiz Inácio Lula da Silva's cabinet. From there he headed to Washington to attend the White House Summit on Malaria. Afterwards he left for San Francisco, where he made a presentation about ending poverty to the founders of Google. That same day, a Friday, he flew home to New York. Over the weekend he attended a dinner with the secretary-general of the United Nations.

What keeps him going at such a frenzied pace? Is his crusade to eradicate poverty fueled by his failure in Russia, as some have suggested? Was his apparent shift from one end of the political spectrum to the other a way of atoning for, compensating for, his errors of judgment? Sachs dismisses such talk out of hand. "If you haven't noticed," he snapped, "people are dying—it's an emergency."

It isn't easy to reconcile the former Dr. Shock with the new, humanitarian persona of Jeffrey Sachs, yet Sachs himself sees no conflict. Again and again he insists that his work in the developing world is no different from his earlier work in Bolivia and Poland. One way or another, he is an emergency physician— a "clinical economist" is how he puts it—and Africa is the patient in cardiac arrest. In essence, using shock therapy to resuscitate a nation's economy, and prescribing humanitarian interventions to save someone's life, depend on the same model of thought. His goal, he explains, has always been "to take on complex challenges and bring to bear expertise in economics and other disciplines to find workable solutions."

More than once, discussing his humanitarian work, Sachs referred to *Bury the Chains,* Adam Hochschild's inspiring account of how, in the late eighteenth century, twelve determined idealists set Britain's antislavery movement in motion. If, at the time, writes Hochschild, "you had stood on a London street corner and insisted that slavery was morally wrong and should be stopped, nine out of ten listeners would have laughed you off as a crackpot. The tenth might have agreed with you in principle, but assured you that ending slavery was wildly impractical." After all, slavery had existed for millennia: the ancient Greeks and Romans had slaves; the Incas and Aztecs had slaves. As Hochschild notes, "Slavery had existed before money or written law."

Have poverty and inequality not existed for millennia? Sachs understands his mission, his vocation, in huge, abstract terms—human rights, social justice, and truth. His ultimate goal is to change the world—to "bend history," as he once said, quoting Robert F. Kennedy.

"Look," Sachs elaborated, "this is not the great titanic battle of morality that I'm on. I'm not saying the only way for the rich and the poor to live together is if the rich cut their living standards by half, give up their cars, understand modern life is a false contrivance and a false consciousness that is destroying the planet and is enslaving and impoverishing the poor and that we have to move away from globalization in the corporate world which owns politics and dominates. . . ." His voice trailed off.

"I don't believe that stuff anyway, but that's not the kind of battle that this is about," he added. "We're just talking about one percent of our income in the world to avert potential calamity!"

Sachs was becoming impatient. He'd put together a detailed blueprint for ending extreme poverty in Africa by pursuing dozens of "science-based" interventions simultaneously; he'd also shown that his plan was "eminently affordable." He'd pestered governments, major international donors, the UN, and African government officials to adopt his strategy. *The End of Poverty* was a best seller, and people were lining up, sometimes for hours, to hear Sachs speak. *Time* magazine added him to its list of the world's most influential people. There was even a Jeffrey Sachs fan club, a registered not-for-profit organization that, having purchased the domain name sachsforpresident.org, was dedicated to drafting him as the next president of the United States. At Columbia University, you could buy T-shirts stenciled with the words JEFF SACHS IS MY HOMEBOY. When it came to putting his theories into practice, however, he'd made very little progress.

In contrast to the celebrities and college students and like-minded idealists who embraced Sachs's agenda, most devel-

opment experts dismissed it as reductive and, ultimately, unworkable. Yes, countless people in sub-Saharan Africa are alive
because of foreign aid. What no one really knows, however,
is whether foreign aid actually leads to long-term economic
development. Or which of the many humanitarian initiatives and interventions have a lasting impact on poverty. Or
whether foreign aid, by creating economic dependence, does
more harm than good. "How do you know what would have
happened without the aid?" asks the development economist
Esther Duflo. "Maybe it would have been much worse. Or
maybe it would have been better. We have no idea.

"We're not any better than the medieval doctors and their
leeches," Duflo continues, comparing leeches to theories promoted by development economists. "Sometimes the patient
gets better. Sometimes the patient dies. Is it the leeches? Is it
something else? We don't know."

Sachs doesn't ignore his critics; they energize him. "We live
in an age of hand-wringing and cynicism—that's the kind
of world we're living in right now. It's weird. And it's unproductive," he said. "Just get out there and solve the problems.
They're not so hard."

In Sachs's view, if the history of international development
is a history of failure, it's because too many people in the field
are complacent, or incompetent, or not accountable. "People
generally view systems as unchanging. They have very static
views of things. They don't really see how change comes about,"
he said. "Maybe it's having had the good experience of hearing,
as I have many, many times, 'Impossible, impossible, impossible, impossible, impossible—obvious.' If you've gone through
that over a period of twenty-five years, it helps you to filter out
a lot of what you're told. Everything seems impossible until it
becomes inevitable."

Tired of hearing the word *impossible,* Sachs decided to take
matters into his own hands. "It all started with a conversa-

tion I had with Gerry Lenfest about ending poverty in Africa," he recalled. "We spoke for a long time. Then he asked, 'How much would it cost?' Gerry just took out his checkbook and said, 'Here's five million dollars. Go for it.'"

H. Fitzgerald ("Gerry") Lenfest, an American entrepreneur and philanthropist, made his fortune when Lenfest Communications, the cable TV company he founded, was sold to Comcast for $6 billion in 2000. He and his wife, Marguerite, have promised publicly to give away at least half of their wealth during their lifetime. So far, among other acts of generosity, their foundation has donated $100 million to Columbia University, $10 million to Teach for America, and $5.8 million to save the historic ship SS *United States* from the scrap heap. It has provided scholarships to poor students in rural Pennsylvania and funded scientific research projects designed to protect the oceans. Giving money to help Jeffrey Sachs save Africa was uncharacteristic: at the time, the Lenfests didn't know very much about Africa or the world of economic development, but they admired Sachs and shared his commitment to helping the poor.

The Lenfest Foundation's $5 million was more than enough for Sachs to test his theories in one or two villages in sub-Saharan Africa. "What we're trying to show is that with just a few interventions and not a lot of money, lives can be transformed," explained Sachs. "It's what MTV would call Extreme Village Makeover."

Every year for five years, Sachs's "Extreme Village Makeover" would allocate $120 per person in those villages to implement the "interventions" outlined in *The End of Poverty:* high-yield seeds and fertilizer, mosquito nets, better schools, improved health care and sanitation, bore wells and protected springs, diesel generators, and so forth. In order to bypass corrupt government officials, the project would hire its own teams of highly trained locals and deliver aid directly to the villages.

The ongoing results of the five-year project would be tested and monitored by academics at Columbia University, their goal being to demonstrate that Sachs's systematic, scientific approach to ending poverty could be used on a grand scale—in which case, millions upon millions of rural Africans would be rescued from the poverty trap and lifted to "the first rung on the ladder of development" (Sachs's phrase).

Sachs named his makeover experiment the "Millennium Villages Project," a reference to the UN's Millennium Declaration of 2000, in which every UN member state promised to "spare no effort to free our fellow men, women and children from the abject and dehumanizing conditions of extreme poverty." He viewed his project as a proof-test of the UN's declaration's stated goals—eradicating extreme poverty and hunger, achieving universal primary education, empowering women, reducing child mortality, improving maternal health, combating disease, and ensuring environmental sustainability by 2015. Perhaps, however, it would be more accurate to say that the Millennium Villages Project was a hugely ambitious social and economic experiment, a petri dish in the laboratory of Dr. Jeffrey Sachs.

The first Millennium village was officially launched in 2005 in Sauri, a remote cluster of farming communities in western Kenya; in no time at all, Sachs declared his work in the village a success. Less than a year into the project, he called for a fifteenfold increase in foreign aid to Kenya, from $100 million to $1.5 billion a year, to fund Millennium villages all across the country.

The results of Sachs's interventions in Sauri *were* encouraging. Thanks to the introduction of fertilizer and high-yield seeds, the production of maize there tripled from one harvest to the next. The incidence of malaria fell by two-thirds after the villagers were given free mosquito nets. As well, attracted by the free school lunches provided by the Millennium Villages

Project, more children than ever were attending the Bar Sauri Primary School. "This is a village that's going to make history" was how Sachs described Sauri in *The Diary of Angelina Jolie and Dr. Jeffrey Sachs in Africa,* an MTV documentary produced a few months after the launch of the Millennium Villages Project. "It's a village that's going to end extreme poverty."

Sachs was convinced that his work in Sauri could be replicated, not only across Kenya but across all of rural Africa, one village at a time. If he could somehow raise $120 million, he'd launch a dozen model Millennium villages, encompassing half a million desperately poor people in ten sub-Saharan countries. Then, once his approach was validated, surely it would be embraced by development experts, by big international foreign aid donors (USAID, the United Kingdom's DFID, etc.), and by African governments. The result would be billions of dollars in foreign aid dedicated to establishing Millennium villages everywhere on the African continent.

In early 2006, Sachs made an appointment to see George Soros, whose Open Society Foundations were primarily dedicated to fighting totalitarianism, not to ending extreme poverty in Africa. Since the early 1980s, Soros's foundations had given away more than $7 billion to support dissident movements, to promote independent media, and to protect human rights. Its mandate was shaped by Soros's childhood: born in Budapest in 1930, he had survived the brutal occupation of Hungary, first by Nazi Germany, then by the Soviet Union. The purpose of his foundation, Soros once said, was "to help to build a country from which I wouldn't want to emigrate."

At a breakfast meeting with Soros, Sachs appealed to the billionaire's conscience: at stake was nothing less than the lives of millions of people. He compared the yoke of poverty to the yoke of totalitarianism. By promoting economic development in Africa, Soros could play a vital role in promoting global stability—after all, countries destabilized by poverty tend to be havens of unrest, violence, and terrorism. "Most of the work can be done in just one year," he assured Soros. "The rest is just footnotes."

Soros's board of directors was not convinced. Even if the Millennium Villages Project worked in a few model villages, as some directors argued, it could never be taken to scale. Others said it was a "top-down" (as opposed to a "bottom-up") approach to development; devised by technocrats in New York, it relied far too heavily on outsiders. A few of Soros's directors dismissed the project as nothing more than an overpriced monument to Sachs's ego. "Almost unanimously," Soros told me, "everybody was opposed to it, because we don't believe in magic bullets."

Soros wasn't blind to Sachs's shortcomings. "There's a certain messianic quality about him," he noted, "and it needs to be kept under critical control." That said, Soros is a gambling man, and investing in the Millennium Villages Project appealed to his instinct as a speculator. In 1992, famously, he made $1 billion by betting against the British pound before it collapsed. Two years later, trading currencies in Japan, he lost $600 million—in a single day. As for betting on the outcome of the Millennium Villages Project: in Soros's opinion, the project offered an attractive "risk-reward ratio." "I would not consider the money necessarily badly spent if the venture did not succeed," he said casually, "because, you know, nothing ventured, nothing gained."

Soros proceeded to override his board of directors. In September 2006 his foundation announced that it would invest $50 million in the Millennium Villages Project. It was a huge amount of money—easily the biggest single donation Sachs would receive from any source—and together with other, smaller sums that Sachs had raised, would get him close enough to the $120 million he needed to launch his five-year experiment in ten countries: Ethiopia, Uganda, Kenya, Tanzania, Malawi, Rwanda, Nigeria, Ghana, Mali, and Senegal.

"I don't know whether I want to describe it as investment or speculation," Soros said. "It's somewhere in between." Pausing, he stood up from his chair, poured himself a glass of mineral water, and looked out the windows of his midtown Manhattan office. "Even though it's a large amount of money—fifty million dollars—I thought there was really very little downside," he went on. "As a humanitarian action, it was a good investment on its own. But if it succeeded, then of course you'd get a reward that would be way out of proportion to the investment made."

Part Two

We have no water. We have no oil. We have no minerals. We have only animals. If you say to me, "One day you will grow crops," I will ask you, "From where will you get water?" If you say to me, "One day there will be industry," I will ask you, "From where will you get water?"

—Ahmed Maalim Mohamed

Chapter 4

It Doesn't Get Harder Than This

When Jeffrey Sachs first heard about Dertu, it wasn't on the official map of Kenya or any other map he'd seen. He wanted each of his Millennium villages to represent a different agro-ecological zone, and someone, perhaps a well-connected government official from North Eastern Province, proposed Dertu as an exemplary semiarid, nomadic pastoralist community. It is located somewhere in North Eastern Province, a degree or so above the equator and not far from the Somali border. Insofar as Dertu existed, its reason for being was a borehole—a water well drilled in 1997 by UNICEF in an otherwise arid, inhospitable stretch of land.

Thanks to the borehole, Dertu had become a crucial stopping-off point for the region's nomadic pastoralists. All day and sometimes through the night, they arrived with their caravans of camels, long-horned cattle, donkeys, and sheep. You could tell they were approaching by the clouds of dust that rose and drifted across the dry savanna—camels piled high with bundles of twigs, cooking utensils, wooden milk bowls, plastic buckets, woven-grass mats, and small children; donkeys loaded down with yellow jerry cans secured with braided-leather ropes.

There was no economy to speak of in Dertu. Here and there the nomadic herdsmen passing through would trade or sell livestock, and a modest business was established to sell camel's milk; otherwise, the only economic activities were gun running and cattle raiding.

After the collapse of the Somali Democratic Republic in 1991, guns, smuggled across the poorly guarded border, had become as common in the region as drought. Foreigners who visited the region (humanitarian aid workers, mainly) were advised to travel with armed escorts. The U.S. embassy in Nairobi had designated the entire North Eastern Province "restricted without prior authorization." A report issued by the Institute for Security Studies cautioned against "highway banditry and hijacking, raiding and stock thefts, robbery and looting, intimidation, physical injury and mutilation, rape, and murder."

Over the course of a decade or so, gradually, a ragtag community of ethnic Somalis settled in the vicinity of Dertu's water hole. Their dome-shaped *aqals,* designed to be temporary and mobile, became semipermanent structures. Having abandoned their lives as nomadic herders, they were living on handouts from humanitarian aid agencies: bags of cornmeal, rice, and pasta supplemented their accustomed diet of camel's milk and *nyiri nyiri.*

A small mosque and a primary school were constructed in Dertu in the early 2000s. As soon as the surrounding population numbered a few thousand, the World Bank, together with UNICEF, funded a "dispensary" to provide the people with basic health care. A rough adobe structure with no power or running water, the dispensary was staffed by one overwhelmed nurse and, like most dispensaries in rural Kenya, was chronically short of even the most rudimentary medical supplies. In life-threatening cases, patients died.

Ever since the Shifta War of the 1960s, Dertu and the surrounding region have existed in a permanent state of catastrophe: wars, droughts, famines, floods, pestilence, tribulations, biblical woes. Natural resources are scarce and getting scarcer. The limited supply of firewood, water, and vegetation is strained by the growing numbers of refugees from Somalia. The sprawling Dadaab refugee camps, not far from Dertu, opened in 1991 in a space designed to accommodate 90,000 people. By the

2000s, with interclan warfare still raging in Somalia, the camps housed an estimated 300,000 refugees who, over time, settled permanently in an area entirely unsuited to human settlement.

Camels, which outnumber humans in North Eastern Province, only make things worse, devouring entire trees, top to bottom, and depleting the water supply, whatever the source. The water table keeps sinking: in one decade alone, it has dropped from 160 to 200 meters below ground. Every year 650 hectares of pastureland disappear in North Eastern Province. With few trees and plants to anchor the soil, the place becomes a dust bowl in the dry season.

Scare resources fuel violence. Competing for water and grazing rights, the province's various Somali clans and subclans have a history of beating, raping, mutilating, and murdering one another. Tribal elders intervene, settling disputes by forcing one clan to pay *diyal* or blood money to the other. (In Dertu, fifty camels is the standard compensation for homicide—less if the victim is a woman.) Before long, the cycle of violence starts all over again.

"What we're talking about here is a community that is barely surviving," Sachs remarked. "Violent poverty, natural hazards, conflict, degradation of the environment—objectively speaking, it doesn't get harder than this."

Sachs had read all about Dertu, and for him the place represented an irresistible challenge: "I mean, what we are starting with here is a baseline that is not only below normal standards, but below *minimum* standards." If his theories on ending poverty could work here, in one of the most deprived places on earth, they could work anywhere.

It was Ahmed Mohamed's job to lift the people of Dertu out of extreme poverty. Hired by the Millennium Villages Project in March 2006, one year after completing his Ph.D. in Belgium,

Ahmed was responsible for implementing what he referred to, admiringly, as "the Great Professor's Ideas"—the Great Professor being Jeffrey Sachs.

Step by step, intervention by intervention, an official *Millennium Villages Handbook* prescribed the course of action to be followed by "change agents" assigned to each village. A 147-page, single-spaced document written by twenty-nine academics, mostly from Columbia University, the handbook features dozens of flow charts, protocols, organizational tables, benchmarks, timelines, and hopeful objectives. As Dertu's designated change agent, Ahmed set out to eradicate extreme poverty by following the *Millennium Villages Handbook* to the letter.

In early 2006 he recruited a team of five educated Somalis from other NGOs and got to work. He'd had no training or experience in economic development, but he was full of optimism. With so much money flowing directly from New York into Dertu—a massive infusion of over half a million dollars during the first year—he could accomplish a great deal. Imagine the potential impact of such largesse!

"With just a few interventions—ambulances, mobile clinics, a cell network—you could make a *huge* difference," Sachs assured Ahmed when they met. "With improved inputs, veterinary care, better breeding, a farmers' cooperative, tapping the Tana River . . . There's a tremendous amount to be done."

For all that, Dertu was perhaps the most challenging of all the Millennium villages. Just getting basic supplies there from Nairobi took weeks, sometimes months. Early in Ahmed's tenure, a mechanical part that was needed to repair one of the well's generators took four months to arrive. When the part did arrive, no one in Dertu knew what to do with it (skilled labor being practically nonexistent among camel herders). Eventually, at considerable expense to the Millennium project, a mechanic was summoned from downcountry.

The closest "city," the chaotic frontier town of Garissa, was only sixty miles south of Dertu, and yet the drive took four hours or more on a good day. When the rains came, the dirt track deteriorated into "soup," as the locals call it, and the drive could take an entire day. Drivers heading to Dertu rarely made it out of second gear as their trucks bounced along the narrow track, swerving to avoid ruts and boulders and thornbushes. (There's a good reason for the stacks of spare tires carried behind and on the roofs of Land Rovers in North Eastern Province.)

Without proper roads, how do you reach a nomadic population spread thinly over 750 square kilometers (around 300 square miles)? Ahmed and his staff spent months trekking into the bush, spreading the word, encouraging cooperation, and convincing skeptical elders to support the Millennium Villages Project. Because there were no staff quarters in Dertu, Ahmed and his team slept outside, or else they commuted across the rough terrain, back and forth to Garissa, sharing the project's one vehicle. It wasn't long before the vehicle, a cheap pickup truck, had to be written off.

Ahmed faced challenges, one after another, that the authors of the *Millennium Villages Handbook* hadn't anticipated. Entire chapters had been devoted to improving agriculture yields, boosting school enrollment, and promoting gender equality. But nothing in the handbook told the change agents how to reduce crime. Ahmed hired police escorts to protect his team from banditry and tribal clashes. He also hired security guards (two for night, two for day) to guard the Millennium project's compound. Nevertheless, shortly after the Millennium Villages Project was established in Dertu, Ahmed's health coordinator, Fatuma Mohamed Shide, was clubbed senseless in a fight between two Somali subclans.

Nor did the handbook address the subject of natural disasters. By the time Ahmed accepted the job with the Millennium Villages Project in 2006, the water well in Dertu had dried up. Since 2002, the entire Horn of Africa had been suffering from drought. The situation was so dire in Dertu that Oxfam was delivering water once or twice a week in tanker trucks. With every visit, each household received a twenty-liter (5.3-gallon) allotment of water. But twenty liters was not nearly enough; many people had to walk hours, sometimes days, in search of water. Herds of cattle died. Dertu's undernourished camels stopped producing milk.

Ahmed received approval from the higher-ups in New York to spend part of his budget on imported water. Day after day, for months, tanker trucks paid for by the Millennium Villages Project kept the people of Dertu alive.

At last, in October 2006, the heavens opened and the rains came: a drop or two at first, then the deluge. Rushing to save themselves from the floodwaters, the people of Dertu lost everything they had, which, God knows, was little enough to begin with. Whatever headway Ahmed made in his first few months on the job was washed away by the floods.

At the local dispensary, cases of malaria surged from 50 per month before the rains to 450 in December. Severe diarrhea, brought on by contaminated water, spread fast, and there were no IV fluids to treat dehydration. Then, as though the people of North Eastern Province hadn't suffered enough, a three-year-old girl in the region was diagnosed with polio—Kenya's first reported case in twenty-two years. With the dirt roads impassable to vehicles, the UN deployed helicopters to drop food aid and medical supplies across the province.

It wasn't long before Rift Valley fever began spreading, transmitted from animals to humans. In Dertu alone, in a single month, six people were diagnosed with the disease; all but one died. From one day to the next, North Eastern Province was crowded with teams of medical workers: doctors and epidemiologists from the Centers for Disease Control, from Doctors Without Borders, from the World Health Organization. Until the outbreak could be contained, the sale of camel milk was strictly off-limits. A ban was placed on the sale of all animals.

For seven weeks the livestock market in Garissa, the biggest, most important livestock market in the area, was shut down. Without the sale of camel milk or livestock to sustain it, the limited economy of North Eastern Province came to a standstill. The market price of brides, a key economic indicator in North Eastern Province, declined sharply, with the result that a wife could be had in exchange for four scrawny cattle. "In these times," Ahmed remarked, "men can marry up to four women cheaply."

Kenya's government stayed aloof from the disasters in North Eastern Province. Flood, disease, drought: they weren't the government's concern. In 2006, in the midst of the drought, members of Kenya's parliament rewarded themselves with yet another increase in compensation. In a country where the per capita income was $770 a year, they were already earning about $100,000 a year—a salary that included tax-free perks: $10,000 a year for entertainment; $11,500 for housing; $12,000 for gasoline and auto maintenance; $5,000 for "extraneous expenses"; and on and on.

Once the floodwaters started to recede, a group of Dertu's community leaders gathered to air their grievances and share their frustrations. (The *Millennium Villages Handbook* states clearly that community participation is critical to the project's success: "Create opportunities for critical mutual and collective reflection and learning. . . . Host or facilitate quarterly, biannual or annual stakeholders review meetings for monitoring and scaling-up.")

"Our needs are many," cried one of the men, a tall Somali wearing an embroidered kufi. Sitting cross-legged under one of the few shade trees in Dertu, Ahmed nodded sympathetically. He's a tall man, serious and imposing, who looks older than he is. In Dertu, everyone called him "Dr. Ahmed."

"It is only God and us who know the kinds of problems we have here," said a woman named Sahlan Bath Hussein, her face framed by the long purple *hijab* she wore over a white cotton gown. She was thirty-three years old and the mother of five children. Now and then, she explained, her husband showed up in Dertu with money or gifts or bags of grain for her; otherwise he lived with his other wife close to the Dadaab refugee camps.

To support herself and her children, Sahlan had opened a tea shop, a wooden shack in the center of town where she made chapatis on a three-stone fire and served chai while her eldest child, a girl of thirteen, looked after the younger children. Month after month, coin by coin, Sahlan had set aside money to pay for medical emergencies and school fees; like many rural Africans without access to commercial banks, she had buried her money in the ground for safekeeping. The floods carried away her "soil bank," her life savings.

"We suffered through the drought," Sahlan continued. "We lost many animals, even our donkey. And now the flood has caused even more problems. We cannot eat our cattle or drink our milk, and the little we had has been washed away by the rains."

Dertu's one shopkeeper, Abdi Hussein, had seen his business collapse. In good times, his store—a small lean-to with merchandise consisting of flip-flops, hair combs, bags of sugar and cornmeal, Sunpop soda, and bars of Star Beauty soap— could bring in as much as 4,000 Kenyan shillings (Ksh) a month, about $55. Since the flood, sales had collapsed to just over 500 Ksh a month, less than $7. "What can I do?" Abdi asked Ahmed rhetorically. "I pray only that it will be better soon. *Insha'Allah*." God willing.

Ahmed understood that the people of Dertu wanted change. "Please bear with us," he said. The Millennium project's planned "interventions" were firmly on track, he assured them, but economic development does not happen overnight.

Already Ahmed and his staff had given out mosquito nets and had vaccinated thousands of camels, cattle, sheep, donkeys, and goats. Using basic materials donated by the Millennium Villages Project and UNICEF, they'd encouraged the people of Dertu to dig and build fifteen pit latrines. To reverse the baleful effects of deforestation and erosion, and to create wind and sand barriers, they'd handed out five thousand acacia seedlings and taught people how to plant and care for the trees. A demonstration farm was under way, sorghum and maize were planted, and eighty-four hoes and eight spades were given out to herders willing to learn about agriculture.

"I can promise you," said Ahmed, "it won't be long before your lives improve."

In early 2007, as buds appeared on the shrubs and the desert grasses grew high, Ahmed set out to convince the people of Dertu of the benefits of hay. "If you gather and dry the tall grass now," he explained, "you will have food for your animals the next time the drought comes." The people were not impressed by his ideas about drying the tall grass. "God has brought us this grass," one man objected. "It is not ours to cut."

Like the people of Dertu, Ahmed is both Somali and Muslim. He'd grown up in these parts; he was the son of a herdsman; he was one of them. For all that, he was viewed as an outsider in Dertu. His pleated dress pants, his starched shirts, his trim beard—those things set him apart. And more than once it was pointed out that while he was Somali, he was descended from a different sub-subclan than the people of Dertu. That alone was a reason to mistrust him.

In Saudi Arabia, Ahmed reasoned, devout Sunni Muslims cut grass; if God didn't object to Saudis cutting grass, surely He would permit the Sunni Muslims of Dertu to do the same. No one was moved by this logic. "It is God's gift," someone repeated. "The more you cut, the angrier God gets—it is a bad omen."

"Time is running out," Ahmed said gently. "The fires are coming with the winds from Somalia, and those fires will consume all the grasses if you do not cut them first."

An old woman named Mama Abshira confronted Ahmed, poking her finger in his face. He was interfering in their way of life, she said. Others jumped in. Soon everyone was arguing. There was a blur of confused shouting. "Please," begged Mama Abshira. "For heaven's sake, don't cut our grass."

Ahmed has a natural talent for diplomacy. When arguments broke out, he would smile agreeably and then, patiently, find a way to settle them. But attitudes are deeply ingrained in Dertu and people are suspicious of change. "The environment is changing, yet the people are not understanding," he told me. "They believe the rains have failed because of their sins or because they did not properly celebrate a festival. I cannot convince them that droughts are part of the long-term way of life."

Convincing people to use mosquito nets was almost as difficult as convincing them to make hay from grass. Wherever you look in Africa, you see the devastating effects of malaria: children in comas, men and women sapped of energy and unable to work.

Controlling malaria was a top priority for Jeffrey Sachs, who convinced Sumitomo Chemical to donate $2 million worth of long-lasting insecticidal mosquito nets to the Millennium Villages Project. By reducing the incidence of malaria and other mosquito-borne diseases, mosquito nets would not only save lives, he argued, they would also improve economic productivity. In other words, an investment in malaria control was an investment in Dertu's future prosperity.

Ahmed and his team distributed more than three thousand of Sumitomo's high-tech mosquito nets to protect the community from malaria and other mosquito-borne diseases. To make very sure that the nets were used properly, as intended, Ahmed issued a stern edict. "This is for human life," he told the people of Dertu, "donated by someone to ensure your survival. If we see you put it over a goat, we will withdraw it."

Traditionally, nomadic pastoralists rely on smoke to keep mosquitoes from attacking their livestock. However, using smoke as a mosquito repellent means that someone has to rekindle the fire every hour or so throughout the night. "It is easier to simply use the nets to protect the animals," said Ahmed, explaining why in Dertu some nets were being diverted from a child's bed to a herd of kid goats. "And in a pastoral community, the livestock have more value than humans."

Chapter 5

Every Problem Has a Solution

In January 2007 Sachs traveled to Ruhiira, an isolated village in the highlands of southwestern Uganda that had been named a Millennium village six months earlier. There wasn't much of anything in Ruhiira. No electricity or running water. No paved roads. It was a place of lack, of deprivation, and thus was typical of Sachs's model villages.

The soil, at one time rich and fertile, was depleted from years of abuse. The surrounding hills had been stripped bare of trees. Without firewood at hand, villagers were forced to use rootstalks as cooking fuel. *Matoke,* a green banana that is boiled and then mashed, is the staple food in these parts. You won't starve living on *matoke,* but you won't thrive: in Ruhiira, four in every ten children are chronically malnourished, their growth stunted for lack of nutrients.

The first time he arrived in Ruhiira, Sachs was alarmed. As Dr. William Nyehangane, the district's health officer, informed him, the total annual budget for health care in the area was $1.90 per person. "Unbelievable!" said Sachs. "Did you hear that? One dollar and ninety cents. *One dollar and ninety cents.* Unbelievable."

At an absolute minimum, for a basic health care system to function, Sachs had calculated that a country must spend $40 per person annually. In much of sub-Saharan Africa, health care budgets are around $20 per person. Yet here the annual health care budget was less than $2 per person. In Ruhiira, where malaria was the number one cause of death for children under five, where TB was rampant, and where the odds were one in thirteen that a woman would die during pregnancy or childbirth, there was really no health care at all.

The Kabuyanda Health Center, the closest hospital to Ruhiira, was hours away by wheelbarrow, the conveyance most often used to transport the sick from one place to another. Located twenty miles off the national electric grid, the health center had no power. Once, for a short time, two solar panels were mounted on the roof. They disappeared. As for the nineteen-kilowatt generator parked outside the building like a totem, there wasn't enough money in the budget to buy diesel fuel.

Without electric power, how do you provide standard medical treatment to people who are dying? Without running water, how do you wash the blood from floors and beds and open wounds? How do you sterilize surgical tools or keep your hands clean or store blood or refrigerate vaccines?

As he made his way through the hospital, Sachs looked distraught. "How many beds are there here?" he asked the young doctor on staff, Stephen Mucunguzi.

"Twenty-eight."

"Twenty-eight for a hundred twenty-five thousand people?" repeated Sachs, trying to grasp the implications of such numbers. "Aren't they filled, filled, filled?"

Dr. Mucunguzi showed Sachs the operating theater, a bare cement room built in 2002 that had never been used for surgery. There'd been one roadblock after another, the doctor explained: surgical equipment had been ordered but had taken three years to arrive. By the time it did arrive, the only doctor on staff had quit, leaving the hospital with no doctor at all for five months. Finally, in late December 2006, Dr. Mucunguzi had come on board, but only after the Millennium Villages Project offered to supplement his official $350-a-month salary.

In any case, the operating theater had been so shoddily

constructed that without major repairs it couldn't possibly be used for general surgery. The windows wouldn't close. The air vents were broken. There were no floor tiles, no medical scrubs, no surgical gloves. The government promised to deliver drugs to the hospital every three months, but they never arrived on time; when they did show up, the supply was barely enough to last a fortnight.

"We are hoping it will be working in a month," said Dr. Mucunguzi.

Sachs looked skeptical. "And running water?" he asked.

"Well, we plan to put in a water tank. We need a maximum of one month to improve the system."

"So," said Sachs, questioning the young doctor, "today is January fourteenth. Could we really try to have this working by March first? No later."

"Yes, yes."

"I think it would be good for us to have a goal."

Back outside, squinting under the midday sun, Sachs shook his head in disbelief; he was personally offended by the situation. "They can't go on like this," he said. "You have one hundred forty out of a thousand children dying before their fifth birthday. The mothers carry their children ten kilometers, and they're dead in their arms before they get to the clinic—they're dead in their arms, or they're in a coma."

Elementary school children raced after Sachs as he walked down the dirt road, waving happily. "How are you? How are you?" they cried, repeating the one English greeting universally taught in East African schools. Just outside the hospital a group of women wearing ankle-length *gomesi*, with high puffed sleeves and wide sashes, were singing, presumably in Sachs's honor. Sachs moved along briskly. "This can't go on," he continued. "This is a death sentence. This is how we allow fellow human beings to die, by doing nothing. I don't get it, I just don't understand it—I've tried, but I can't understand what we are doing."

Uganda's fertility rate is among the highest in the world. At the current rate of seven children per woman, Sachs reckons the population will double in the next twenty years, from around 35 million to 70 million—this after having already doubled in the previous twenty years. Meanwhile, the amount of farmland is shrinking. "Not only has the land been cleared and deforested, but the arable land can't keep pace with the population, so people are getting hungrier and hungrier," he said, stepping into his UN-issued Land Rover. "They're trapped in poverty. They can't find fuel wood. The nutrients in the soil are depleted. And next year they'll be trapped even deeper in poverty—because they'll have another child and two years after that, another child, and at this rate you can't get out of poverty."

Back at the center of town, on the other side of Ruhiira's low-lying hills, local dignitaries and journalists were waiting for Sachs to arrive. Unsteadily, he made his way down a steep footpath—loose dirt and small stones—toward Ruhiira's main water supply, a stagnant, muddy water hole. Girls and women in bare feet, babies strapped to their backs, were bending over the brown water filling plastic buckets and jerry cans. Young children were transporting the water up the slope, balancing twenty-liter jerry cans on their small heads. Some of the girls were dressed in torn party dresses, pink tulle with ruffles, that might have been sent to Africa by, say, a church in Tulsa, Oklahoma.

"Look at this!" exclaimed Sachs, in a rage. "It's completely unprotected! You're getting runoff of excrement. There are bugs floating on the surface. This is dramatic. People should not be condemned to drink this kind of water. This kills. Massively. This is a massive killer."

Meanwhile, one after the other, onlookers were following Sachs down the footpath: villagers, local politicians, government officials, and at least three members of Uganda's parliament, brushing dust from their Sunday suits. A half-dozen men wearing brand-new United Nations caps joined the group. A clutch of journalists arrived: a writer for *The Guardian* had flown in from London, along with a photographer for Agence France-Presse, a correspondent for Nation Television Uganda, and an eager representative for *UNDP News,* the in-house publication of the United Nations Development Program.

Nearby, being filmed for the BBC, was Sachs's good friend George Osborne, a British member of Parliament and a rising star in the Conservative Party. (In 2010 he would be appointed Chancellor of the Exchequer.) "We're here at the only water source for the village," he intoned in a plummy accent, looking right into the camera. "And as you can see, the mothers there, some of whom are pregnant, are picking up water which they've then got to take up the hill."

Sachs hadn't come to Ruhiira to predict doom; his goal was to sound the alarm, to call the world's attention to the poverty trap, and to gather support for his proposed solution. There was a solution to poverty, he was certain of that, and the solution was "basic" and "very simple," and it was "amazing" how fast it could work.

"Thank you for bringing us to this place," he began, addressing the villagers off the top of his head, without notes. "We are honored that you have taken us into your community." The crowd hushed respectfully.

"We have seen how we can work with you to improve the agriculture, with new crops and ideas to improve your income." A translator repeated his words to the crowd in the local Bantu language, Runyankole.

"And we have seen the bed nets in your houses. Do you have bed nets in your houses?"

"Yes!"

"All right!" responded Sachs. He was getting fired up now. "And are they working? Do they help?"

"Yes!"

"We are happy to see that. We went to the school, and we saw how the school-feeding program has started, and we're very proud of what you have done with that. And we went to the health center to see how it is being expanded, with more health workers in the community. Why do I mention all these things? Because for *every* problem you have, there is a solution! We want to help you find the solution!"

The people clapped. Then they began to cheer. Sachs was pleased with himself and grinned. "In five years we are going to end hunger in this community," he continued. "In five years we are going to bring malaria completely under control. In five years we will have hospitals and clinics through the *whole* community. In five years you will have beautiful crops. Step by step, poverty will become something of the past!

"Tomorrow we will be in Kampala meeting with your president, and we will tell him what remarkable progress you have made here. Because we now have the evidence—you are the proof of what can be accomplished! We will tell the president what you have done, and we will talk to him about expanding the project all across Uganda. And then we will go to Kenya, to Djibouti, to Ethiopia, and we will tell all the people what is happening here. We will tell them that we *can* fight disease! That we *can* fight hunger! That we *can* end poverty in our lifetime!"

Now, in a traditional Ugandan gesture of approval, the equivalent of a standing ovation, the villagers stretched out their hands toward Sachs and began wiggling their fingers. Everywhere you looked, like the gentle rain from heaven, fingers wiggled and fluttered. The people of Ruhiira were raining blessings on Jeffrey Sachs.

One day later, as promised, Sachs was in Kampala meeting with Yoweri Museveni, the longtime president of Uganda.

While Museveni swiveled left and right in his black leather executive chair, Sachs was making an impassioned presentation to him about the Millennium Villages Project. Museveni's support was urgently needed, Sachs told him. The situation was dire. People were dying. With the president's backing, the project could be expanded, village by village, all across Uganda. "The idea is a poverty eradication effort, but focusing on practical investments," Sachs informed him. "The idea is six goals with strict timetables."

Museveni gestured to an assistant: he wanted tea.

"First," Sachs explained, "we want to help the farmers have a bumper harvest of food. The key is fertilizer, so in Ruhiira, to start out, we've done a universal distribution to every household of fifty kilograms of fertilizer and about ten kilograms of high-yield maize seeds."

"Mmmmm," murmured Museveni in reply. "Mmmmm."

"And they're having a bumper harvest," Sachs went on, "and it's really incredible actually. Because of the fertilizer and the good seeds, it looks like they're going to get six tons. The crops are eight feet tall right now. It's really incredible."

Museveni appeared restless and kept on swiveling. His tea arrived. "Mmmmm," he said, reaching for the sugar. That same week his government's peace talks with Joseph Kony, the deluded leader of the insurgent Lord's Resistance Army (L.R.A.), had collapsed, yet again. For the past twenty years, the L.R.A. had terrorized northern Uganda: 1.5 million Ugandans had been displaced, their villages burned to the ground. Tens of thousands of civilians had been butchered, their limbs hacked off by bayonets, their heads smashed with rifle butts. An estimated twenty-four thousand children had been abducted.

Even more troubling to Museveni, perhaps, was the fact that he was no longer the West's favorite African leader. For many years after seizing power in 1986, he had been a "donor darling," which is to say that Uganda had received a disproportionate amount of foreign aid. Modern and principled, devoted to democracy and reform, Museveni was widely viewed as the model for a new generation of African leaders. He spoke eloquently about ending poverty and sectarianism. He denounced African leaders in general for their corruption. "The Honorable Excellency who is going to the United Nations in executive jets, but has a population at home of ninety percent walking barefoot, is nothing but a pathetic spectacle," he railed in his swearing-in address.

After a time, however, some observers began to ask themselves: Wasn't Museveni just another African "Big Man"? In 2000, he'd ordered an executive jet for himself, a $30 million Gulfstream IV. And in 2005, just before the national election, he had abruptly amended Uganda's constitution to abolish presidential term limits—with the result that he was able to run for an unprecedented third term. During the election, his opponents were mostly kept out of sight, independent media outlets were shut down, and uncooperative journalists were detained. Museveni won handily.

Meanwhile, Uganda remains one of the most corrupt countries in the world. A study prepared for Transparency International concluded what most Ugandans already know: that the majority of their country's elected officials are guilty of "influence peddling, vote buying, nepotism, sabotage, bribery, diversion of public resources, and embezzlement." Year after year, as much as half of all the money in government coffers—somewhere between $100 million and $950 million a year, depending on estimates—is looted.

Now, in his office in Kampala, swiveling in his chair, Museveni seemed distracted. Sachs had moved on to the subject of Ruhiira's water supply. "The only water is way down in the valleys, so people walk kilometers down pretty steep paths to get to a miserable, unprotected water basin," he reported. "It is shocking, I have to say, the water situation. We went down a steep slope to a pond that they had dug, and they just collect, you know, the runoff, and it's muddy, the excrement from the animals is coming in, bugs are coming in. Completely unprotected! And that's their water hole! And we saw the women there, a pregnant woman, baby on her back, with a jerry can trying to get water out. It was shocking, actually."

"Mmmmm."

"We're trying to figure out whether we can pump some water in," Sachs said eagerly. "I have a donor who's the world's largest manufacturer of PVC piping, and he said he'll give a huge amount of piping if we can find a way to pump. So I think we can get that solved."

"That water," Museveni remarked offhandedly. "They boil it. As long as you boil that water—"

"I don't know about that," interrupted Sachs. "There's no fuel wood to boil anything."

"Mmmmm."

Sachs circled back to the subject of the Millennium Villages Project: with the right interventions, success was almost guaranteed. "My impression, Mr. President, is that this will all happen within one year," he assured Museveni. "And it shows to me a pretty basic point, which is that when we're talking about extreme world poverty, it shouldn't take a lot of time to make a difference. Just a couple of years could make a *huge* difference—with the right targeted investments, starting with agriculture, getting inputs to the farmers, getting basic health care, getting school feeding programs, and—it's a bigger budget item, but I'd say, you know—making sure there's a graded road and electricity connection, that will change the *whole* rural landscape."

Museveni was interested in the root meaning of the word *Ruhiira*. "Bantu grass, that's what *Ruhiira* means," he said, stirring his tea. "That's what *Ruhiira* means."

"Yeah," said Sachs, hurrying to the crucial matter of

Uganda's farm productivity. "Your country's fertilizer use is about the lowest actually in the world right now. It's essentially zero. And what we saw in Ruhiira, they're going to get, in maize, six tons per hectare probably. This is really a bumper crop—not just a crop, a bumper crop! It's phenomenal! And it's because they never had fertilizer before."

Sachs was urging Museveni to offer bags of subsidized fertilizer and high-yield seeds to every small-hold farmer in the nation. "Go for the big scale!" he said dramatically. "Why wait? There's no reason to wait."

Museveni cleared his throat. "I use fertilizers once in a while," he remarked, referring to his own farm, his own personal situation. "I'm trying to remember, when I grew maize, I harvested eight hundred bags."

"Eight hundred," repeated Sachs, politely.

"Yes, eight hundred—eight hundred bags. I must have been using like fifty acres. The bag is one hundred kilograms."

"That's eighty tons over fifty acres," said Sachs, running the numbers off the top of his head.

"Mmmmm." Museveni, reaching for the calculator on his desk, started tapping the keys: "That's one point six . . ."

Sachs was way ahead of him. "Times two point five would be—that would be four tons per hectare."

"Four tons?" asked Museveni, puzzled by the figure.

"Per hectare," repeated Sachs.

"Ah, okay," agreed Museveni. "That's what I harvested. Yes."

"You're a master farmer: you got four tons," said Sachs, complimenting the president on his crop yield and eager to return to the matter at hand. "But the average here is less than a ton," he pointed out, referring to Uganda generally.

Museveni seemed mildly interested. Who would have thought that his nation's small-hold farmers were so unproductive? "Mmmmm," he remarked. "That's very low."

"But with fertilizer, you get four tons," Sachs added, hoping to seize the day. "If you had all the farmers *quadrupling* their yields, do you know what kind of growth that would mean for this country? That's like a twenty-five percent increase of GNP!"

Museveni settled back in his chair. On the wall behind his desk was a single framed photograph, of Museveni himself. "Yes, I see," he said, still sipping his tea. "But there are other things to consider, Professor. You know, in these countries of Africa, we have many other problems. This is not India or China. There are no markets. There is no network. No rails. No roads. We have no political cohesion."

The meeting with Sachs was over. The president had other commitments. Downstairs, his driver was standing by.

Chapter 6

Everything Is Written

Change came slowly to Dertu. Ahmed worried that time was running out. There was so much to do. Convincing people to cut hay or use mosquito nets was one thing; changing social conventions was something else altogether.

More than 80 percent of Dertu's population is illiterate. Most men have three wives, and women, on average, have nine children. One woman in Dertu, Amina Abdi, had given birth to six children; all died in childhood. Another woman, Adey Mohamed, had ten children; six died before the age of five. How did they die? I asked. Adey shrugged: "I am a Muslim. I am a strong believer. If death happens, no one can prevent it. When a child is born, God has already set for him a fixed time of death. Everything is written." She paused, then added: "Why are we put on earth if not to have children?" Even Fatuma Shide, whose job as the Millennium project's health coordinator involved teaching people family planning and "gender empowerment," had given birth to ten children; two died shortly after birth.

One evening, sitting under the moonlit sky in Dertu, I found myself talking about children with Ahmed and two members of his senior staff, Idris Sahal Kolon and Abdi Sheikh Mohamed. The khat leaves we were chewing stuck to the roof of my mouth like bits of cheap toilet paper. "The short-term goal is that children take care of you when you get old," Idris said, unraveling the logic of large families. "The long-term goal is increasing the population of the clan to protect against tribal invasions and to maintain the dynasty."

Idris and Abdi were startled to learn that I have only two children and, worse, that I don't plan to have more. "Only two!" Idris exclaimed. "Please have more children. Have five or six. Do not waste yourself. Please."

"Bill Gates, if he is so rich, why does he not have more children?" asked Abdi, whose own father had twenty-four. "America is called the land of plenty, but why do you not give birth? This Oprah Winfrey. Why does she not have children? Bill Clinton—he has only one daughter. I sympathize for him."

"Our former president has eight children," chimed in Idris, referring to Daniel Arap Moi.

"He is blessed with children *and* power," added Abdi, suggesting that one is linked to the other.

"You should have as many children as possible," said Idris. "Do not fear. God will take care of your children. God will be sure you can afford the medical bills. God will help you pay for the school."

"A Somali man can think only to have more children," Ahmed said, shaking his head. "One man in Dertu has twenty-one children. He always tells me, 'Dr. Ahmed, I am father of twenty-one and I am not yet sixty!' He is proud of this."

For Jeffrey Sachs, the pattern makes good sense: people make a rational economic decision to have large families. Because child mortality rates in Dertu are among the highest in the world, parents naturally assume that a high percentage of their children will not survive. Giving birth to too many children is a kind of insurance policy, a hedge against the risk of loss: parents *overcompensate*.

In Dertu, children collect water, gather firewood, and herd camels, among other necessary chores. They represent cheap labor. But as living standards improve and households gain access to running water and gas stoves, children will become less economically valuable. At the same time, with better health care, more children will survive. The end result, according to Sachs, will be that fertility rates drop. In his view, prosperity is the most effective form of birth control.

Intuitively, Ahmed knew that the people of Dertu would be better off if they had fewer children—children were a liability, not an insurance policy. But to him the issue wasn't about economics; it was about life and death. Pregnancy is risky everywhere; in Dertu, however, where just about every woman gives birth at home in her *aqal,* sometimes far into the bush, childbirth can be a death sentence. Even by the dismal standards of rural Africa, maternal and infant death rates in Dertu are shocking. When something goes wrong, when labor is prolonged, or the baby is trapped in the birth canal, or the mother is hemorrhaging, her family typically summons a traditional birth attendant, whose medical artillery consists of herbal potions and prayer.

Late one afternoon, while the village nurse, a young man named Mohamed Malele, was preparing to go home for the day, a nomadic herdsman appeared at the dispensary pleading for help. The herdsman's wife had just given birth, and she was bleeding badly. Please, asked the man, could Mohamed return with him to his homestead?

When Mohamed arrived at the *aqal,* the woman was lying on the ground, moaning and barely conscious. Her sarong was soaked through with blood. Two other women (neighbors? relatives?) crouched over her. The newborn baby was wrapped in a cotton sarong. A young girl, about ten years old, was feeding the infant camel's milk from a pink plastic cup.

By the time the men carried the woman to the dispensary in Dertu, it was dark. Someone held up a plastic flashlight while

Mohamed looked around for a dilator and a pair of clean latex gloves. Scattered on a utility cart were dirty tweezers, an open bottle of amoxicillin tablets, and an empty box of syringes. On the floor of the dispensary, a cardboard box was overflowing with soiled gloves and used needles.

Mohamed needed water. He tried the tap at the sink; nothing but air came out. He sent the herdsman to fetch water from the tank outside, but the on-and-off valve had been put somewhere for safekeeping, in order to prevent people from stealing water, and now no one could find it. Holding a roll of gauze, Mohamed soaked up the woman's blood. Her placenta was not fully expelled, he concluded. He tried detaching it manually. Meanwhile, lying on the vinyl examining table, the woman kept drifting in and out of consciousness. The wind had picked up, and sand was blowing into the room through the open windows.

By morning, the woman was dead. Her family came to collect her. Hastily they buried her, then returned to their homestead deep in the bush. No one seemed especially startled by her death. In this place, life was a game of chance. One day you're sifting grain outside your *aqal,* and the next day you're dead. *Everything is written.*

In his monthly reports, e-mailed to the Millennium Villages' head office in New York, Ahmed listed his many accomplishments in Dertu. He was making progress, even if it wasn't at the pace he'd hoped for. At the dispensary, he had installed a generator just big enough to power a microscope (to diagnose malaria and tuberculosis). He'd purchased a propane refrigerator to store vaccines and antivenin. A small laboratory had been built, and Ahmed had hired a lab technician whose monthly salary of 25,000 Ksh ($350) was paid by the Millennium project. Novartis, the Swiss pharmaceutical company, donated Coartem, the newest and most effective antimalarial drug. Other essential medicines were being sent from New York and Nairobi. Once a month, for a day or two at a time, nurses came from Garissa to set up temporary open-air health clinics in the bush around Dertu. They immunized children, treated the sick, and educated pastoralists in basic health and nutrition.

At Dertu's primary school, Ahmed and his team enclosed the grounds with a tall fence to keep out warthogs and to protect the children from hyenas and jackals. They built a new classroom, installed a solar panel, and wired up two lightbulbs so the children could work after sundown. One of the Millennium project's core interventions called for Ahmed to establish a school-feeding program that provided the children with a free lunch of beans and *ugali,* a thick cornmeal porridge. The results were obvious and immediate: not only did the feeding program reduce malnutrition; it also encouraged parents to send their children to school. From fewer than 300 before Ahmed's arrival, the student population had now grown to 450.

To better serve nomadic families, Ahmed recruited an itinerant teacher: Abdullahi Bari Barow, the son of a nomadic herder, who had grown up not far from Dertu. In exchange for a camel and a monthly salary of 15,000 Ksh (about $200), Abdullahi moved with the pastoralists from place to place, wherever they set up camp. He would untie the blackboard from the back of his camel, establish his classroom under an acacia tree, and proceed to teach reading, writing, basic math, and basic English to 110 pupils (more or less) between the ages of three and twenty-eight.

For all his sound ideas, Ahmed was confined by his limited budget, which was strictly controlled from New York—with the result that Ahmed started writing letters to various NGOs, requesting money for this worthy project or that one. Pointing out that sleeping quarters would encourage nomadic herders to keep their children in school, he convinced UNICEF to build a dormitory. To provide emergency transportation from the bush to the dispensary, he asked the Danish International Development Agency to donate thirty two-wheeled donkey carts, whose passengers would include women with life-threatening birth complications (cord prolapses, hemorrhages, obstructed labor); children stung by scorpions; herders who'd been bitten by black mambas, spitting cobras, puff adders. A Swedish woman donated enough money to build a basic maternity ward in Dertu. CARE provided funding for an additional schoolteacher. USAID donated four beds to the health clinic. The UN's Food and Agricultural Organization gave $20,000 to plant a tree nursery.

Meanwhile, Ahmed was lobbying local government officials to grade and widen the dirt road between Garissa and Dertu. "Where the money will come from I don't know," Ahmed said cheerfully, "but I wrote a letter to the minister of roads requesting one million shillings to build us a good road!"

To gauge progress, the Millennium Villages Project used standard metrics, measuring such things as infant mortality, maternal deaths, fertility rates, malnutrition, access to safe water, improved sanitation, primary school attendance, and so forth. At Columbia University in New York, a team of experts worked full-time gathering and organizing these data as they came in from the villages. It was time-consuming work.

For one thing, the quantity of data was enormous: just to create a baseline against which improvements could be measured, the Millennium project had devised ten different household surveys, each with dozens of questions that had to be asked by fieldworkers. For example: Do you practice birth control? How many times have you been pregnant? Did you give birth with the help of a traditional birth attendant or a health professional? In the past year, has anyone in your household not had enough to eat? How often in the past year has someone in your household been treated for malaria? Do you own a mosquito net? Do you use fertilizer? Do you own a radio? Do you own livestock? Does anyone in your household attend school? Beyond the household surveys, researchers had compiled reams of demographic and medical data: blood and stool samples were tested for parasites; head and arm circumferences were measured to assess malnutrition. They had obtained birth and death records; on and on.

Back in New York, all the data collected in the field had to be analyzed and plugged into spreadsheets. Someone had to make sense of handwritten notes, compare inconsistent medical records, discard questionable results, and send back incomplete surveys. It took eighteen months just to sort through the first round of data, never mind the follow-up data that continuously came in from the villages.

For all that, Ahmed viewed the metrics with skepticism. In rural Africa, record keeping is generally sloppy. Besides, when questioned by outsiders, villagers don't necessarily tell the truth; sometimes they frame their answers to please the questioner. One villager, pregnant with her fifth child, freely admitted that she'd told a surveyor that she had two children. Why didn't she tell the truth? I asked her. "You are a *mzungu*," she said, using the Swahili word for a white man, "and we know that *mzungu* do not approve if we have many children."

Ahmed had his own way of evaluating the success of the Millennium Villages Project: he counted the number of corrugated tin roofs in Dertu. In Africa, tin roofs are a sign of material wealth—a "status symbol," he called them. One year into the project, by the summer of 2007, the number of tin-roofed structures in Dertu had climbed from six to about thirty. Soon they numbered nearly one hundred. Approaching Dertu, you could see them from at least a mile away, shining like beacons.

From the beginning, the goal of the Millennium Villages Project had been to support the pastoralists' traditional nomadic way of life and, at the same time, to provide basic health and education, ensure access to clean water and sanitation, improve the quality of livestock, and build roads linking people to markets. Encouraging nomads to become "pastoralist dropouts" (as they're known in academic circles) was no one's objective. Nevertheless, the money pouring in from the Millennium Villages Project encouraged more and more pastoralists to abandon their nomadic life and settle in and around Dertu. A growing number of residents were immigrants from other, poorer communities. "Modern life encourages sedentary life," remarked Ahmed.

Tin roof after tin roof, Dertu was turning into a village. Some people opened tea shops and simple restaurants. Others hawked batteries, flip-flops, and khat. Others sat around, waiting for handouts and the odd job from the Millennium project. With so much commercial activity in town, Abdi Hussein, Dertu's first shopkeeper, now complained that he suffered from too much competition.

Inside people's *aqals*, there were growing signs of material wealth: tin bowls, plastic cups, the odd bar of soap, hair oil, powdered milk, plastic sandals, even basic furniture. Abdullahi, the itinerant schoolteacher, built for his wife and newborn daughter a one-room "semipermanent" house made of mud and corrugated tin. A sheet of vinyl flooring had been placed over the sand. The room was dominated by a brown ultrasuede sofa that Abdullahi had bought in Garissa.

Madame Sofia Guhad, the school principal, was the proud owner of Dertu's first television set, a twelve-inch model bought in Nairobi for 25,000 Ksh, about $350 or a month's salary for her. One evening she asked me over to watch TV. Even before I entered the school compound, I could hear high-pitched sounds that turned out to be love songs performed by a Somali pop singer named Kaskey. Dressed in an orange tracksuit, he was surrounded by a wild pattern of red flames that darted here and there and spun around like a barber's pole. A festive crowd had gathered in front of the flickering TV screen outside; no one seemed bothered by the noise and fumes coming from Madame Sofia's secondhand diesel generator. The crowd laughed and clapped and sang along with Kaskey.

Darkness fell, and the generator coughed and ran out of fuel. Madame Sofia's guests headed home. Flashlights were turned on and off. I could hear a truck braking, a baby crying, and the musical ringtone of a cell phone. Someone was listening to Radio Mogadishu on shortwave. Sitting on a bench outside Sahlan's tea shop in the center of Dertu, men were chatting and drinking chai and chewing khat.

Inside, kneeling over an open fire, Sahlan was cooking *ugali*. Business was good; some days she served as many as fifty people, not all of them locals. Sahlan's husband (who lived with his other wife near the Dadaab refugee camps) no longer herded camels as he once had. Instead, he'd bought himself a *matatu* (a minibus) and now made a decent living driving people between Dertu and Dadaab. He had become more generous with Sahlan. And she in turn treated herself to a few indulgences, among them, a bottle of musk perfume. Her face was fuller than it had been. I noticed her new *hijab,* black with sparkling sequins.

Now that Dertu had begun to prosper, Sahlan dared to imagine a better future. Maybe everything wasn't written in stone after all. She envisioned sending her children to secondary school and living in a house with a tin roof. She'd buy herself a comfortable chair and a jar of face cream. Her children would support her in old age, sending remittances from their good jobs in the city. "There are many things that were with us before that are no longer," said Sahlan, referring to life in Dertu before the Millennium Villages Project. "There was insecurity, but now we are at peace, and when there is peace there is development. Our life was a nomadic one, but now we are settled. We have a school, we have a dispensary. Now we are dreaming of what more will come to us."

The most startling change in Dertu was the advent of mobile telephony. The village was so remote, so far off the grid, that mobile telephones represented a triumph of technology and of determination. At some point in 2007, Jeffrey Sachs persuaded his friend Carl-Henric Svanberg, the CEO of Ericsson, to donate his company's know-how and equipment to the Millennium Villages Project.

In response, and honoring its commitment to "corporate responsibility," Ericsson constructed a sixty-six-foot-high wind- and solar-powered cell tower in Dertu. The company then donated solar-powered cell phone chargers and gave out free handsets to six of the village elders. Meanwhile, responding to Sachs's goal of bringing Internet connectivity to rural Africa, Sony donated laptop computers to Dertu's primary school; a special modem would use the cell tower to connect the people of Dertu to the World Wide Web.

The day the network was launched, Svanberg and his wife arrived in Dertu by helicopter. "One of my strongest memories is from the day we launched the network in Dertu," he recalled when he retired as CEO of Ericsson. "Their chief, one of the camel drivers, came up to me and said, 'Today our village is reborn.'"

The dollar value of Ericsson's donation was around $250,000 (more if you reckon the cost of Ericsson's time), and its impact was immediate. Within a few months, at least one-quarter of the households in Dertu had put together enough money to buy cell phones. When solar-powered cell phone chargers proved to be slow and inefficient, one enterprising local bought a diesel generator, connected it to dozens of power strips, and charged a few shillings for each cell phone battery he recharged.

Sachs was right: it's remarkable how much can change in a

short time. Even Ahmed's far-fetched request to the minister of roads had been granted, and now, thanks to the freshly graded (though not yet paved) road between Garissa and Dertu, the sixty-mile drive took two hours instead of four. Whereas trucks had once bypassed Dertu on their way through North Eastern Province (the preferred route was via Habaswein), they were now driving through the center of town. As well, a regular bus service now passed through Dertu on the way from Garissa to Sharitabak. Sometimes at night, when cooler temperatures made driving more comfortable, so much traffic rumbled through town that it was hard to sleep. The truck drivers spent good money in Dertu, paying for food and lodging and also, it was rumored, for prostitutes.

"We have made a big gain," boasted Ahmed. "When I first arrived, our problems were the size of Mount Everest; now they are the size of Mount Kenya. When I came, Dertu was dark; now I see lights. When I came, the school had three hundred pupils; now we have seven hundred twenty-nine. When I came, there were six or seven tin roofs; now we have one hundred. I feel happier by far. If we continue, we will meet our goals."

Ahmed still measured progress by counting tin roofs; in addition, he now counted piles of garbage. Dertu had become a dump site, a sure sign of newfound prosperity. (In really poor rural places there's almost no trash: where no one buys toothpaste, there's no empty tube to throw away.) The ditches between people's *aqals* were filled with crushed boxes of McVitie's Ginger Nuts biscuits, mangled tubes of Close-Up toothpaste, bald rubber tires, chunks of molded Styrofoam, empty boxes of Sportsman cigarettes, torn flip-flops, broken Bic pens, tin cans, juice cartons, and polyurethane bags.

In response to the growing problem of litter, Ahmed established an official Garbage Committee. A meeting of the elders was called, and right away six or seven young men volunteered to be sanitation workers. Ahmed presented them with a check for 60,000 Ksh ($850) to purchase wheelbarrows, rakes, and other tools of the trade. I was asked to take a photo of the group. Standing in front of a thornbush, two members of the Garbage Committee are holding out Ahmed's check and smiling.

One morning three land surveyors appeared in Dertu—outsiders dispatched by the government of Kenya to create an official town plan. Blueprints in hand, tripods in place, they hammered rough wooden pegs into the sand, marked off official boundary lines, and made notes on their blueprints. They then proceeded to rope off big parcels of land: for a secondary school here, a hospital there, a church, a cemetery, and many mosques. There'd be playing fields, parking lots, bus stops, a well-stocked library, a community center, a botanical garden, and even, eventually, a university. The wilderness would be made like Eden.

For the most part, Ahmed was excited. Like tin roofs (or piles of garbage), the presence of land surveyors was a clear sign of progress. At the same time, the vision of a city rising from the desert made him anxious. Above all, he worried that he couldn't satisfy the community's unrealistic demands—demands that he, in his enthusiasm, had helped fuel.

In a twenty-page report sent to his bosses in New York, Ahmed wrote about "too much expectations from the Project" (what people expected from the Millennium Villages Project, that is). Those expectations included "construction of houses for all individuals in the village, a visit to the village by the UN Secretary General, and diversion of the River Tana to Dertu village for irrigation purposes."

The Millennium Villages Project aimed to teach self-sufficiency. At the same time, confusing matters, the people of Dertu had been dependent on international food aid since the great *lafaad* drought of the 1970s. Instead of using traditional coverings (woven-grass mats and hides), people in and around the village were now covering their *aqals* with plastic tarps from the UN Refugee Agency and with burlap grain bags stamped with the blue logo of the UN World Food Program. In the small commercial center of the village, empty tins of vegetable oil from USAID were hammered flat and made into doors.

Month after month, accustomed to the ritual by this time, people lined up for rations from the UN: a four-liter (one-gallon) tin of cooking oil, enriched porridge for the children, bags of rice and cornmeal. A good number of locals (no one knew how many) quietly maintained a second residence in one of the nearby Dadaab refugee camps, where they received additional food aid and essential goods—tarps, charcoal, blankets, and so on. Once a month, thanks to UNICEF's Cash Transfer for Orphans and Vulnerable Children program, between fifty and one hundred of Dertu's children (or their guardians) received 500 Ksh ($7) each.

"Our people have refugee syndrome," Ahmed said reflectively. "There are so many handouts here. Free food, free medications, free water, free education. And now we come in and talk to them about empowerment. Are you seeing the problem? The concept is very hard."

Chapter 7

It Will Be Sweet Like Honey

Ahmed kept a well-thumbed copy of *The End of Poverty* in his office and could recite certain passages from memory. "At the most basic level, the key to ending extreme poverty is to enable the poorest of the poor to get their foot on the ladder of development," Jeffrey Sachs had written. "The development ladder hovers overhead, and the poorest of the poor are stuck beneath it. They lack the minimum amount of capital necessary to get a foothold, and therefore need a boost up to the first rung."

With the Millennium project's core interventions in place (medical supplies, classrooms, pit latrines), the people of Dertu were no longer struggling just to stay alive. Arguably, they were on the first step of the development ladder. The next step, as Ahmed understood it, was to help them discover practical, creative ways to earn a living and escape the poverty trap. The whole purpose of foreign aid, he reminded his staff (quoting the Great Professor), was to "jump-start" the process of capital accumulation, economic growth, and household income. Sooner or later the money Dertu was receiving from the Millennium Villages Project would dry up. When that happened, how would the local population manage to sustain itself? What were the options? For all the progress Ahmed had made, there was no real economy in North Eastern Province—nothing that offered people long-term, stable employment.

"We have no water. We have no oil. We have no minerals. We have only animals," Ahmed said. "If you say to me, 'One day you will grow crops,' I will ask you, 'From where will you get water?' If you say to me, 'One day there will be industry,' I will ask you, 'From where will you get water?'"

For the past fifty years or so, ever since Kenya achieved independence, development experts have been confronted by a huge stumbling block: there isn't enough water or arable land in the country to meet the needs of its fast-growing population. In the arid North Eastern Province, where it hardly ever rains and rain-fed agriculture is out of the question, the only long-term solution is to divert water from the region's one dependable water source, the Tana, Kenya's longest river. From the fertile highlands of Mount Kenya, the Tana runs 440 miles, along the dry western fringe of North Eastern Province, toward Kenya's tropical coastline, and into the Indian Ocean.

Over the years, supported by massive amounts of foreign aid and goodwill, one failed irrigation project after another has attempted to supply North Eastern Province with water by diverting it from the Tana River. The village of Bura, about 120 miles south of Dertu, is the site of the most infamous irrigation project in Kenya.

Launched in 1977 by the World Bank, the Bura Irrigation Settlement Project proposed to "settle the landless, create employment, and contribute to foreign exchange earnings by producing cotton and food (maize)." The project would divert the Tana, build pumping stations, dig 34 miles of canals, create water distribution and drainage systems, and clear and level 16,500 acres of barren land.

The Bura project represented far more than a simple irrigation scheme; it was an "integrated rural development project"—a popular approach to development in the 1970s and early 1980s, whereby all the root causes of poverty were to be eradicated at one time. Plans for Bura included building a commercial center and twenty-three surrounding villages, all from scratch. Roads, houses, and latrines were constructed, along with six primary schools, a secondary school, a health center, a police station, a telephone repeater station, and a clubhouse with a swimming pool. Approximately 65,000 of North Eastern Province's poorest inhabitants were to be moved from their mud huts and *aqals* and resettled in Bura.

So ambitious was the Bura project that by the early 1980s it was swallowing up fully one-quarter of Kenya's total public investment in agriculture. You can probably guess what followed. An internal report from the World Bank, published in 1990, devotes forty single-spaced pages to the folly. One undertaking or another was "doomed," "inappropriate," "erroneous," "problematic," "inadequate." We read about "cost escalation," "lack of technical knowledge," "managerial difficulties," "frequent breakdowns," "lack of financial viability," and "poor performance."

Even if you overlook charges of incompetence, the Bura project was ill-fated from the start. It didn't make economic sense. No matter how many thousands of gallons of water the Bura project managed to divert from the Tana, agricultural yields in North Eastern Province could never justify the cost of irrigation. By the time the Bura project was officially abandoned in 1987, more than $100 million had been wasted. Adjusted for inflation, that's approximately $200 million today.

To Ahmed, the failure of the Bura Irrigation Settlement Project confirmed the obvious: "Pastoralism is the only real future for us—all other paths are doomed to fail."

In his view, the only long-term solution to the problems of North Eastern Province was to accept its natural order, its traditional way of life, and make the region self-sustaining. He wanted to preserve Dertu's nomadic pastoralist economy. At the same time, the economy would diversify into related areas such as leather tanning, livestock trading, and large-scale milk production. In turn, economic diversification would link Dertu to the regional and even the global economy.

Slowly, encouraged by the Millennium Villages' office in New York, Ahmed put his plan into action. His top priority was to establish a livestock market in Dertu. As it was, pastoralists who wanted to sell their animals had only two options:

1. They could sell their animals to one of the few ambitious, hard-nosed traders who ventured upcountry; in which case, they might receive half of what they'd get in Garissa.
2. They and their livestock (camels, cows, goats, donkeys) could undertake the sixty-mile trek from Dertu to the weekly livestock auction in Garissa. On their way they might be robbed at gunpoint by cattle raiders. Once they arrived, they would be exploited by *dilal,* middlemen who knew very well that anyone who'd walked from Dertu was unlikely to return home empty-handed, no matter how little he received for his livestock.

One way or the other, invariably, pastoralists were shortchanged. Dertu was at the bottom of the market chain, and bush traders and *dilal* were voracious bottom-feeders. A goat might sell in Dertu for 1,200 Ksh ($15), be resold in Garissa for 2,000 Ksh, and be sold again to a slaughterhouse in Nairobi for 4,000 Ksh. Camel milk fetched twice as much in Garissa as it did in Dertu. Not surprisingly, the big money was made by those who were rich enough to own trucks or livestock trailers: the average *dilal* in Garissa made between 15,000 and 20,000 Ksh (between $185 and $250) on a single market day. To put things in perspective, that was more or less what people in Dertu earned in an entire year.

Sachs railed at that sort of market inefficiency. The farther away a herdsman lived from a market, the more likely it was he'd be exploited. In theory, the problem shouldn't have been hard to solve. With better roads, pastoralists living in the hinterlands would have better access to markets. As soon as people had cell phones, they'd inform themselves of current market prices before leaving Dertu for Garissa; they could also arrange the sale of their animals ahead of time. The best solution of all, Ahmed argued, would be to bring the livestock market to Dertu.

Setting aside a huge parcel of land not far from the water hole, Ahmed invested months of work, and tens of thousands of dollars, to establishing Dertu's livestock market. More than one million Ksh ($12,000) was spent on fencing—on holding pens for camels, cattle, goats, sheep, and donkeys, for example. There were weighing stations, an auction stand, water troughs, and racks to hold branding irons. In order to channel water from the watering hole to the market, a distance of about one mile, Ahmed hired a crew of laborers to dig trenches. Each worker was paid a day rate of 300 Ksh ($3.50). Technical experts sent to Dertu by Kenya's Ministry of Water and Irrigation installed and connected high-quality PVC pipes to an immense 24,000-liter (6,340-gallon) water tank. The entire venture was underwritten by the Millennium Villages Project.

One section of the livestock market would be given over to commercial stalls. As envisioned by Ahmed, the stalls would sell tea, snacks, animal feed, veterinary medicines, and gasoline to traders who'd arrive in Dertu from across the Horn of Africa. Eventually, if things went as planned, Dertu would have a slaughterhouse and a tannery. Paved roads would fan out in all directions, like interstate highways.

"The travelers will come with vehicles," Ahmed said, "and they will need a garage and fuel and somewhere to rest. The livestock market will be our milking cow. It will be our engine. It will be sweet like honey."

*   *   *

The Millennium Villages Project Livestock Market opened officially on Jeffrey Sachs's first visit to Dertu in the summer of 2007. Together with his wife, Sonia, Sachs made his way from Garissa in a convoy of heavily armored UN vehicles, tinted windows rolled up tight, air-conditioning set to high. The entire village turned out to mark the occasion; hundreds of people assembled in the midday sun, waiting for the arrival of Sachs and his party. A dozen or so regional government officials in well-polished shoes were seated in a row of plastic chairs beneath a sagging blue-and-white-striped tent that, at every moment, threatened to collapse.

"Thank you for having us in Dertu today," Sachs began, addressing the expectant crowd. "We are so grateful to be here." Draped over his left shoulder was a red-and-white-checked kaffiyeh, a gift from the village elders. The welcoming committee presented him with a traditional wooden staff. A *macawis* (Somali sarong) was tied around his waist. Someone took photographs. A group of local men performed a Somali dance, and Sachs joined in, hopping from one foot to the other and clapping and smiling.

It was time for speeches. "We went to see the school—what a wonderful school," he enthused. "We went to see the clinic. And we went to see the new Millennium livestock market. People will come from many, many kilometers away to your market! It will be the most important market in the region!"

The crowd roared with pleasure and appreciation. Women sprang to their feet and began ululating. He continued, "Dertu will become the center of the economy in the region!"

I'd heard Sachs give several versions of that speech in various African villages. And yet in Dertu he was just as enthusiastic, as convincing, as ever. Like other charismatic speakers, he never fails to inspire. "A few days ago, in New York, I told the secretary-general of the United Nations, Secretary-General Ban Ki-moon, that I was coming to Dertu, and he said to send his good wishes to all of you," he told the crowd. "And yesterday, when I arrived in Nairobi, I spoke to Kofi Annan, the former secretary-general, and I told Mr. Annan that we were coming to Dertu, and he also sends good wishes to all of you."

At the mention of the Ghana-born Kofi Annan, the crowd went wild.

"This is very good for Dertu," Sachs went on, his voice louder so he'd be heard above the thrashing tent flaps. The wind had picked up. The tent was swaying. "Two secretary-generals saying hello to you! Now I will go back to tell them all of the wonderful things you are doing here! I will tell them how much progress Dertu is making!

"Every time you take a step forward, we will be with you to help! As fast as you go, we'll run along with you! We will help build more classrooms. We will build more dormitories. We will make sure all the children have a meal at school. And when more children go to school, we will help build a secondary school. So I want to ask the children: Do you like being in school?"

Haa! Haa! Haa! Yes! Yes! Yes!

"We will help get a maternity ward at the clinic. And with all the wind you have here, we can turn that wind into electricity, and Dertu can provide power to everyone."

Haa! Haa! Haa!

"We will come back again to see all the progress you are making. We will always have Dertu in our hearts." With that, Sachs and his party climbed into their air-conditioned SUVs, waved goodbye, and left.

From Dertu, Sachs's procession headed back to Garissa, where he was scheduled to meet Kiritu Wamae, the district commissioner for North Eastern Province. It had been a long day. Sachs looked hot and dusty. His hair was pasted to his head. His khakis and button-down shirt were badly wrinkled. Despite the oppressive heat, the district commissioner was wearing a dark suit and tie, and the overhead fan in his office was idle. On his desk, like a relic from the Brezhnev era, was a bank of four push-button telephones.

"You have to think how you want Garissa to look ten years from now," Sachs told the district commissioner. "Perhaps you'd like to be a major center for livestock trading. This is already a regional livestock center, I realize—but have you considered what it would take to be a *highly productive* livestock center? You could market camel milk—not just out of jerry cans, but in bulk, with pasteurization plants. What about a meat-packaging plant with refrigeration? What other areas are there for cash earnings? I believe that for the communities along the Tana River, we can get donors to provide investments to create irrigation systems."

Transforming the lives of people in a remote village was important, but it wasn't enough. What mattered to Sachs was taking his project to scale. One day, viewed from space, the African continent would be one vast Millennium village. Of course it would take time, but in the interim, what Sachs feared most was the loss of momentum. "It's like an airplane," he once said, referring to the Millennium Villages Project. "If the climb rate's not high enough, you'll never take off."

Sachs's project had to expand quickly. He hoped to have as many as one thousand Millennium villages by 2009; for the time being, however, it was important that the project expand beyond individual villages, first to surrounding villages, then to entire districts or provinces. The reason he was meeting with the district commissioner was to convince him to turn all of North Eastern Province into one huge Millennium district with Garissa at its core.

"I want you to dream a little bit," Sachs said. "What would

a model district look like? Once you have the answer to that, then together we can figure out how to get there from here. We need financing from the government and donors and also from private investors—but to get those investors we need a plan to sell them. This is a sales job."

Encouraged by Sachs's optimism, Kiritu Wamae had several ideas. Camel milk could be pasteurized; camel hooves could be made into buttons; and camel bones could be ground into animal feed. "We have a lot of gypsum, so also making cement is a possibility," the commissioner informed Sachs. "Myrrh could be used for perfumes and medicines. And agro-processing: along the Tana, there is potential to irrigate twenty-four thousand acres, but only two thousand acres are now irrigated."

"What's the chance of getting investors from the United Arab Emirates?" asked Sachs.

"Well, the Emirates are not investing here, but they are in Somaliland," answered the district commissioner, referring to the breakaway state in northern Somalia.

"Somaliland!" Sachs laughed in disbelief. "They're investing in Somaliland but not here? You should be able to compete against Somaliland—you actually have a country!"

Sachs had other good ideas. "Maybe you need a paradigm shift," he said. "Maybe you need to find out what the market needs and produce for that. Maybe, instead of looking to sell overseas, in Europe or the Middle East where the health barriers are high, you should find ways to sell to other parts of Africa. It's a big market. The better ideas we have, the more funds we can raise."

"We have not marketed North Eastern Province properly," conceded the district commissioner. "We need to market so people know that North Eastern is not a security threat for investors."

"I think we need to create an investor roundtable here—I'd like to try to attract foreign investors to Garissa. If you hosted an investor roundtable, I could bring people here. Could you do that?"

"Please."

"What about tourism?" asked Sachs. "You know, camel safaris for people who want to learn about Somali culture."

Pasteurization plants, camel safaris, and money pouring in from the Emirates: for Sachs, no idea was too far-fetched. He's never cynical. On the contrary, what drives him is an absolute conviction that the world can be changed for the better.

The district commissioner nodded happily in agreement. "The hirola antelope is endangered and is found only in North Eastern Province," he observed. "We have giraffes and lions. It would be possible to have tourism. There are ostriches. When it is winter [in Europe], people can come and enjoy our animals and our weather."

"That's wonderful!" enthused Sachs, standing up. "Here's my card. E-mail me anytime with ideas. And let's get that investor roundtable on the calendar, okay?"

Part Three

It just blows my mind how little money has been spent on malaria research. What has prevented the rich world from attempting this? I just keep asking myself, Do we really not care because it doesn't affect us? Is that what it is?

—Bill Gates

Chapter 8

A Pipe Dream

Jeffrey Sachs likes to say that malaria represents the great divide between rich and poor. Illustrating the point to his students, he superimposes two color-coded maps: a map of the world's poorest countries, and a map of countries with the highest burden of malaria. With few exceptions, the colored zones on both maps are nearly identical. The poorer a country, the more likely it is that its people will suffer from malaria.

In an academic article published in 2001, "The Economic Burden of Malaria," Sachs and a colleague used cross-country regression analysis to show that even if you control for all sorts of other factors (economic policy, geography, life expectancy, initial poverty levels), countries with high rates of malaria grow substantially more slowly than do countries without malaria. There's a corollary to this conclusion: as soon as a country has malaria under control, its rate of economic growth starts to increase.

It's obvious, when you think about it, that a nation's pro-ductivity and wealth can be sapped by malaria. The Italian government concluded as much a century ago. "Fever destroys the capacity to work, annihilates energy, and renders a people sluggish and indifferent," a prefect for the Sicilian province of Girgenti wrote in 1908. "Malaria shackles the development of industry and agriculture."

In the West, an all-out offensive against malaria-transmitting mosquitoes got under way in the early part of the twentieth century. To destroy their breeding grounds, government agencies started from the bottom up, draining swamps, wetlands, bogs, and marshes—anywhere that stagnant water accumulated. They dug canals and trenches and made certain that screens were installed on windows and doors. They distributed massive quantities of quinine, an antimalarial drug made from the bark of the cinchona tree, and of chloroquine, quinine's synthetic substitute.

By the 1950s, malaria had been eradicated in the United States and most of Europe. In poorer countries it was brought under control in the 1960s, thanks to the chemical compound dichloro-diphenyl-trichloroethane, the insecticide better known as DDT. Between 1955 and 1969, the World Health Organization's Global Malaria Eradication Program, underwritten with billions of dollars from the United States, established hundreds of DDT training centers in infected areas, distributed hundreds of tons of DDT, and sprayed and fogged millions of homes, inside and out. The program was a triumph. In India, for example, where malaria had killed 800,000 people a year, fatalities by the 1960s dropped to zero.

Following the publication of Rachel Carson's widely influential book *Silent Spring* in 1962, however, DDT became suspect. It was poisoning the environment. The death of birds, of animals, and possibly of human beings could be traced to the widespread use of the pesticide. In 1963 the United States stopped funding the Global Malaria Eradication Program. Research grants dried up. Finally, in the 1970s, DDT was officially banned in the United States and most of Europe.

Meanwhile, the malarial parasite had developed a resistance to DDT, and also to the antimalarial drug chloroquine; in self-defense, it mutated into an even deadlier species. In some countries where malaria had been more or less eliminated—Sri Lanka, for example—the disease resurfaced. In sub-Saharan Africa, a region that had been bypassed by the Global Malaria

Eradication Program, malaria continued to claim millions of lives every year. The hopeful goal of eradicating malaria world-wide was nothing more than a pipe dream.

"All you have to do is fly over the Amazon basin or go up the rivers of Surinam," an epidemiologist told *The New York Times* in 1966. "How are you going to find the people to treat? There are 20,000 aborigines in Malaya. They live in lean-tos. They're here one day; the next day they're gone. Now how in hell are you going to eradicate malaria in people you can't even find?"

By the early 2000s, malaria prevention was once again a fashionable humanitarian cause. Among its most ardent supporters were Bill Gates and his wife, Melinda, whose foundation has since then spent hundreds of millions of dollars to support medical research on malaria.

"It just blows my mind how little money has been spent on malaria research," Gates told a reporter in 2005. "What has prevented the rich world from attempting this? I just keep asking myself, Do we really not care because it doesn't affect us? Is that what it is?"

That same year, in a speech given at the World Economic Forum, in Davos, Switzerland, the president of Tanzania informed his listeners that countless Tanzanian children were dying of malaria. Suddenly the actress Sharon Stone stood up, reached for a microphone, and raising a clenched fist in a sign of solidarity, called on the audience to support the cause. "Just stand up! Just stand up!" she cried, tears welling in her eyes. "People are dying in his country today, and that is not okay with me."

In a single decade, between 1997 and 2007, thanks in no small part to the Gates Foundation, global funding for malaria control soared, from almost nothing to nearly $800 million. No one was naïve enough to claim that malaria could be "eradicated"—the goal now was to "control" and "prevent" the spread of the disease. Roll Back Malaria, a new global partnership started by the World Health Organization (together with UNICEF and the World Bank), aimed to cut deaths from malaria in half by 2010. Thanks to the new insecticide-treated mosquito net developed by Sumitomo Chemical, there was good reason to believe that the timeline was realistic.

In contrast to older mosquito nets, bed nets treated with insecticide kill mosquitoes on contact. Study after study has shown their effectiveness: the distinguished Swiss parasitologist Christian Lengeler, one of the world's leading experts on malaria control, has predicted that the number of malaria cases worldwide will drop by half once insecticide-treated bed nets are used by 80 percent of Africa's population.

In more practical terms: distributing millions of mosquito nets to Africa's rural poor is a complicated business. Imagine the logistics of packing, unpacking, sorting, and transporting enormously heavy sacks of bed nets to communities with no paved roads or no roads at all. (Lengeler reckons that the task of moving one million bed nets from one place to another is equivalent to the manual labor of two thousand men, each one pulling a fully loaded cart.) As well, there's the very real problem of looting: safeguarding the mosquito nets requires precise record keeping and oversight, especially in the most remote rural districts. Warehouses have to be guarded. And someone has to teach a largely illiterate population to use the nets correctly.

Even if you ignore that catalog of obstacles, there's the matter of cost. In 2007 some African shops were selling insecticide-treated bed nets for around five dollars apiece. Can anyone living on a dollar a day afford to buy a five-dollar bed net?

To Sachs, the answer to that question is obvious: you cannot expect poor Africans to pay for mosquito nets, just as you can't expect them to pay for polio or smallpox vaccinations or antiretroviral drugs. In his Millennium villages, every household was already receiving insecticide-treated bed nets free of charge. With enough determination (and military precision), he argued, free bed nets could be distributed to every African in need. Refusing to donate bed nets to poor Africans is "unethical," he added; it is "one of the shocking crimes of our time."

But where would the money come from? Who was prepared to underwrite the cost of distributing 300 million bed nets in Africa? Those sorts of questions enraged Sachs: "The amounts of money we're talking about are *insignificant*. I can't tell you how small this is. I've got neighbors down the block from me in Manhattan who could do this without skipping a beat. Do you know what the Christmas bonus was on Wall Street this year? *Twenty-four billion dollars!* Do you know how much that is? That's four billion bed nets."

Repeatedly he'd point out to anyone who would listen that the cost of preventing malaria in Africa was equal to just "one Starbucks coffee a year" for every person in the rich world. On other occasions, he'd weigh the "truly tiny" cost of 300 million mosquito nets against America's colossal military budget: "One day's Pentagon spending could cover every sleeping site in Africa for five years with antimalaria bed nets."

In the summer of 2007, Sachs headed to Tanzania's biggest city, Dar es Salaam, to meet a group of influential foreign aid donors. His goal was to convince them to underwrite and distribute millions of mosquito nets in Tanzania, a country on the front line in the battle to prevent malaria. Every year epidemiologists count 250 million cases of malaria worldwide;

85 percent are in Africa, most of them in just five sub-Saharan countries, including Tanzania.

The big foreign aid donors had spent years developing a program to control malaria in Tanzania. It was a textbook case of what's known in the trade as a "market approach to development." Starting from the ground up, the donors had created a market for insecticidal bed nets. First they'd encouraged private manufacturers to convert failing textile factories into bed net factories. Then they helped six thousand shopkeepers and street vendors get into the business of selling bed nets. Finally they established a voucher program to subsidize bed nets, so that even the poorest Tanzanians could buy one for $1.50 or so, a fraction of the retail price.

There's more: donors had to make sure that the treated mosquito nets were being used properly. Sometimes people hoard nets and then barter or sell them. Sometimes they use them to catch fish or to protect goats from mosquitoes. It may seem strange to outsiders that people at high risk of malaria have to be persuaded to use a simple, inexpensive device that may one day save their life. Then again, some people may not care deeply about a mosquito bite that may or may not kill them. In much of sub-Saharan Africa, just finding water to get through the day is enough to worry about without fetishizing mosquito nets. In her book *The Fever,* Sonia Shah argues that many Africans don't take malaria all that seriously—they're resigned to it. She compares a rural African's view of malaria to the Western view of the common cold: an inconvenient but inevitable part of everyday life.

To convey the mortal dangers of malaria and to promote the use of bed nets, foreign aid donors in Tanzania spent years and millions of dollars on "social marketing": handing out pamphlets, putting up posters in health clinics and schools, hiring theater troupes, and plastering the country with billboards. *Zinduka! Malaria Haikubaliki!*—Swahili for "Wake Up! Malaria Is Unacceptable!"—was one popular slogan.

And yet by 2007, despite the donors' best efforts, no more than a third of Tanzania's households owned long-lasting insecticidal bed nets. Even fewer people were actually using them. The reason Tanzanians weren't using bed nets, Sachs assured the donors, was the prohibitive cost; even at the subsidized price of $1.50, the nets were far too expensive for poor Africans.

For Sachs, the market approach to development was wrongheaded: it was "simplistic free-market ideology." "Malaria is not a market," he informed the group of foreign aid donors in Tanzania. "It's a pandemic disease and a killer. We're not selling Buicks here—we're trying to keep people alive!"

In his model Millennium villages, Sachs had witnessed at first hand the dramatic effect of handing out free beds nets: it stopped malaria in its tracks. He was sure that similar results could be achieved in Tanzania. The entire country could be covered with 15 million bed nets; at five dollars apiece, that would cost no more than $75 million. Taking into account the expense of setting up and implementing and following through on a program to distribute millions of bed nets all over the country, the cost to donors would be no higher than $200 million.

From the donors' point of view, however, distributing hundreds of millions of bed nets to Africans for free would undermine self-reliance and create a "culture of dependency." It was a "hand out instead of a hand up." The program was unsustainable. "Giving away free bed nets is not development—it's charity," Julie McLaughlin, the World Bank's lead health specialist for Africa, assured me.

In any case, where would the $200 million come from? "If you ask any of us if bed nets should be free, most of us would say, 'Yes, absolutely,'" McLaughlin went on. "Health care should be free too. But there are choices to be made, and you'd think a macroeconomist like Jeff Sachs would know that." Then, for good measure, she added: "Jeff's a televangelist, which seems to go over with some people, but I don't find him all that articulate or charming. And I don't want to be lectured to."

In the weeks leading up to his arrival in Tanzania, a flurry of e-mails sped back and forth between Sachs and the donors. The whole exchange was leaked to me. I counted fifty-nine e-mails, each one longer and more hostile than the one before.

Momentum built up until, at one point, so many people were being cc'd that at least fifty names appeared in the address field, including the regional or local representatives for all the big national development agencies (USAID, DFID, Irish Aid, Denmark's DANIDA, Switzerland's SDC, Germany's GIZ, etc.); global health organizations (WHO, the Centers for Disease Control, the President's Malaria Initiative, Roll Back Malaria, Population Services International); UN agencies (UNICEF, UNDP, UNFPA); multilateral agencies (the World Bank, the Global Fund, the African Development Bank); and major foundations (the Bill and Melinda Gates Foundation, the Clinton Foundation).

The donors regarded Sachs as an intruder; that became obvious to me. They didn't like his ideas and they didn't like his attitude and they didn't like him. A representative for Germany's GIZ (Deutsche Gesellschaft für Internationale Zusammenarbeit) went so far as to accuse "Sacks" (*sic*) of "harassment": "With due respect to his renown[ed] reputation as [an] economist, I myself am a Senior Public Health specialist with 34 years of experience in Africa, and I believe [I am] entitled not to be treated like a young boy."

For his part, Sachs was outraged that the donors refused to admit that their market approach to malaria was unworkable. In his e-mails he described it variously as "profoundly flawed," "misguided," "ill-advised," "ineffective," "inexcusable," "completely ill-informed," "not acceptable," "outdated," "mind-boggling," and "shameful."

The parasitologist Christian Lengeler took the lead in defending the donors. Point by point, his e-mails presented a case for retaining the status quo in Tanzania. Yes, he acknowledged, fewer people were using bed nets than the donors had anticipated and planned for; nevertheless, real progress was being made. Moreover, giving away millions of free bed nets would destroy the private market that the donors had so carefully built up in Tanzania. Local factories would be shuttered. Retailers would go under. And then, in four or five years, when all those free bed nets had to be replaced, where would the money come from?

"A mass net distribution on its own is not the best solution at this point in Tanzania," Lengeler concluded. "On a final note," he added, addressing Sachs directly, "I am not a policy maker and it is not my call to make decisions for the country. And neither is it yours."

"Frankly," Sachs informed Lengeler, in yet another mass e-mail, "I find your approach disreputable as well as economically ignorant." International donors handed out free antiretroviral drugs to HIV/AIDS patients in Africa; why on earth wouldn't they hand out free bed nets?

Sachs didn't stop there: "One day's Pentagon spending would provide for five years of comprehensive coverage for all of Africa. And you are worried about 'sustainability'??!," he wrote. "Get over it. You have everything upside down. The only true lack of sustainability is the millions of lives being lost in Africa as you dribble out bed nets in this ridiculous social marketing campaign."

Chapter 9

Complacency and Fear

On Thursday, July 19, Sachs boarded his flight from Zurich to Dar es Salaam, where he would have forty-eight hours to make his case, in person, to the donors. Even before boarding the plane, he was agitated. At the gate he paced back and forth, like a caged animal. "Yah? Well, he's a punk!" he yelled into his BlackBerry, referring to Lengeler. "He can go to hell!"

Ten hours later, standing in the aisle of the business-class cabin, waiting to disembark, Sachs was at it again: "These deaths are on your hands!" he shouted at a fellow passenger. It was Lengeler.

Lengeler was surprisingly calm. "You are stubborn," he replied with a French accent.

"No!" insisted Sachs. "You're the one who is stubborn—and people's lives are in your hands."

"You do not know the facts," said Lengeler wearily.

"What I know is you're letting people die!" Sachs went on in a rage.

"I do not need to be insulted," said Lengeler.

Sachs wouldn't let up. Passengers were trying to squeeze by him.

His wife, Sonia, intervened. "Come on," she said urgently, taking his arm. "Let's go."

Sachs shook her off. He was red in the face and his hair was disheveled. Lengeler turned his back and walked away.

"Your actions are reprehensible!" Sachs yelled after him, getting in the last word. "I hope you know that!"

VIP Security Detail rushed Sachs out of the Julius Nyerere International Airport and into a black Mercedes (license plate STATECAR 10) with pale blue curtains and two small flags fluttering on its polished hood. Traffic going into the city was backed up for miles. Maybe it was rush hour or there'd been an accident. Looking out the tinted windows of the Mercedes, Sachs could see mopeds and rickshaws and rusted Toyotas and a packed *dala-dala* bus with JESUS LOVES YOU painted across the back. Pedestrians were threading their way around the stalled vehicles, followed by a line of schoolchildren dressed in bright pink uniforms. The air was heavy with exhaust fumes.

Flanked by three military police escorts on motorcycles, STATECAR 10 swerved into the oncoming lane and, with a screech of the tires, roared past the traffic jam, arriving a few minutes later at the Kilimanjaro Hotel Kempinski. The car door opened, and Sachs, ignoring the postcard view of the Indian Ocean, hurried up the red carpet and across the marble floor of the vast lobby barely in time for his first appointment: a meeting with John Murray McIntire, the World Bank's country director for Tanzania, Uganda, and Burundi.

"I know what I'm talking about here, Jim," said Sachs, not wasting a second on small talk. "There's no reason, not a reason in the world, not to cover more people with bed nets."

"Look," replied McIntire, "this government's getting five to six hundred million dollars from us. Two or three hundred million of that is untied budget support, plus more from the donors. So maybe in total there'll be five hundred million in untied budget support. They can spend that on anything they want."

"I'm talking about *advice* here, Jim," Sachs told him. "You have a responsibility to give the country good advice. The current recommendations are retrograde and completely indefensible. I'd like the World Bank to lead the discussion, not just go along with the donors. Christian Lengeler may be a good malariologist, but he's a bad economist. He can go to hell! I'm a good economist!"

McIntire leaned back in his chair casually and crossed his legs. He looked the way a World Bank director is supposed to look. Maybe it was the tasseled loafers. Or the fact that he was wearing a blue blazer with khakis, and a white dress shirt monogrammed on the cuff (JMM). "You need to calm down, Jeff," McIntire advised. "Everyone's committed to the same goal here."

"This is about life and death—that's why I get heated about it!" Sachs told him. "This is just outrageous, Jim!"

"It's John, not Jim."

"From an economic point of view, *John,* I think the whole thing is utterly preposterous."

"You're spending an hour with the president today," McIntire said, trying to wriggle off the hook. "If he wants to chart another course, he should just say, 'This is what we'd like to do.' He doesn't have to follow the donors' advice."

Every year Tanzania is sustained by more than $2 billion in foreign aid. Nearly 40 percent of the government's entire budget is underwritten by foreign aid. Without its international donors, the country would collapse in a heap. How likely was it that the president of Tanzania would disagree with the donors' advice about bed nets or anything else?

It was the great statesman Julius Nyerere, Tanzania's first president after independence, who noted the "neocolonial" relationship between his country and its donors. "The English have a proverb which says: 'He who pays the piper calls the tune,'" he wrote in his seminal Arusha Declaration of 1967, which outlined his vision for Tanzania. "How can we depend upon foreign governments and companies for the major part of our development without giving those governments and countries a great part of our freedom to act as we please? The truth is that we cannot." How independent can an impoverished country be?

Sachs moved on. "Your job—and I mean this only with respect," he said impatiently, "—is to advise this country, not to hunker down!"

"We're not hunkering down," McIntire objected.

"Lengeler is giving advice, and it's bad advice," Sachs insisted. "My advice is much better. And your advice would be too. I'd love nothing more than to have the World Bank lead on this issue. There's nothing mysterious about how to make great progress on malaria. All I want is for you to say that poor people will die unless we spend more! In the end it comes down to saying, 'Let's spend one day's Pentagon spending to cover all sleeping sites'!"

"We agree, Jeff," said McIntire. "It's not rocket science. But when people speak of restraint, they are not complicit in human suffering—they just recognize that the U.S. government would rather spend money on bombers."

"It's complacency," Sachs answered firmly. "The donors are just sitting in the comfort zone. This is how it's been for years: complacency and fear. I can't see any reason why the world can't get its shit together to cover three hundred million sleeping sites in Africa! It's less than a day of Pentagon spending! It's chicken feed!"

Leaving the Kilimanjaro Hotel Kempinski, Sachs moved on to the Swedish embassy, where he was scheduled to address a group of foreign aid donors. By the time he arrived, every seat in the room was taken, and more people kept walking in.

"I know we've had a lot of e-mail exchanges in the last few days," said Sachs agreeably. He'd calmed down since his meeting with McIntire. "But I'd like to speak briefly and more broadly today about how to achieve our goals in Tanzania."

There was nothing brief about Sachs's speech. There never is. Using his Millennium Villages Project as a case in point, he lectured the donors on ways to achieve the goal of ending poverty in Tanzania: Doubling or tripling agricultural outputs. Building a basic health care system. Providing universal primary education. Ensuring access to safe water. Generating electricity. Building roads. Constructing manufacturing centers. Establishing export markets. Attracting tourists. On and on he went, listing one intervention after another—interventions that would, in his opinion, "easily" lead to double-digit growth rates.

Finally Sachs came to the vexed subject of bed nets; that's what the donors had come to hear. "With mass distribution of bed nets we'll break transmission. . . . The economics are absolutely straightforward. . . . I've recommended mass distribution for five years now. . . . This is the lowest-hanging fruit on the planet. . . . This is something that should be done. So what's the problem?" he said. "This is about people's lives! This is urgent!"

Sachs's forehead was damp with perspiration. "Are there any questions?" he asked. Not one. "Any comments?" Nothing. Fifteen seconds, thirty seconds, one minute.

Finally, someone spoke. It was Pamela White, head of USAID for Tanzania. "I don't want to argue with you, Jeff," she said disdainfully, "because I don't want to be called ignorant or unprofessional. I have worked in Africa for thirty years. My colleagues combined have worked in the field for one hundred plus years. We don't like your tone. We don't like you preaching to us. We are not your students. We do not work for you."

The meeting was over. Sachs stood up, pulled his tattered JanSport backpack over one shoulder, and walked out of the Swedish embassy. It was a beautiful day in Dar es Salaam. A light breeze was coming off the Indian Ocean. He took a deep breath of the salt air. "Sometimes," he said to no one in particular, "I wonder why I need a Ph.D. for this."

It was time for Sachs's meeting with Jakaya Mrisho Kikwete, the president of Tanzania. As he approached State House, he quickened his pace. Anyone else might have been discouraged by now, but not Sachs—he knew what had to be done. Taking matters into his own hands, he would lobby the president of Tanzania directly.

"My basic belief, my very strong belief," he said to the president, "is that Tanzania is the best-placed country in all sub-Saharan Africa to make a great breakthrough right now—and I'd like to do whatever I can to help you."

"I appreciate that," the president said sincerely, leading Sachs through the Moorish archways of State House and into the formal drawing room.

"It seems to me, from many points of view, Mr. President," continued Sachs, "from governance, from the peace in the country, from the unity in the country, from the point of view of your resource base, your energy resources, your touristic resources, your agricultural resources, your seaport, your gateway to East Africa, your coastline—when I add it all up, it seems to me you've got all the makings of becoming Africa's first emerging market."

Kikwete settled into an oversize mahogany armchair fitted out with burgundy silk-taffeta pillows. He wore a well-cut khaki suit with fashionable Chelsea boots and a black shirt open at the collar. Behind him, standing at attention, were two guards in red ceremonial uniforms with gold tassels.

By most measures, his country is a wreck. Nothing really works. There are few roads and even fewer doctors. Electric power is always in short supply. People are wretchedly poor. The average annual income is $1,510 per person. Nearly nine in every ten Tanzanians live on less than two dollars a day.

Then again, progress is relative in Africa, and compared to its neighbors, Tanzania is a success. There was good reason for Sachs to be hopeful about the country's future. It's peaceful and not entirely corrupt—less corrupt than Russia, for example, or than its neighbors Kenya and Uganda. The economy, which had grown at an average of 6.7 percent between 2000 and 2006, was doing well: in 2007 it was expected to grow by 7 percent.

Sachs was well along in his presentation. "I was just in Kenya, and you know they gave out three point four million nets," he informed the president strategically, taking full advantage of Tanzania's long-standing rivalry with its northern neighbor. "Keep in mind, Mr. President, that in four years you've only gotten out as many nets as Kenya did in just two weeks. And in Kenya, they're now asking for the balance of the nets they need so they can go back, not just to cover children and pregnant mothers, but to cover every sleeping site in the country. This is what I'd like to happen in Tanzania."

"How did Kenya do it?" asked Kikwete. He was paying close attention.

"Kenya just asked the donors," answered Sachs, making it all sound effortless. "Kenya said, 'We want to do mass distribution. We want to give them out.' And the donors said 'Fine.' They just said, 'Fine.' So all you have to do is say you want to do it here."

"Really?"

"Really," replied Sachs. "We had meetings today with the various development partners, and after a lot of e-mails in the last couple of weeks, they're now all saying, 'Whatever the government wants to do, we're ready.'"

"Are they really?" repeated Kikwete.

"Well, no one publicly said, 'We oppose this,'" Sachs hedged, not wanting to stretch the truth to its limit. "They don't dare. All you have to do is ask for the nets. That's my guess. Now, it may be in the end, you know, disaster could strike, and in the end they turn you down. I don't deny the possibility."

"So how do we do it?"

"If it concurs with you," said Sachs, "I think all that's needed is a clear statement that says the government of Tanzania would like to move to a mass distribution based on the principle that each sleeping site in a malaria-transmission region should be protected by a long-lasting insecticide net—and that you would like to work with the development partners, the donors, to facilitate this approach on an expedited basis. That to me would be the start, just that statement."

"Are you sure?"

"Absolutely," Sachs assured the president. "It's common sense. The donors know, scientifically, that they can't justify their position."

"Well, common sense is not the issue," said Kikwete, smiling. "It's subjectivism."

Kikwete is no fool. He may depend on the donors for foreign aid, but he also knows how the game is played. He's intelligent, charismatic, and enormously popular. (He was elected president in 2005 with 80 percent of the vote.) His English is flawless. After graduating with a degree in economics from the University of Dar es Salaam and rising to the rank of lieutenant colonel in Tanzania's military, he spent a decade as the country's minister of foreign affairs. As president, he continues to woo foreign investors and donors by embracing free-market capitalism.

Kikwete has not only received a lot of foreign aid, but he's received it in the form of "untied" or "direct" budget support. Untied support is a sign of the donors' trust in him; instead of funding specific one-off development projects in Tanzania, they're willing to contribute directly to the country's general budget. Officially, direct budget support is unconditional, no strings attached. In practice, though, as soon as Kikwete antagonizes his donors by spending their money in ways they don't approve of, they'll withdraw their direct support.

"Won't they be angry?" Kikwete asked, referring to the donors. "The thing is, they have the money, and they decide what is best for us."

"Angry? What angry?" replied Sachs, in pretended disbelief. "You're going to end malaria! You'll make heroes out of them! Believe me, they're on a failed course right now. If you push through a mass distribution of nets, you'll make heroes out of them."

Kikwete laughed. He liked Jeffrey Sachs who, by hook or crook, wound up getting exactly what he wanted: insecticide-treated bed nets for all of Tanzania.

Less than one month after Sachs left Tanzania, the World Health Organization issued official guidelines calling for the mass distribution of "free or highly subsidized" insecticide-treated mosquito nets to all Africans at risk for malaria. Everyone in the business was convinced that Sachs was behind the move. He probably was.

Next came a major announcement by UN secretary-general Ban Ki-moon calling on member states to embrace the "bold but achievable" goal of providing universal coverage of mosquito nets across Africa by the end of 2010. The same day Kikwete himself, in his role as chairman of the African Union, issued a press release: "On behalf of the people, leaders and governments of Africa, I welcome and support the Secretary General's call for action. Africa seeks—and actually deserves—

universal coverage of malaria control interventions, with access for all."

Not long afterwards a $200 million grant came through. Funded largely by the Global Fund and the President's Malaria Initiative, the grant would cover all of Tanzania with more than 18 million long-lasting insecticidal mosquito nets. Even Christian Lengeler was impressed. *Mind-boggling* is the word he used to describe the size of the grant. "None of us could have imagined that one country could get two hundred million dollars for a single intervention."

In 2008 Sachs's good friend the philanthropist Ray Chambers, cofounder of the advocacy group Malaria No More, was named the UN's Special Envoy for Malaria. His mission was to mobilize the funds and necessary tools to distribute a staggering 300 million bed nets across sub-Saharan Africa by the end of 2010, the stated objective being to end all deaths from malaria by 2015.

Let's say that universal coverage of bed nets *is* achieved, and that as a result, the rate of malaria transmission plummets. After four or five years, insecticidal long-lasting bed nets start to disintegrate. Unless they're replaced, transmission rates in Africa will start rising. How likely is it that in four or five years, Africans themselves will be able to afford new bed nets? Is it realistic to assume that, when the time comes, groups like Malaria No More or the Global Fund can summon up the resources and enthusiasm to roll out another campaign for universal coverage?

The more his ideas about universal coverage were challenged, the more short-tempered Sachs became. The endless back and forth, the equivocating, the calls for more studies and research and reports, the delays—that's precisely why nothing got done in the field of development! "Believe me," he snapped, "it's over. The debate is over. It's completely in the past. We're in the implementation stage now."

Part Four

I know that if you spend enough money on each person in a village, you will change their lives. If you put in enough resources—enough *mzungu*, foreigners, technical assistance, and money—lives change. I know that. . . . The problem is, when you walk away, what happens?

—Simon Bland

Chapter 10

David Siriri

Henry Morton Stanley referred to Uganda as the "pearl of Africa." Winston Churchill called it a "fairy tale": "Uganda is from end to end one beautiful garden, where the staple food of the people grows almost without labour, and where almost everything else can be grown better and easier than anywhere else," he rhapsodized in *My African Journey.*

> Cotton grows everywhere. Rubber, fibre, hemp, cinnamon, cocoa, coffee, tea, coca, vanilla, oranges, lemons, pineapples are natural or thrive in introduction. As for our English garden products, brought in contact with the surface of Uganda they simply give one wild bound of efflorescence or fruition and break their hearts for joy. Does it not sound a paradise on earth?

By the time of independence in 1962, any ambitious Ugandan wanted to get as far away as possible from the efflorescent land. In their eyes, there was nothing romantic about subsistence farming. With each generation, their *shambas,* their plots of land, had become smaller and less fertile, until people could barely grow enough food to stay alive. Now, instead of tilling the land, Ugandans wanted an African version of industrialized Europe. They wanted to wear a suit and tie and carry a fine leather briefcase.

David Siriri's parents belonged to Uganda's fast-growing,

post-independence middle class. They married in 1968; two years later, on December 14, 1970, their son David was born in the eastern town of Tororo, just a few miles from the Kenyan border. It was a time of hope: the country appeared to be at peace, the economy was one of the fastest growing in sub-Saharan Africa, and all across the nation young people were leaving the countryside to seek their fortunes in town.

Siriri's father was a mathematics teacher at the Kisoko Boys Primary School, just west of Tororo. His mother was a midwife at the local hospital. They weren't rich, but they could envision a promising future for their children. Everything in Uganda was better than it had been. Instead of the mud-and-thatched-grass huts they'd grown up in, Siriri's parents built themselves a three-bedroom "semipermanent" house with a tin roof. Siriri's father was his parents' only son; as a result, he inherited all twenty acres of his father's land, on which the Siriris now grew millet, sorghum, cassava, soybeans, sweet potatoes, kidney beans—more than enough to feed their eight children. As well, they cultivated cotton, a cash crop introduced to Uganda by the colonial government to supply Britain's textile industry.

Theirs was a "very strict Christian household," according to David Siriri. At the family's parish church, Siriri's mother was head of the Mothers' Union, an influential Anglican women's association devoted to upholding Christian values in the home and to teaching children the "habits of obedience, self-control, purity, and truth." David was an altar boy, so pious and hard-working that it was taken for granted that he would one day be ordained as a priest. The family gathered for prayers every evening, Sundays were devoted to churchgoing and prayer, and the children learned to read by using the Bible as a primer. Alcohol, cigarettes, and cursing were forbidden in the Siriri household. "We were instructed to always live our lives according to the fruit of the Spirit," Siriri said, referring to the nine attributes of a true Christian life as described by the apostle Paul: love, joy, peace, long-suffering, gentleness, goodness, faith, meekness, and temperance (Galatians 5:22–23).

When they were not in school or in church, the Siriri children tilled, weeded, and harvested the family farm. David and his brothers managed the ox-plow, with one boy driving the oxen and another steadying the plow. Cotton-harvesting season was especially intense: even the youngest children were needed to pick, clean, and sort the cotton. As they moved through the fields, trailed by long burlap sacks that weighed up to one hundred pounds when full, their hands bled from picking the thorny plants. If the children did not work hard enough, their father beat them with a stick.

It was only later that the Siriris realized that they'd been mistaken about the future. On January 25, 1971, exactly six weeks after David Siriri was born, Idi Amin staged a coup d'état, seizing power from the corrupt and oppressive Milton Obote, Uganda's first prime minister. Thousands of cheering Ugandans thronged the streets of Kampala to celebrate their new president and liberator. "I am not an ambitious man, personally," Idi Amin assured the people modestly. "I am just a soldier with a concern for my country and for my people."

Before long, Uganda was sliding into chaos. Idi Amin was not a liberator; he turned out to be a despot who ravaged the country. During his eight-year reign, his goons and death squads shot or bludgeoned to death an estimated 300,000 to 500,000 Ugandans. By the thousands their mutilated bodies were dumped into Lake Victoria. "Even Amin does not know how many people he has ordered to be executed," Uganda's health minister, Henry Kyemba, told the journalist Russell Miller when Kyemba defected to Britain in 1977. "The country is littered with bodies."

Any hope of prosperity evaporated when Amin ordered the immediate expulsion of all Ugandans of Asian descent, many of whose ancestors had been brought to Africa from India generations earlier, thanks to the British. In Amin's populist rhetoric, Uganda's Asians were "economic saboteurs," when in fact they had propelled the country's economic growth. Amin confiscated, nationalized, and ruined companies the Asians had built. Thereafter investors scrambled to get out of Uganda; exports of coffee, tea, and cotton dropped by more than half; and the economy came to a standstill.

Although Idi Amin was forced out of power in 1979, his absence did nothing to stop Uganda's decline. Instead, the country spiraled into a state of anarchy. In hindsight, it becomes clear that 1970, the year before Idi Amin came to power, had been Uganda's greatest moment of promise.

"My parents had been part of the post-independence professional rush," David Siriri told me. "But unfortunately things turned terribly bad. The period I remember as a child was a horrible one. The scarcity of things—you can hardly imagine! I can remember we had no sugar, no salt, no soap. There was no petrol in the whole country. I remember as a young boy lining up for a whole day to get half a kilo of sugar on the black market. And I remember the war near the end of Idi Amin's days in power. We had to abandon school because the soldiers were all over and they were looting our homes and stealing and killing people indiscriminately. It was a tormenting time."

To save themselves, the Siriri family fled their home and hid in the bush. In their absence, Idi Amin's soldiers ransacked the house, destroyed the farm, and stole the oxen. Afterwards Siriri's mother suffered a stroke. Her brain was damaged and the left side of her body was paralyzed. She was twenty-eight years old. "There was nothing we could do to help," recalls Siriri. "The doctor had abandoned our hospital, there was no medicine, and we couldn't move her to a bigger hospital because there was no petrol and it was too dangerous to move around the country." Left with nothing, the family turned to prayer. "Only by clinging to God could we get out of the terrible situation we were in," said Siriri.

Salvation came in the form of the Christian Children's Fund, an American charity that pioneered child "sponsorship" programs in Africa. Using heartrending footage of starving children, and starring the actress Sally Struthers (*All in the Family*), CCF's television commercials in the 1980s persuaded tens of thousands of Americans to donate seventy cents a day to "help change the life of a child forever."

One of those children was David Siriri. Sponsored by an American family who paid for his tuition and his lunch (a bowl of *posho,* or cornmeal porridge), Siriri returned to the local primary school. A few years later, in the national exam required for admission to secondary school, Siriri received the highest possible grade, outperforming every student in Pallisa District. Once again CCF came through with a sponsor willing to underwrite Siriri's secondary school education, in the town of Budaka.

Meanwhile, like most Ugandans, Siriri's parents were sinking into extreme poverty. His mother was too weak to work, and with the collapse of the Ugandan shilling, his father's salary was almost worthless. Unable to afford oxen or laborers, the family regressed to the most basic subsistence farming. At first, they made a bit of money by renting out their land. Then, acre by acre, they were forced to sell off their one asset.

Only by the grace of God, thought David Siriri, did he go on to university. At the time, there was just one university in Uganda—the esteemed Makerere University, established by the British in 1922 and free to anyone who could pass its entrance exam. The year Siriri applied, he was one of approximately 100,000 Ugandans competing for 2,000 spots. He'd long ago dropped the idea of becoming a priest; now he hoped to be a medical doctor. For one reason or another, however, on that Monday in the summer of 1991 when Makerere announced the results of its entrance exam, he found out that he'd been accepted at the School of Agricultural Sciences. So be it: it was a blessing, a sign from God.

At university, Siriri became his family's main income producer, living so frugally that he was able to send home practically all the money awarded to him for living expenses. By borrowing textbooks from friends, he freed up at least half his 100,000-shilling book allowance. On weekends, by hauling two-hundred-pound bags of corn on his bicycle, he earned another 30,000 to 50,000 shillings—money that paid his younger siblings' school fees.

On earning his B.Sc. in 1995, Siriri ranked first in a class of eighty-one agriculture students. He stayed on at Makerere University, completing a master's degree while working part-time at the World Agroforestry Center. The job paid $300 a month. "Boy, that was a lot of money for me!" Siriri later recalled. "I was living on the bare minimum. I used one hundred dollars to cover tuition for my brothers and sisters, and the rest I saved." Within a few years, he had saved enough to build a permanent house for his parents. He also bought himself a quarter-acre plot of land in a suburb of Kampala. It was his first hard asset.

In 2003 Siriri won a Commonwealth Scholarship to attend the University of Nottingham in the United Kingdom, where he would earn a Ph.D. in agroforestry. Married by that time, and the father of a two-year-old girl, Siriri now supported more people than ever. In Nottingham, he worked in a restaurant six nights a week, from six p.m. until midnight, earning enough money to allow him to send home much of the £750 monthly stipend that came with his scholarship.

Soon after being granted his Ph.D., Siriri was hired to launch the Millennium Villages Project in Ruhiira. What impressed him most was the project's deep pockets: $120 million to end poverty in a dozen villages! "I was used to organizations where you were always having to write proposals for more money," he said. "But in this case, the money was already in place— enough to last for five years! I'd never heard of that before."

What did concern Siriri was his job description; it was vague.

"I spent a week in Nairobi at an orientation workshop," he said. "The principles of the Millennium project were explained to us—the objectives, the template. They emphasized the holistic, integrated nature of the project. I understood that we were working on a hypothesis; that on a hundred and twenty dollars per person per year, you can get people out of poverty. But to be honest, the project was not well defined. The objectives of the project were clear—what was less clear was how to achieve those objectives."

Chapter 11

A Green Revolution

From the moment he arrived in Ruhiira in 2006, David Siriri recognized that the easiest way to increase household income was by cutting out as many *matoke* middlemen as possible. Every farmer in Ruhiira grows the green *matoke* banana, and traditionally those farmers sold their *matoke* to "banana boys"—enterprising traders who trekked far into the hills, climbing the steep footpaths that lead from one remote farm to another.

Sebuuma Sadati, age fifteen, was one of Ruhiira's many banana boys. Enrolled off and on at the local primary school, he hoped eventually to complete grade seven. In the meantime, he'd staked out his turf on one of Ruhiira's isolated hills, buying *matoke* from farmers at 3,500 to 4,000 shillings ($1.50 to $2) a stalk. Buying as much as he could carry, usually five stalks, Sadati would push his overloaded bicycle for twenty miles along the dirt road to a collection center in the town of Mbarara, where he resold his produce to brokers at a markup of 1,000 shillings a stalk.

You had to be strong to work this job, and you had to be able to protect your turf from competitors. Sometimes, to fend off other banana boys, Sadati pulled out his panga machete—but only as a theat. All things considered, it wasn't a bad job, and as far as Sadati could tell, the pay was good: for a full day's work, he could earn 5,000 shillings, or $2.50.

Sadati and his fellow banana boys were the first link in the *matoke* market chain; then, as *matoke* made its way north, from Mbarara to Kampala, four more middlemen got involved, each one taking a cut of the profits until finally, at grocery stores in Kampala, the *matoke* sold for 10,000 shillings a stalk. "A typical, inefficient exploitive market chain" is how Erastus Kibugu, country director for TechnoServe Uganda, described the disorderly sale of Ruhiira's *matoke* to me. "And the farmers are the most exploited of all."

Backed by TechnoServe, an American NGO whose slogan is "Business Solutions to Poverty," David Siriri encouraged individual *matoke* farmers to join cooperatives and sell their crop, in bulk, directly to buyers from Kampala. By carrying their *matoke* bunches to a central location in Ruhiira, and selling them to traders by the truckload, the farmers were now selling their *matoke* at an average of 8,000 shillings ($4) a bunch, twice what they earned by selling to banana boys. It helped too that Siriri had trained the farmers to increase the space between *matoke* plants—with more sunlight, *matoke* grown in Ruhiira was bigger and healthier than ever.

Almost overnight you could see the impact of higher earnings from *matoke*. In the village center, wedged between Newkars Tea House and Classic Saloon & Barbers ("All Hair Styles"), there was now a bar with a pool table. At 1,600 shillings, a bottle of Pilsner Lager was still a luxury for most villagers. But the local moonshine, a banana gin known as *waragi*, sold fast at 500 shillings (25 cents) a glass. No one seemed to mind that *waragi* is illegal in Uganda, or that thousands of Ugandans are poisoned each year by toxic *waragi*.

Siriri didn't approve of alcohol; he had never tasted beer, let alone hard liquor. Nevertheless, it was a sign of Ruhiira's increased prosperity that on almost any day of the week a dozen men or more could be found hanging around outside the bar, idly drinking *waragi* and shooting pool at 500 shillings a game. The bar's owner was earning as much as 6,000 shillings a day from pool games alone, all because of the villagers' increased earnings from *matoke*. He couldn't believe his luck, he told me, grinning widely.

Siriri too was pleased with the surge in earnings from *matoke*. As he was the first to acknowledge, however, *matoke* alone could never be profitable enough to support the people of Ruhiira. To actually end poverty—to make a decisive difference in household incomes—the people would have to diversify their crops. "Agriculture," Jeffrey Sachs told his staff in one of their meetings, "is the economic pillar of this whole project. Without gains in agricultural yields, nothing else can be accomplished."

As a Ph.D. student, Siriri had focused on ways to reduce soil erosion and improve yields. To regenerate leached soil, he'd proposed planting tree fallows (as opposed to natural fallows) and had conducted experiments to discover which species had the greatest impact on fertility. In Ruhiira, where the depleted soil had led to years of declining agricultural yields, Siriri set out to put his academic studies to good use.

In Ruhiira, farms were so small (officially, 0.32 acres per household) that the people could barely grow enough food to feed themselves. Agricultural practices were outdated. No one used chemical fertilizers or high-yield seeds. There was no irrigation. As for tractors, or even ox-powered farming implements: for the small-hold farmer in Ruhiira, a hand hoe was as far as it got.

Jeffrey Sachs was determined to change all that. Just as he had persuaded the world to distribute mosquito nets to people in malaria-prone areas, so he set out to bring fertilizers, high-yield seeds, and irrigation not only to Ruhiira but to all of rural Africa. "It's a little more complicated than distributing bed nets," he told me, "but it's not the most complicated thing we'll ever do on this planet. In fact, it's relatively straightforward."

As a model for Africa, Sachs pointed to India, where until the late 1960s the subcontinent couldn't grow enough food to feed its exploding population. India was heading toward mass starvation, warned Paul Ehrlich in his best-selling book of 1968, *The Population Bomb.* And yet by the early 1970s, thanks to an initiative financed by the Rockefeller Foundation, modern agronomy was introduced to the Indian subcontinent: high-yield and disease-resistant wheat seeds, fertilizer, irrigation, training. In a single decade, between 1967 and 1977, rural poverty fell from 64 percent to 50 percent—and then to 34 percent in 1986. India was saved by the so-called Green Revolution, "one of the most important triumphs of targeted science in the past century," according to Sachs.

Sachs was proposing nothing less than a Green Revolution for Africa. "The good news to me is that there's absolutely nothing wrong with African agriculture that can't be quickly improved," he said in a speech delivered in London in 2007. "There's overwhelming systematic evidence that you can improve yields by a factor of two or three . . . and that productivity won't take a generation to double, but could be doubled actually from one growing season to the next."

Improving yields for small-hold African farmers would end malnutrition. It might also eliminate the need for emergency food aid. For Sachs the ultimate goal of a Green Revolution for Africa was economic growth. "It's like hitting the sixty-four-billion-dollar jackpot," he continued enthusiastically. "If you can double agriculture productivity in a few years, you're talking about ten or fifteen percent aggregate GNP growth in a very short period of time. As a macroeconomist, I can tell you I believe absolutely seriously in that. Easy!"

In meeting after meeting, he lobbied the World Bank and international donors to subsidize agricultural inputs in Africa. In articles and in chapters of his books, he argued that fertilizer and hybrid seeds were the answer to extreme poverty. He lectured on the subject. In the United States, he noted, farmers receive $15 billion a year in subsidies. In Europe, the figure is around $70 billion. Why, even the average European cow is better off than the average African farmer: a Swiss dairy cow receives an estimated $4,000 a year in subsidies! And yet when it comes to African farmers, railed Sachs, we balk at subsidies of any kind.

It did not escape Sachs's notice, of course, that whether they were opposing mosquito nets or opposing agricultural subsidies, donors and development experts tended to fall back on the same stale talking points. Some experts insisted that subsidies would smother ambition and create a culture of dependency. Others worried about sustainability: Given the lack of credit available to poor Africans, how would farmers finance inputs once their subsidies were withdrawn? Still others were skeptical of Sachs's claim that Africans don't use fertilizer because they can't afford it.

In her study of agricultural inputs in western Kenya, the development economist Esther Duflo found that nearly every farmer intended to use and could afford to buy at least a small amount of fertilizer; by the time planting season actually arrived, however, only one-third of the farmers actually followed through. Yes, they understood the economic benefits of using fertilizer, she reported, but most of them chose to spend their money on other things. The gap between intention and outcome was not unlike an American worker choosing not to invest in his company's retirement plan, despite the obvious long-term benefits. In the language of behavioral economists, Duflo's African farmers displayed "present-biased preferences"; in other words, they preferred immediate gratification to future rewards.

As usual, Sachs had no patience for such theories. "For every problem," he'd say again and again, "there is a solution." The great thinkers of the Age of Enlightenment—Thomas Jefferson, John Locke, Adam Smith, Immanuel Kant, Sir Francis Bacon—those were the men Jeffrey Sachs looked to for inspiration, men in whose footsteps he believed he was following. He shared their optimism and confidence. Like them, he was sure that logic and reason triumph over ignorance and superstition.

Sachs never doubted that Africans would use mosquito nets to protect human beings. He was equally certain that, given the opportunity, farmers would buy fertilizer. "The Enlightenment commitment to reason is not a denial of the unreasonable side of human nature," he wrote in *The End of Poverty,* "but rather a belief that despite human irrationality and passions, human reason can still be harnessed—through science, nonviolent action, and historical reflection—to solve basic problems of social organization and to improve human welfare."

He was determined to end poverty—to put people on the ladder of development—and the fastest way to achieve that goal was to increase agricultural yields. In Sachs's villages, farmers would initially receive fertilizer and high-quality seeds free of charge; as soon as their yields increased, they would gladly invest their own money in inputs, or so Sachs presumed. Season by season, based on that premise, the Millennium Villages Project would scale back its subsidies, from 100 percent to 50 percent to 25 percent and downward. On paper, and in Sachs's fertile mind, success was assured.

Southern Ugandans don't much like corn—"school food" or "prison food" is what they call *posho* or *ugali,* the cornmeal porridge popular in other parts of East Africa. Nonetheless, maize was the crop that Jeffrey Sachs and his staff in New York decided was best for the Millennium villages. It was nutritious, drought-tolerant, and relatively easy to grow. It could be eaten fresh, or dried and ground into cornmeal.

And so, during the long rains of September 2006, David Siriri dutifully distributed 32 tons of high-yield maize seeds and 221 tons of fertilizer to more than 7,000 households in Ruhiira. A smaller number of households, around 850, received high-yield, disease-resistant kidney bean seeds. The entire cost of the inputs, just over $300,000, was paid by the Millennium Villages Project. To prove the effectiveness of modern agricultural practices, Siriri set up forty-eight demonstration farms and sent teams of agricultural extension workers across Ruhiira's hills to teach farmers modern "Sasakawa" planting methods.

At harvest time in February 2007, the results were fantastic: average maize yields had increased from 1.8 tons per hectare to 3.7 tons, resulting in a bumper crop of 3,840 tons of maize. Not only were villagers well fed, they also had excess maize that, in theory, could be sold or safely stored for the lean years. All well and good, except for one fact: locally, there were no storage facilities to keep the surplus maize safe from vermin, pests, and disease. "Maize is everywhere! Under the beds, in the living rooms, in the kitchens—everywhere!" exclaimed Tumushabe Boneconcila, a widow and the mother of nine children. "And the rats are everywhere too."

Rats! They ate their way through bags of maize, chewed holes in plastic jerry cans, and gnawed on stacks of mosquito nets. In this remote, landlocked corner of the world, without any roads or trucks to link farmers to markets, what could be done with all that corn? Selling *matoke* was easy compared to selling maize. For one thing, *matoke* is in constant and high demand all across the country. For another, most of the country's *matoke* is grown in the hills of southwestern Uganda, where Ruhiira is located, so traders have no choice but to buy their produce there. Finding markets for other crops was more complicated, Siriri discovered. Even if a buyer for Ruhiira's excess maize was found, the cost of transport alone would wipe out any profit.

Meanwhile, the people of Ruhiira were desperate for cash; they couldn't afford to sit around waiting for the right opportunity to sell their maize. And so they did what poor farmers in remote regions have always done with bumper crops: they dumped their excess maize all at once, with the result that market prices collapsed. Most farmers were forced to sell their maize for far less than the cost of inputs. Others, unable to find buyers at any price, left the maize to rot.

Scrambling to justify the project's $300,000 investment, Siriri managed to find buyers in neighboring Rwanda willing to buy 50 tons of maize at 250 shillings a kilogram, about 35 percent above break-even point—but 50 tons was only a fraction of Ruhiira's total yield that season. The villagers were unhappy. What was the point of growing maize? they demanded. Why grow a crop you didn't like to eat? A crop that was hard to sell? Furthermore, compared with *matoke* bananas, which grew everywhere, with or without chemical fertilizers, growing maize was hard work. "The Millennium project encouraged us to grow maize," groused a farmer named Paul, when I met him in Ruhiira, "and so I did. But the maize, it takes four months to harvest—*matoke* you can harvest every month. And it took me so much work to look after the maize that I didn't have time to harvest my *matoke* properly."

"We wasted money on maize seeds and fertilizer," Siriri acknowledged. "It is money I wish we had not spent."

It occurred to Siriri that there was more to advancing Ruhiira's agricultural prospects than simply increasing yields. Every intervention, it seemed to him, had unintended consequences: time and again, by solving one problem, he created another. To solve the problem of storage, Siriri was pushing ahead with plans to build an enormous grain warehouse in Ruhiira. Going forward, farmers wouldn't have to sell their surplus right away; instead, they could store it securely until prices were higher or until buyers had been found. That was a step in the right direction, thought Siriri. Now all he needed was to find someone to buy the beans and maize.

Chapter 12

Awaire, Awaire

It was 2008. Almost two years had passed since the Millennium Villages Project had started, and in the villages, harvest by harvest, people's lives were slowly improving. There were many noticeable changes: new classrooms and health clinics, better roads, safer drinking water, ample supplies of staple foods, the growing use of cell phones . . . The speed of change gave people hope: if all this could be accomplished in so short a time, imagine where they'd be in another three years. It was natural to suppose, as Sachs did, that the rate of progress would continue along a sharp upward line until, after five years of interventions, extreme poverty would be a thing of the past.

In Ruhiira, where the Millennium Villages Project had so far invested $3.5 million, the operating theater at the Kabuyanda Health Center was finally up and running. There was still no running water, but the floor had been tiled and the windows sealed. Diesel fuel was now available for the generator. Staff quarters had been constructed: a simple concrete block comprising three rooms. And here and there on the hospital grounds, shrubs and flowers had been planted.

A new, young doctor had joined the staff. Dr. Martin Buhamizo was a recent graduate of Uganda's Mbarara University, where he'd earned a degree in medicine and surgery. Despite other job opportunities, he'd accepted the posting at Kabuyanda Health Center largely because the Millennium project offered him a monthly salary of 1.5 million Ugandan shillings, about $750, double the government wage for doctors in Uganda.

Early one morning Dr. Buhamizo arrived at work to see a crowd of people outside the operating theater. One woman was lying on the ground. Another was on a makeshift stretcher, a wooden plank tied to a wheelbarrow. The diagnosis for both women was obstructed or prolonged labor. Their babies were in breech, or else they were wedged sideways behind the pelvic bone, or else the mothers' pelvises were too small, a common problem among malnourished women. One way or another, the babies were trapped in the birth canal.

Asking the nurse to bring a handheld Doppler monitor, Dr. Buhamizo quickly assessed the situation. Tall and lean, he was wearing a spotless white lab coat with a ballpoint pen clipped to the breast pocket. *"Atwire arwaire obwire buriingwa?"* he asked one of the women's relatives, gently—"How long has she been like this?"

There was a lot of back-and-forth in Runyankole, the local Bantu language. The women, first treated in their villages by traditional healers, had followed the usual instructions for obstructed labor: they had chewed plant roots and stuffed their cervixes with the leaves of a local weed (*orucwamba*) to induce contractions. Only when it became clear that the women were dangerously ill did someone bring them to the health clinic. Now their babies were in distress, their heart rates low and dropping. Deprived of oxygen, they were almost certainly asphyxiating. "The mothers, they always come too late," Dr. Buhamizo remarked. It wasn't a judgment, just a fact.

While the women were being carried into the operating theater, Dr. Buhamizo grabbed two jerry cans of diesel fuel from his truck and filled the generator tank. The generator was working today, and thank goodness for that, said Dr. Buhamizo. The last time it broke down, more than two weeks went by before he found a mechanic to fix it. He had learned to improvise. "I am a GP, a gynecologist and an obstetrician, a pediatrician, a pathologist—and a mechanic too," he told me.

Less than forty-five minutes after arriving at the clinic, Dr. Buhamizo had managed to deliver the babies. One was a severely premature girl no bigger than the palm of his hand. The other, a boy, was unconscious. *"Maama,"* said Dr. Buhamizo, *"awaire, awaire"*—"He is not well."

The boy had a fatal neural-tube defect known as anencephaly—his brain and skull were grossly malformed. A nurse swaddled the infant and handed him to his grandmother; within an hour he was dead in her arms. Lying on the operating table, covered in blood and a green-and-brown sarong, his mother murmured something. This was her ninth child, the second to die at birth. She urgently needed a blood transfusion, but that was out of the question: for one thing, the hospital's refrigerator wasn't working, and the refrigerator wasn't working because the solar inverter was broken.

Everything was in short supply. The staff at Kabuyanda was skeletal, with just half the number of health care workers required to operate a hospital of this size, according to the government's own guidelines. Meanwhile, it had been five months since the government had last sent drugs and basic medical supplies. Oral rehydration solution and surgical gloves were out of stock, and any day now, Dr. Buhamizo feared, he'd be out of antiretroviral medication and antidiabetic pills and suture thread too.

By this time, more people had arrived at the hospital, and Dr. Buhamizo was trying to deliver another child. It was not yet noon. "The head is completely stuck!" he cried out. His white lab coat was smeared with blood. It was suffocatingly hot in the operating theater. In a corner of the room, a plastic bucket was overflowing with bloody gauze and used needles and disposed placentas.

By the time the baby made it out of the birth canal, he was

limp and gasping for air. His Apgar score, which rates the health of a newborn from zero to ten (ten being perfect), was two. He weighed less than 1,400 grams, about three pounds. Dr. Buhamizo and the nurse tried to resuscitate the baby, and for a short while, his Apgar score climbed. Then his blood pressure fell precipitately, and he went into shock.

Dizzy, I pushed my way out of the operating room. In America, in a hospital with a neonatal intensive care unit, perhaps something could have been done to save the child. Since Jeffrey Sachs's first visit to Ruhiira in early 2007, the Kabuyanda Health Center had certainly improved. Nevertheless, in Ruhiira, the Millennium project's staff was stretched to capacity, budgets were tight, and there was a limit to how much could be accomplished. In the hospital ward, where all twenty-eight beds were occupied by two people or more, two brand-new state-of-the-art incubators were wedged into the corner, wrapped in plastic. Donated by General Electric—"from America," a nurse said proudly—the two machines were a sign of GE's commitment to helping the world's poorest people and to the Millennium Villages Project. For all GE's good intentions, there wasn't enough electricity in the health center to power the machines.

By the time Dr. Buhamizo emerged from the operating room, the sun was setting. He'd been working ten hours straight. "Sometimes it's too much," he said. "Sometimes you get pushed past your peak and it's too much." Walking across the grounds of the hospital, we passed families camping outside while relatives were in the hospital. A few women were washing clothes in yellow buckets. A pot of *matoke* was cooking on an open three-stone fire.

The generator was out of fuel. "We always run short of fuel," he said. "They give us eighty or one hundred liters a month," he added, referring to the Millennium Villages Project, "but it's never enough.

"It's never enough," he repeated, "but it is so much more than we had before. Without the Millennium project there would be no drugs, there would be no surgical equipment, there would be no way to operate the generator—I would be redundant most of the time. They say funding will continue, but someday it will stop, and when the funding stops, most likely everything we have done will be put to waste. I do not see how we are going to continue after they have left."

How would they continue? "I know that if you spend enough money on each person in a village, you will change their lives," Simon Bland was saying. "If you put in enough resources—enough *mzungu,* foreigners, technical assistance, and money—lives change. I know that. I've been doing it for years. I've lived and worked on and managed development projects."

A senior officer with Britain's Department for International Development (DFID), Bland had spent thirty years working in the field of development. He'd run DFID's offices in Russia, in Ukraine, in Somalia, and in Kenya, implementing and overseeing countless development projects in many of the world's poorest places. Now he was trying to decide whether DFID should back Jeffrey Sachs and his Millennium Villages Project. His main concern was "sustainability"; what would happen when funding for the Millennium Villages ran out?

Broken water pumps, half-finished health care clinics, abandoned housing blocks, roads that lead nowhere, dams that have collapsed—Africa is strewn with the remains of well-meaning development projects, Bland pointed out. "The problem is," he said, "when you walk away, what happens?" Who will fill the potholes and mend the pipes and pit latrines? Who will buy fuel and supply spare parts for the generators? Who will pay Dr. Buhamizo's salary?

Jeffrey Sachs had designed the Millennium Villages Project with a timeline of five years; at that point, according to
his model, the villages would be self-sufficient. To quote an
internal memo distributed to Sachs's senior staff: "Sustainability within the Millennium Villages Project has one precise
meaning: When the five-year MV funding stops . . . the MVs
should be able to continue their economic progress without a
loss of momentum, a drop in living standards, or a decline in
social services."

But what if Sachs's model was unrealistic? What if, after all,
economic development did not advance along a straight upward
line but instead, like the stock market, flatlined? By 2008, even
Sachs could see that a five-year timeline was overly ambitious.
People in the villages were healthier and better nourished than
they had been. Nevertheless, the long-term goals of the Millennium Villages Project—to set people on the path of sustainable
economic progress, to teach them self-sufficiency, to lift them
out of extreme poverty—were as elusive as ever. As for scaling
up, that goal too remained unfulfilled.

Revising his timetable, Sachs announced that the Millennium Villages Project would extend for ten years instead of
five. This change in timeline was by no means an admission of
failure; it was a minor adjustment, he told me, a "course correc-
tion." "There is no blueprint for what we're doing—our ideas
continue to evolve all the time," he said. "The main thing is to
add another block of time to really get the income levels sig-
nificantly raised. The plane is flying and it's gaining altitude—
now we just need to ensure a smooth flight." But where would
money for the second block of time come from?

"Rick and I went to see Jeffrey Sachs," recalled Tom Ryan.
"We sat down with him, and we asked him the simple ques-

tion: 'What's your funding horizon? You know, looking ahead, where are you getting the money to pay for this?'" Sachs had raised $120 million to fund the first five years of the Millennium Villages Project, but surely he couldn't rely on funding from a few wealthy individuals and charitable foundations forever.

Ryan's boss, Rick Schaden, was the majority shareholder of Quiznos, a chain of sandwich shops based in Denver. Since 1991, when he and his father bought the eighteen-store chain, Schaden had overseen the expansion of Quiznos to five thousand franchised shops. Now in his midforties, he had entered the stage of his life where he was starting to think about sharing his wealth. Embarking on what he called a "personal discovery," he read *The End of Poverty* and decided to write a check for $3 million to help fund Sachs's model villages. "Rick loved the idea of a systemic solution to a worldwide problem," Ryan told me, "the idea that instead of giving these people fish, you're teaching them how to fish."

The more involved he became in the Millennium Villages Project, however, the more Schaden suspected the project was flawed. "We talked to them about their vision and we feared for them, actually," continued Ryan, who was chief marketing officer for Quiznos. "They were raising money from high-net-worth individuals, and they were doing a great job of it— you know, they'd raised one hundred twenty million dollars, fifty million of it from George Soros. But that's not a sustainable approach. And we realized pretty quickly that these guys are going to have an uphill struggle."

Rather than depend on the whim and bank accounts of a few very rich people, the Millennium Villages Project needed "to mine channels of consumer giving," argued Schaden and Ryan. Selling the end of poverty was not unlike selling sandwiches: it required a strong, identifiable brand, glossy brochures, and a catchy tagline. "That's our vision," said Ryan, "because, to us, it's better to get ten dollars a year from the twenty percent of the Americans who like this cause than three million dollars from fifteen Rick Schadens. The math is much better. And it's sustainable."

Working pro bono, the Quiznos marketing team proposed a confident new tagline for the Millennium Villages Project: "Extreme Poverty Ends Here." Next, drawing up a road map for the Millennium project's senior staff, they put together a so-called brand book that described the project's "manifesto" in clear, compelling language that would inspire people to donate to the cause. The brand book included a list of adjectives to be used by fund-raisers: "dignified," "hopeful," "meaningful," "authentic," "optimistic," and "confident." It also set out a list of adjectives to be avoided ("gloomy," "shocking," "sad," "hopeless," "bureaucratic," "corporate," and "institutional"). One chapter explored the "psychographics" of potential donors: the sorts of people most likely to give money to the Millennium Villages Project were "earthy," "cultured," "compassionate," "inquisitive," and "fashionable."

Meanwhile, Quiznos's advertising agency, Nitro Group, created an airbrushed brochure for the Millennium project. The cover featured a single photograph—a young African boy in profile, barefoot, silhouetted against the soft orange glow of an African sunset. Inside, printed on vellum, we read: "Extreme poverty ends here. It has to." Now, full-page photographs: barren trees in a sun-drenched desert; a child's pleading, outstretched hands; a dandelion, its seedpods scattered by the wind; sheaves of amber wheat. "Imagine, for a moment, if all the simple fundamentals of life were taken away from you."

Moving along: more sunsets, jagged rocks, an African man with a child strapped to his back, panoramic views of the savanna. "The human spirit is resilient and powerful. It cannot be contained by extreme poverty." Now, the kicker: "Together, with you, we can assure that by 2025, extreme poverty ends here. It has to. And it will."

Schaden and Ryan convinced Sachs to hire a chief marketing officer, whose $350,000 salary would be paid for by Schaden. His name was Peter Kaye, and according to his bio, he was "a strategist with a passion for making a difference." Since graduating from Harvard Business School in 1994, he'd helped to brand such consumer products as Nestlé's Butterfinger candy bar, Dannon's Fruit-on-the-Bottom yogurt, Diet Sprite, and Johnnie Walker. His latest assignment was to make a difference by branding poverty.

For all that, Jeffrey Sachs was not convinced by the plan to mine channels of consumer giving. What Rick Schaden didn't seem to grasp was that the Millennium Villages Project wasn't like Doctors Without Borders, or Oxfam, or Operation Smile—it was about something much bigger than helping individuals. Sachs's main goal was to convince policy makers to alter their approach to economic development in Africa. His aim was to end global poverty once and for all; he was shaking up the establishment, and clearly he could not depend on philanthropic donations in increments of ten dollars, nor even increments of $50 million. "Going slow and steady does not win the race," he told me categorically.

Sachs's model for ending poverty in Africa was predicated on a huge increase in foreign aid, the "big push" that he had called for in *The End of Poverty*. He was establishing an innovative blueprint that the big international donor agencies—USAID, DFID, the whole UN establishment—would one day embrace and roll out everywhere. His goal was a massive scaling up of the Millennium project.

"Getting money from USAID and DFID is our equivalent to an initial public offering" is how Jeffrey Walker, chairman of Millennium Promise, the charity that funnels money to the Millennium Villages Project, explained it to me. "It's the ultimate leverage of our ideas—mission accomplished!"

With enough foreign aid, the Millennium Villages Project could be franchised like an international chain of fast-food restaurants. "The model works," said Walker, "so now the question is how to take it to scale. Is it McDonald's? Can we have our version of Hamburger University, where we train people in our methods of development and send them out to launch Millennium villages?" He seemed to think so.

Very well, but where would the "big push" in foreign aid come from? Who would bell the cat? You didn't have to be a cynic to question a model whose outcome depended on promises made by rich countries to the developing world. As long ago as 1974, at the UN World Food Conference in Rome, 135 nations adopted the Universal Declaration on the Eradication of Hunger and Malnutrition. "Today we must proclaim a bold objective," announced U.S. secretary of state Henry Kissinger in a rousing keynote address, "that within a decade no child will go to bed hungry, that no family will fear for its next day's bread, and that no human being's future and capacities will be stunted by malnutrition!"

More recently, at the 2005 Group of Eight summit in Gleneagles, Scotland, the G8 leaders promised to double aid to Africa, from about $25 billion to $50 billion a year by 2010. As Sachs pointed out repeatedly, $50 billion was about equal to $100 a year for every sub-Saharan African—roughly in line with the Millennium Villages Project's budget of $120 per person.

"The way I look at it, it doesn't cost anything to ask for money," said Sachs. "So I advise Africa's governments to come right out and demand money from the donor agencies—and then demand it again. And again. That's what I do. I write a letter. Then another letter. Then an op-ed. And then I throw a tantrum. In the end, the money may appear—if only so they can get rid of me."

*   *   *

Africa's leaders weren't holding their breath. "Professor Sachs advises us that we shall get more money from the donors," said Ezra Suruma, Uganda's minister of finance, planning, and economic development. "I thank Professor Sachs for his optimism and for his goodwill. I am glad he is optimistic that the problem of poverty can be solved."

Pouring himself a cup of coffee from the silver urn in his office in Kampala, he continued: "Not everyone is as optimistic as Jeffrey Sachs. I enjoy optimistic people. But I'm sorry to say that while we were going through our budget last week, we had to cut our health spending because the donors cut their allocation. So from where I sit, the situation is not so rosy."

An economist who received his Ph.D. from the University of Connecticut in 1976, Suruma has had a long and distinguished career in Uganda as a professor, as a banker, and since 2005 as finance minister. In 2009 he was named Africa's "Finance Minister of the Year" by the British trade magazine *The Banker,* whose editors commended Suruma's "prudent fiscal policy."

"I went to the World Bank last year and told them we have a crisis," Suruma said. "I told them, 'It is a matter of urgency—please help us.' " Then, smiling, he added: "We are still waiting."

Chapter 13

Capitalist Philanthropy

By 2008 the strategy behind the Millennium Villages Project was changing radically. Sachs no longer seemed convinced that the project's original plan of interventions—the "quick wins" he had anticipated in agriculture, health, and education—would be enough to lift people up and out of extreme poverty. Increasingly, he concerned himself with business development. Now commercial agriculture was more important to him than increased yields for small-hold farmers. Instead of lobbying only the big international donor agencies for more money, he was now lobbying venture capital investors. In brief, he was moving away from a model in which the end of poverty depended on foreign aid.

"We've realized that we need much more of a business arm to this," he said, speaking to me by cell phone on his way to catch another international flight, this time from New York to Addis Ababa. "Staple crops and tomatoes and sweet potatoes and all that stuff is fine—but it ain't going to make you rich. What we need is commercial agriculture. And I'm pretty much convinced that any kind of high-value crop, for example, depends on better water control than we have right now. We can't really get to the next stage without drip irrigation and microdams and refrigeration and storage and better clones and larger nurseries and paved roads. And we just need to get electricity into these villages—I think the end of poverty definitely depends on universal access to electricity. Basically, we can't get to the next stage without things that cost a lot of money.

"What we've been doing in the Millennium Villages Project is essentially making grants," Sachs said, echoing what his critics had been saying all along: in its current form, the Millennium Villages Project was not development, it was charity. "Going forward, the big difference, technically, is that we'd make loans or equity investments, as opposed to aid, to get the villages up and running." He continued, "So I envision this year, if things pan out, we'll raise some tens of millions of dollars for this. That's ambitious, but I think it can be done."

In early 2008, to accomplish his goal of making "loans or equity investments, as opposed to giving aid," he hired a director of business development, Rustom Masalawala, who at one point had been a portfolio manager for the Acumen Fund, a nonprofit venture fund that supports small businesses in poor countries with the aim of earning "social returns" (rather than financial returns). Instead of demanding returns of, say, 20 or 30 percent on investments, Acumen is willing to accept 5 to 10 percent. Under Sachs, Masalawala would convince social investment funds like Acumen to underwrite business ventures in the Millennium villages.

By then it had become fashionable to say that business was the solution to Africa's problems. A few months before Masalawala was hired, the cover of *Business Week* asked, "Can Greed Save Africa?" Evidently it can: according to the businessmen and politicians featured in the article, private investment is a sure path to sustainable economic development. "We are capitalists and opportunists," boasted the head of one British company investing in Africa. "We are doing this to make money. That's the only way to help."

In effect, Masalawala's job was to keep the Millennium Villages Project going after the original $120 million of philanthropic funding ran out—and it *was* running out. "The idea is to create real, rising income in the villages. And once you create that income, people can pay for the basics like education and health themselves," he said. "It's a fundamental difference in approach. These ventures are not cheap, but they're probably the only way you will see sustained change. And if we get it right, we'll have a very powerful model to show the world."

Masalawala's desk in New York was cluttered with product samples he'd brought back from a recent visit to the Millennium villages: banana flour, ground cardamom, honey, fruit preserves. There were myriad opportunities to make money. "We'll bring in cardamom seeds and plant them in the valleys of Ruhiira," he said. "There's a processing plant not far away where we can have the cardamom made into powder. The numbers are huge: the local price for one hundred grams is four thousand Ugandan shillings. That's less than two dollars. In the United States, we pay ten dollars or more for the same thing!"

Ginger offered even bigger profit margins. Then there was pineapple. Masalawala was confident that he could raise $850,000 from the UN Industrial Development Organization to establish large-scale production of fresh and dried pineapple in Ruhiira. Demand for pineapple in Europe was big and getting bigger every day.

Masalawala imagined other business possibilities: banana cake mix, cocoa, palm oil, shea butter, chicken eggs, goat meat, sunflower seeds, fruit juice, myrrh, ecotourism. Sold under the brand name "Millennium Farms," the products could be marketed like Fair Trade coffee and Max Havelaar bananas and roses, and be sold to consumers willing to pay a premium to help improve conditions in the developing word. "In my opinion, every Millennium village has two or three opportunities for very-high-value transactions over the next twelve months," he assured me.

"As soon as we have business plans, we can take them to investors in New York," he went on. "It's an ambitious idea. Each one of these is a complicated business plan. It's all about local execution. You need to be hard-nosed about it. You need to make sure they run the business like entrepreneurs. But it can be done."

"Moving up the value chain" is what Sachs and Masalawala called the strategic move from subsistence crops to cash crops. And now David Siriri too adopted the management jargon used by his higher-ups in New York. He talked about "market linkages" and "input credits" and the "aggregation of produce," and he devoted more and more of his time to the study of agribusiness. His job, as he understood it, wasn't simply to provide a safety net for the people of Ruhiira, but to help them earn a living by preparing them for the efficiency of a cutthroat global economy. "They need to stand on their own two feet, the sooner the better," he said. "We need to wean them from pampering."

The first step to launching business ventures, Siriri decided, was identifying and training entrepreneurs. Knowing how to run a business is not intuitive, particularly when it is not an integral part of the culture. "In Uganda, business is seen as a last resort; it is for people who have no other option," said Richard Happy, a Ugandan accountant hired by Siriri to be Ruhiira's enterprise facilitator. "Having a government job or being a farmer has far more status, so we have to work hard to change attitudes."

Starting a business requires a long-term outlook, but thinking long term is not easy for people living in extreme poverty. "If your only concerns are immediate needs, you think in the immediate term," said Happy. "One year is the farthest horizon you get here." That perspective was something else he intended to change.

Emmy Byamukama was one of the aspiring entrepreneurs who enrolled in the Millennium project's "Entrepreneurship Development and Business Skills Training Program." Unable to support his family on his monthly salary of 200,000 Ugandan shillings (less than $100) as a schoolteacher, Byamukama had quit his job to start a backyard poultry farm. Consulting an old manual (*Small-Scale Poultry Keeping: A Guide to Free-Range Poultry Production*), he taught himself the basics of the trade: how to breed laying hens, how to prevent disease, and how to build a simple chicken coop using wooden poles and wire mesh. He and his wife, Beatrice, bought a few local hens and a rooster and began selling eggs to friends and relatives.

Now Byamukama wanted to expand: he planned to sell eggs to shops and hotels in Mbarara, the biggest town in southwestern Uganda, and eventually as far away as Kampala, a good six-hour drive from Ruhiira. Encouraged by Richard Happy, he dreamed too of one day exporting his eggs to Rwanda or Kenya.

Thanks to the Millennium Villages Project's entrepreneurship program, Byamukama learned "The Five 'P's of Marketing": Product, Place, Price, Promotion, Positioning. He learned basic financial accounting and terminology ("The *break-even point* helps you determine the level of operation where your business makes no profit or loss"). He was taught to "brainstorm" and to "think outside the box" and to be "proactive." During a session designed to highlight the dangers of working with the wrong equipment, he was blindfolded and then instructed by Happy to build a tower of fifteen small wooden blocks. Not surprisingly, this was a difficult task: Byamukama's tower never got higher than four blocks before collapsing.

Of the two hundred people who initially signed up for the two-week course, seventy-six made it through successfully.

One of them was Emmy Byamukama, who had put together a thoughtful, handwritten business plan for Twimukye Poultry Farm, as he'd named his company. Drawn on the cover was the logo he had designed, a simple oval (an egg) resting on the initials TPF. He had come up with a English slogan: "Buy and taste you will never regret." Potential customers, competitors, suppliers, a marketing plan, equipment needed—every detail was included. A full page of the business plan was devoted to his "Goals & Objectives," primarily "to supply quality products to my customers." He set out a list of potential dangers:

1. Diseases—bird flu—which have no vaccine;
2. Farm is not near veterinary services;
3. Farm is not near customers;
4. Farm is not near permanent source of water, hence a problem;
5. Thieves.

Looking ahead, and assuming he could raise the necessary capital to buy one thousand laying hens, Byamukama projected that within a year he would earn a monthly net profit of 76,200 Ugandan shillings ($35) on sales of 403,200 Ugandan shillings ($200). It wasn't much, but it was a promising start.

Jeffrey Sachs was enthusiastic about the possibilities of poultry farming in rural Africa. He had convinced Tyson Foods to help launch "poultry enterprises" in various Millennium villages, and already an executive from Tyson's corporate headquarters in Springdale, Arkansas, had traveled to Ruhiira to work on a feasibility study.

Meanwhile, from New York, Rustom Masalawala was urging David Siriri to plant cardamom, ginger, and pineapple—crops with real potential to earn money for the people of Ruhiira. Siriri had encouraged people to plant vitamin-rich vegetables such as carrots, spinach, and sweet potatoes in their *shambas.* And more than three hundred households were being trained in the art of backyard vegetable gardening. All well and good, Masalawala told him, but if the goal was to increase people's incomes, Ruhiira needed cash crops—crops that could be exported.

Masalawala was in talks with two companies who were keen to buy spices from Ruhiira, he said. He was working on a business plan, drafted for him by interns from MIT's Sloan School of Management, in which he projected that with a modest initial investment of $45,000, dried ginger alone would generate for Ruhiira annual revenues "in the hundreds of thousands of dollars" and, by 2010, more than $1 million. Any day now, Masalawala assured Siriri, he'd be presenting the business plan to social investment funds in New York.

Sachs had another good idea: he'd convince the World Food Program (WFP) to buy Ruhiira's surplus crops of corn and beans in bulk. More and more, the WFP had become involved in economic development. Instead of doling out food aid, the program aimed to establish markets and improve agricultural yields in poor countries by buying food from small local farmers. Already the WFP was purchasing around $50 million a year of maize and beans from small-hold farmers in Uganda. Now, backed by the Gates Foundation and USAID, a new pilot program known as Purchase for Progress (P4P) promised to at least double that figure.

Thanks to Sachs's persistence, the WFP agreed to expand its P4P program to Ruhiira, committing to buy 150 tons of kidney beans at the next harvest, in 2008. A "forward contract" guaranteed the sale at 20 percent above market prices. If all went well, Siriri understood, the WFP would commit to buying as much of Ruhiira's surplus crops as he could supply.

*   *   *

For commercial agriculture to take strong roots in Ruhiira, the village had to move away from rain-fed agriculture by improving its water supply. With access to irrigation, farmers could cultivate two or three cash crops a year instead of one. According to Rustom Masalawala, the end of poverty depended on nothing less than three crops a year.

Some of the other Millennium villages had already introduced methods of irrigation. In Toya, the Millennium village at the southern edge of the Sahara in northern Mali, where the dry season lasts for nine to ten months, the project spent $40,000 to buy two huge diesel-fueled pumps to draw water from the Niger, West Africa's great river. Traditionally, Toya's farmers had planted floating rice in the lowlands, where they depended on the annual floodwaters for irrigation. Now, thanks to the water pumps, the village had two rice crops a year instead of one.

Ruhiira's situation was more complicated than Toya's, however. For one thing, Ruhiira has no river. For another, because practically every tree has been chopped down for firewood, rainwater shoots down the steep slopes in torrents, collecting in stagnant ponds on the valley floor. Some people in Ruhiira traveled six kilometers (3.7 miles) a day to fetch water from the valley. "I can tell you," attested Siriri, "walking six kilometers on a flat area is very different than walking six kilometers on a hilly area like Ruhiira—it's a lot of hard work."

Improving Ruhiira's water supply was vital; everyone agreed on that. But how to go about it? "It's very complicated," said a young American engineer named Brett. The Millennium project had sent him to Ruhiira, and now, standing with me at the top of a ridge, looking down the steep path to the village's main water supply, he kept shaking his head. "It's three hundred vertical meters from that water source in the valley to the hills where people live." He pointed somewhere in the distance. "So from an engineering standpoint, it's hugely complicated. Ideally there would be four pumps and three diesel generators with twenty to thirty kVA—those are *big* generators. Plus we need PVC pipes—ninety kilometers of PVC pipes. It's complicated."

Siriri understood the complexities of Ruhiira's water supply better than anyone. Even before the Millennium Villages Project had arrived here, a Christian mission called Africa Community Technical Service, or ACTS, had devoted five years to the task of bringing clean water to this part of Uganda. Rather than depend on expensive electric or diesel generators, ACTS had designed a simple gravity-flow water supply system. Single-handedly, a team of enthusiastic volunteers from western Canada—engineers, surveyors, technicians, construction workers—had built the system from the ground up. As soon as their work was completed, they went home—whereupon something went very wrong. The flow of water became inconsistent. Many of the taps installed throughout the village went dry. Either there wasn't enough water pressure, people surmised, or the system wasn't sufficiency robust. In any case, no one in Ruhiira knew how to fix it.

On his first visit to Ruhiira in early 2007, Jeffery Sachs had been shocked to see the village's main water source: the floating bugs, the runoff of excrement, the mud. "Our problem here, sir, is water," the local member of parliament, Alex Bakunda, had told him at the time. "Water, water, water."

Since then Sachs had managed to convince JM Eagle, the world's largest manufacturer of plastic pipes, to donate $150,000 worth of PVC pipes to Ruhiira. The pipes were ready to be shipped, and would be, just as soon as engineers figured out the logistics of piping water up and over the hills. As it turned out, however, the estimated cost of transporting the PVC pipes from any one of JM Eagle's manufacturing plants in the United States to Ruhiira was almost as high as the value of the pipes themselves: around $120,000, according to Siriri's research. To complicate matters further, JM Eagle's pipes and fittings were incompatible with Ugandan pipes and fittings, which are manufactured to British standards. Siriri wasn't complaining—he was grateful for JM Eagle's help—but all in all, he reckoned, it would be easier and more efficient if JM Eagle simply made a cash donation that allowed him to buy the pipes locally.

While the New York office was struggling with the problem of incompatible PVC pipes, Masalawala came up with an inspired idea: Why not use donkeys to transport water from Ruhiira's valleys up to the hills where people lived? "Rather than sit around waiting for piped water to happen, I am convinced we can do the job with pack animals," he said. "Did you know that just four donkeys can carry eight hundred liters at a time? We could create water-filling stations at the top of the cliffs and have people collect their water there for a small fee. We'll prove that people can make money on their crops even if they have to pay for water."

In short order, eight donkeys arrived in Ruhiira.

Jeffrey Sachs, his wife, Sonia (in black), and Ahmed Mohamed (front center) celebrate the opening of the short-lived Millennium Villages Livestock Market in Dertu. © *Nina Munk*

Abdi Hussein, Dertu's first shopkeeper, waiting for customers. In good times, his store brought in as much as $55 a month. © *Guillaume Bonn*

Amina Abdi, a resident of Dertu, inside her traditional Somali *aqal*, a dome-shaped hut made of soft twigs, grass mats, and cowhides. © *Guillaume Bonn*

Ahmed Mohamed in Dertu's Millennium Villages Project compound. "I can promise you," he told the people, "it won't be long before your lives improve."
© *Nina Munk*

Attracted by Dertu's relative wealth as a Millennium village, nomadic pastoralists, immigrants, squatters, and refugees began settling in town. Soon the once-pastoral landscape resembled a shantytown. © *Nina Munk*

In the arid bush near Dertu, a nomadic Somali herder sought grazing land for his most prized possession. The more camels a Somali has, the greater his wealth and status in the community.
© *Nina Munk*

As Dertu began to prosper, Abdullahi Bari Barow, the itinerant schoolteacher, built for himself and his wife this "semi-permanent" house with the ultimate rural African status symbol: a tin roof. © *Nina Munk*

In the summer of 2011, with another drought gripping the Horn of Africa, everywhere in Dertu animal carcasses littered the parched land. © *Nina Munk*

At Sahlan Bath Hussein's tea shop, the author (center), Sahlan (right), and Sahlan's daughter (left) take a break.
© *Nina Munk*

Once a month, to immunize children and treat the sick, the Millennium project set up temporary open-air health clinics in the bush around Dertu. © *Nina Munk*

In Ruhiira's commercial center there were growing signs of economic activity: bicycles, diesel generators, and new shops. Yet David Siriri couldn't help but wonder how much of that activity would continue once the Millennium project had run its course and he had moved on. © *Nina Munk*

On one of Ruhiira's many hilltops, a farmer stands above his *matoke* banana plantation.
© *Nina Munk*

David Siriri inspecting the soil in Ruhiira's moist valley, where he hoped to plant such high-value crops as cardamom and ginger. "Agriculture," Jeffrey Sachs told his staff, "is the economic pillar of this whole project."
© *Nina Munk*

Sebuuma Sadati, one of Ruhiira's "banana boys," on the road to Mbarara, where he would sell his *matoke* at a markup of 1,000 shillings (or $1) a stalk. © *Nina Munk*

In Ruhiira, children traveled as many as six kilometers a day to fetch water from the valley below. "Our problem here is water," the local parliamentarian told Sachs. "Water, water, water." © *Nina Munk*

Overcoming years of obstacles, one hundred kilometers (sixty-two miles) of donated PVC pipes finally arrived in Ruhiira. In July 2011, piped water began flowing from forty public taps. © *Guillaume Bonn*

Outside Ruhiira's Omwicwamba Primary School, Jeffrey Sachs is surrounded by local dignitaries, journalists, and villagers.
© *Guillaume Bonn*

Angelina Jolie and Jeffrey Sachs in New York, at a screening of MTV's *The Diary of Angelina Jolie and Dr. Jeffrey Sachs in Africa.* © *Andrew Kent/ Getty Images*

Part Five

What can we do? We cannot enforce. We try to explain. We want to empower. But no one can come and change them if they do not want to change themselves.

—Ahmed Maalim Mohamed

Chapter 14

Setbacks

Writing business plans was not one of Ahmed Mohamed's strengths. Still, his supervisors in New York had warned him that in order to keep money flowing into Dertu, he had to come up with a big idea that would appeal to a social investment fund in America. So in the spring of 2008, he got to work.

"Business Plan for Small-Scale Milk Processing and Marketing in Dertu" was the title of Ahmed's proposal—though, honestly, it reads more like an academic research report than a business plan. Under the subheading "Investment Rationale," Ahmed wrote: "There are large quantities of milk produced by the pastoralist[s] which exceed the consumption and [a] large amount of it goes into waste (spoilage). The excess milk if processed, cooled and stored will contribute to the nutrition and income of the people of Dertu and the region especially in dry seasons."

From New York, Rustom Masalawala returned Ahmed's business proposal with dozens of disheartening questions and comments. Among them: "There is no such thing [in this plan] to suggest a Return on Investment—we need to have a P/L or an Income Statement and a Cash Flow [Statement] in a standard format that industry accepts." And: "You need to talk about how you will compete in this space and why our product will be superior." And: "No one will fund the project if we do not have a clear idea of what equipment we want to buy and how we plan to use it."

Ahmed and his deputy, Idris, then spent weeks writing a more detailed, more confident business plan. Boldly, they took stabs at guessing the potential size of the market for camel milk. They drew up a Profit and Loss Statement. Then, dutifully, respectfully, they sent the business plan back to New York. Again Masalawala deemed it unsatisfactory: "You have talked about selling thousands of liters of milk a day in the P/L and here your total quantity adds up to no more than 100 liters or so," he wrote. "This is completely inconsistent and needs much more explanation."

Ahmed and Idris tried again. And again Masalawala demanded major revisions: "I am sure this will feel frustrating but unfortunately these are the standards investors set before giving out money."

Eventually, fed up with the charade, Ahmed ignored Masalawala's increasingly insistent e-mails. "This is the fourth email that I am sending you—the other three have received no responses at all," wrote Masalawala. "I am now wondering if these mails are getting through to you—or if there is some other specific reason for the lack of response." In fact, there was a specific reason: things were going badly in Dertu.

Dertu's aging borehole had broken down, and not for the first time. In this instance, however, the situation was especially dire: it was the dry season, and both generator-driven pumps had given out at once. There were no spare parts in Dertu, and no one had the skills to fix the pumps. And so, in a panic, Ahmed spent $1,500 of his budget to have a 9,000-liter (3,778-gallon) tanker deliver water to Dertu until one of the pumps could be replaced.

But 9,000 liters wasn't enough water for the thousands of thirsty people and animals that congregated in Dertu. Fighting broke out among the villagers. The driver of the water truck was beaten by an angry mob. A sixteen-year-old boy, accused of cutting in line, was stabbed to death. "It traumatizes me," Ahmed said. "This is about life and death. A human being is only orderly when things are in plenty."

Meanwhile, yet another famine threatened the region. "Horn of Africa: Exceptional Food Security Crisis" was the headline of a 2008 bulletin issued by the Red Cross. A combination of drought, poor harvests, and soaring food prices had combined to create "the perfect storm," as Sachs referred to it.

In an urgent e-mail to his bosses in Nairobi, Ahmed requested permission to buy a new pump. "This is to inform you that the two boreholes in Dertu suddenly broke down," he wrote, "and the local community are in critical/emergency water crisis. There is not even a drop of water at the village. Lives are in danger (both human and livestock). The stories narrated are very pathetic, e.g. pastoral mothers who left their young ones some 20–30 km away to get water by donkeys could not hold back tears when they found out that there is no water at the borehole to help their dear ones and themselves."

Ahmed needed 400,000 to 500,000 Kenyan shillings ($5,000 to $6,000) for a new pump. The Millennium project's Nairobi office was of course sympathetic, but in responding to Ahmed's request, they noted that repairing the pumps was no more than a short-term solution to Dertu's water problems. "I usually liken boreholes to babies who do not show signs of illnesses until they are critically or fatally sick," one of the coordinators responded knowingly. "This happens all the time with boreholes but investors never learn."

Back in 2006 the project had concluded that Dertu's population could be sustained only if multiple water sources were available—shallow wells, roof catchment systems, and huge water-pan reservoirs to harvest rainwater, for example. The project had allocated $23,000 to "empower the local community to manage these water resources," and yet with the exception of a few water tanks at the school and the clinic, no long-term solution had materialized.

Besides, the Nairobi office wanted to know, didn't Dertu's Water Users Association have its own money to buy new pumps? For each camel that drank at the borehole, herders had to pay six Ksh, money that was supposed to pay for fuel, maintenance, and repairs. Where had this money gone? Ahmed had no idea why the Water Users Association lacked money to replace the broken pumps; he only knew that the people of Dertu needed water desperately. If money was being embezzled, as some had begun to suspect, he knew nothing about it.

Everything in Dertu was proving more expensive than the Millennium Villages Project had planned for: fuel, staple foods, building supplies. The value of the U.S. dollar had fallen and prices had soared since the project's launch in early 2006. Ahmed was almost out of money; he faced budget cutbacks in the coming year, and the people of Dertu felt cheated. More and more of his time was now devoted to pleading for additional funding from the Millennium Villages Project and from any other donor he could think of.

Construction of the boys' dormitory at Dertu's school had been completed, but there was no money left over to buy mattresses. At the health clinic, the new maternity ward was two-thirds complete, but the contractors refused to finish the job unless they were paid more than the sum they'd originally agreed to. The laboratory technician demanded a raise of 10,000 Ksh a month, about $120—and when his demand was not met, he quit, with the result that there was no lab technician in Dertu for almost a year and the clinic's microscope, donated by the Millennium project to diagnose malaria and TB, gathered dust, literally, and sand. Dertu's one itinerant schoolteacher now had 392 students, and there was no budget to hire another teacher.

There were other setbacks. The project's attempts to diversify Dertu's food supply had been for nothing. For Dertu's demonstration farm, Ahmed had planted row after row of sorghum, a cereal crop more tolerant of drought than corn, but the seeds were devoured by a swarm of Red-billed Quelea— "locust birds," as they're known in Africa. They darkened the land like storm clouds, huge ominous flocks swooping in to devastate the fields. As for the eighty-four hoes and eight spades that Ahmed had given out to promote farming in Dertu, they disappeared without a trace.

A "kitchen gardening" program, meant to encourage the women of Dertu to grow kale and tomatoes in burlap sacks, hadn't worked either. The high saline content of Dertu's groundwater was to blame, someone said. The women had received no proper training, someone else explained. Somalis didn't like kale, another person told me.

One way or another, Dertu's agricultural experiments were not a success. "Dertu should be green by now," observed Ahmed. "We've given away five thousand seedlings, but people don't understand the importance of trees. There is not a culture of tree plantings."

For the first time since I'd known him, Ahmed looked discouraged. I arrived in Dertu one day just as he was leaving for Nairobi. The purpose of his trip was to raise money to buy six hundred goats, part of a "restocking" program to donate livestock to Dertu's poorest residents. The Millennium Villages Project had promised the goats long ago, but by this time there was no money for them in the budget, and the people of Dertu were resentful. "The community is on our neck," Ahmed said. "They say, 'You build, but you never complete.'"

In its annual report for 2008, the Millennium Villages Project stated that Dertu's livestock market was generating $14,000 a month in "profit"—a dreamlike figure that should have been questioned in New York, if anyone had paid close attention to the numbers. In reality, the livestock market never generated a cent.

Persuaded by Jeffrey Sachs's sweeping vision, Ahmed did everything in his power to rally support for the livestock market in Dertu. He met again and again with the village elders. He hosted six town hall meetings for the community. And to encourage their interest and participation, he invited the district commissioner and other local dignitaries to visit the market. Despite Ahmed's efforts, however, Dertu's livestock market was formally abandoned a few months after it opened.

What went wrong? Again, the answer depends on whom you speak to. Explanation A: The bigger, more established market in Garissa made a market in Dertu superfluous. B: The market was undermined by local politicians who wanted a cut of the profits. C: Various clans and subclans feuded for control. D: Herders wanted to sell their goats and sheep whenever the spirit moved them, not only on weekly market days. E: The community hadn't been properly trained or "sensitized."

Development is complicated and full of natural and cultural pitfalls. The explanation that makes the most sense may be the most obvious one: in planning for Dertu's livestock market, the Millennium Villages Project ignored the idiosyncrasies of Somali nomadic pastoralists. Economically speaking, the core assumption behind the founding of the livestock market was the so-called Rational Man theory, the classical economic model that presumes that people act in their own best interest. A simple, rational cost-benefit analysis would suggest that it is better all around to sell livestock in Dertu rather than in Garissa. After all, time is money.

But what if, for the people of Dertu, time was not money? In that case, spending three or four days trekking to and from the livestock market in Garissa might not be a wasteful or an uneconomical use of time after all. "These pastoralists, they will travel even four hundred kilometers to get an extra hundred shillings," said Ahmed, who was trying hard to understand why his people were resisting change. "Time is not a factor."

There's something else, a cultural fact that had long confused outsiders in the Horn of Africa: the whole concept of selling one's livestock is antithetical to Somali values. Somalis hoard camels, even when it makes no good economic sense to do so.

Now and again, when they need money, people in Dertu will sell their goats or sheep. Ahmed liked to refer to those animals as a nomad's ATM, by which he meant that in a place with no commercial banks, they served as a quick source of cash. But in the eyes of Somalis, camels are very different from goats and sheep. Camels are slaughtered, sold, or traded only on the most important occasions—a wedding, for instance. Camels are used as dowry. In the case of tribal killings, they're paid out to a victim's family as *diyal*.

One much-cited study, published in the *American Journal of Agricultural Economics,* concludes that in much of rural Africa, the actual number of animals that a herder owns is more important to him than their underlying monetary value; the animals are "an end in themselves." To quote a 1928 report by a colonial administrator in Kenya: "It is the old story of the vicious circle. The natives amass stock until the country will no longer carry it, a period of drought or disease occurs, heavy losses are incurred and the process of amassing stock again commences."

"What can we do?" asked Ahmed, rhetorically. "We cannot enforce. We try to explain. We want to empower. But no one can come and change them if they do not want to change themselves."

Chapter 15

Insha'Allah

Is poverty the result of cultural values? Religion? Jeffrey Sachs has no patience with that sort of thinking—in his view, it's nothing more than a form of cultural imperialism. "Virtually every society that was once poor has been castigated for being lazy and unworthy until its citizens became rich, at which point their new wealth was 'explained' by their industriousness," he wrote in *The End of Poverty*. "What look like immutable social values turn out to be highly malleable to economic circumstances and opportunities."

According to Sachs, as soon as people are lifted out of poverty, they move beyond superstition and outdated rites. To a large extent, the success of the Millennium Villages Project depended on Sachs's idea of progress. As Ahmed understood it, mounting the development ladder was like boiling a frog: you proceeded gradually, one step, one rung at a time. "If you put a frog in boiling water, he will jump out," said Ahmed, "but if you put the frog in cold water and slowly warm it up, you may be able to get the frog to the point where you can eat it."

Ahmed believed in Sachs's idea of progress. Sometimes, however, he felt he was losing his bearings. The more he tried to effect change in Dertu, the more often he was assured that the future was in God's hands. The Arabic phrase *Insha'Allah*, "God willing," is used all the time in Dertu, in almost every situation.

Ever since the Millennium Villages Project arrived in

Dertu, the village dispensary had been stocked with free contraceptives—birth control pills, condoms, injectables, you name it. And yet no more than five or six women or men in the village used birth control of any kind. Meanwhile, female genital cutting continued to be an almost universal practice.

Few people in Dertu will speak openly about genital cutting; they know it's illegal in Kenya, just as they know that "Europeans" consider it barbaric. For the record, Sheikh Abdirahman Guliya, Dertu's imam, discourages complete infibulations—the most extreme form of genital cutting—in favor of a simple ceremonial "nick." At least, that's what he told me. In all events, infibulation is a normal and accepted practice in Dertu.

When a girl is six or seven years old, her clitoris and labia are sliced off with a knife or razor blade, and the surrounding area is stitched tight with sewing thread or string from sisal sacks. All this is done without anesthetic. After the operation the girl's legs are bound together with cords of camel leather, and she is kept in isolation for seven days while the wound heals.

Soon after she arrived in Dertu, Fatuma Shide, the Millennium project's health coordinator, was present at a ritual circumcision in the village. Yes, as a child her genitals had been cut, but she had retained no memory of the procedure. Seeing it years later, at first hand, made her ill.

"The girl was seven years old," Fatuma reported. "Four old ladies were holding her down by the legs and arms, like a goat being taken for slaughter. The little girl was screaming and crying and trying to bite the old ladies. I saw her flesh being cut with a razor blade, the clitoris, and inside they were cutting and cutting. The blood was coming out between her legs. The blood was coming out everywhere. I had to look away, I was crying, and the old ladies they saw me crying, and they said, 'You are a coward.' I am not able to erase the scene out of my head. I still feel the pain."

In Dertu, as in North Eastern Province generally, an uncircumcised girl brings shame upon her family. She'll never find a husband, for one thing, since the purpose of genital mutilation is to guarantee and demonstrate a girl's virginity. I knew all this, and yet I hadn't fully considered what it really meant until, one day, I was invited to a wedding in Dertu.

As is customary, the celebration would last all day and all night. When I arrived in the early afternoon, a large crowd was gathered in the homestead, outside the hut where the bride and groom would spend their wedding night. Chanting loudly and stomping their feet, a dozen men danced around in a tight circle, banging their wooden staffs on the dry ground. A woman was beating an overturned plastic bucket with two sticks. I could hear the wailing of conch shell trumpets. Soon the dancers were surrounded by onlookers, clapping and singing. Old women shrieked and ululated.

Allahumma salli ala Muhammadin wa ala aali Muhammadin—Oh Allah, shower blessings upon Muhammad and upon the family of Muhammad. *Kamaa sallaita ala Ibraheema wa ala aali Ibraheem innaka hameedun majeed*—Just as you showered your blessings on the family of Abraham. You are the Praiseworthy, the Glorious.

The dancing ended at dusk, and the wedding feast began. A camel bull had been slaughtered for the occasion. Someone brought us a tin bowl with shredded pieces of camel meat in ghee, and deep-fried squares of *kac kac*. To wash down the camel meat, I was offered a ladle of warm, smoked camel's milk.

Just after nightfall the bride arrived. She was veiled almost completely, her eyes darkened with kohl, and her hands and fingernails were stained orange with henna. Escorted by a dozen ululating women holding up a silk canopy, she was led into the matrimonial hut. Inside was a small wooden bed. A large carpet had been placed over the sand. Soon she was joined by her husband and by the two women who would serve as "witnesses." Officially, the ancient ritual would go on for three days.

I tracked down the one woman at the wedding who I knew spoke good English, a Kenyan nurse named Irene: "Why do they need witnesses?"

"To see that the girl is pure," she answered.

"You mean, they'll examine her to see that she's a virgin."

"They will use the penis," said Irene, pronouncing the word very slowly, *pee-niis,* in case it wasn't understood. "Without a stick, how can you know how deep the river is? Without a stick, how do you know the vessel can receive?" The entrance to the bride's vessel had been sewn up years ago. Now the groom had to prove his worth, and his bride's worth, by breaking the seal and plumbing the depth of the river.

Until he managed to penetrate the bride fully, the couple would remain in the hut. As soon as it became clear that the bride's vessel could receive, the two witnesses emerged from the hut holding up their evidence, a bloodstained sheet. At which point the festivities resumed.

Would this rite of passage become a thing of the past, once Dertu was lifted out of poverty? Ahmed wasn't sure. The people of Dertu, as far as he could tell, were in no hurry to embrace Western ideas of modernity. "*Mzungu* come and *mzungu* go," Madame Sofia once remarked: life went on, and the people of Dertu would do what they had always done, *Insha'Allah.* Was it Ahmed's job to convince then to abandon their way of life? To what end? Apart from encouraging a dependence on aid, what had the *mzungu* ever done for the people of North Eastern Province?

Part Six

I said to him, "Jeff, to be honest, we are not ready for input credits. We need to keep subsidizing. These are peasants, living hand to mouth, and you are telling me to extend to them a one-million-dollar line of credit that must be paid back? That's a very tall order indeed!"

—David Siriri

Chapter 16

I Am Thinking We Are Not Ready for This

In June 2008 the Millennium Villages Project held its annual five-day conference in Bamako, the capital of Mali. More than 150 people—all the senior staff from New York, four or five staff members from every Millennium village, and a number of the project's major benefactors—were in attendance. A month or so before the meeting, a memo had been sent to all participants announcing that business development would be the central theme of the meeting. "By the end of the conference," the memo stated, "it is expected that we will have completed and approved strategic plans for sustainability of private sector enterprises that will include details on priority commercial agriculture initiatives, microfinance initiatives, and market linkages."

At the Azalai Hotel Salam, on the left bank of the Niger River, Jeffrey Sachs opened the first plenary session of the conference with a hard-nosed talk about money. Despite his best efforts, the "big push" in foreign aid hadn't come to fruition. And he still hadn't managed to convince international donors to underwrite agricultural inputs in Africa. According to several participants, he was blunt in his assessment: the time had come—more quickly than expected—for the Millennium Villages Project to make the transition from subsistence agriculture (or sub-subsistence, as the case might be) to commercial agriculture. The project could not afford to continue giving grants.

By nearly every measure, the Millennium Villages Project

was losing money on agriculture. It didn't help that the cost of inputs had soared. In less than eighteen months, the price of diammonium phosphate (DAP) fertilizer on the world market had increased almost fivefold, from $250 to nearly $1,200 per metric ton by that summer of 2008. At these prices, there was no way to justify the expense of fertilizer—not if the objective was self-sufficiency.

To make the point clear for his audience, Sachs displayed on an overhead slide a chart of each village's "value-cost ratios," which are commonly used to calculate the economic return of fertilizer. In most of the villages, the ratio was far below the minimum of 3 to 4 needed to justify the cost of fertilizer. In Ruhiira, the ratio on beans was a dismal 1.25; on maize, 1.26; on sorghum, 0.64. "If the value-cost ratio isn't good, it can't work—period," he said.

The villages would not be lifted out of poverty on rain-fed agriculture alone; that was a given. Now, however, it had become clear that even with the help of fertilizer, yields were not high enough to make a difference. To "move up the value chain," farmers in the villages needed to increase productivity by double or even triple cropping; they needed high-value crops; above all, they needed irrigation. "What we need," Sachs said, "is to think big."

One member of the audience raised his hand. "Excuse me, Professor," he began hesitantly. "I am thinking that we are not ready for this. The biggest problem we are having is subsistence farmers who are trying to get enough food to feed themselves. So I am asking, why are we thinking big now?"

It was then that Sachs began to yell. "We don't want you to think big or small," he bellowed. "What we want you to think is RICH! What we want is to maximize opportunities!"

"We need business plans from all of you," Rustom Masalawala chimed in. "It's all about execution and the speed of execution. 'Make it and they will come' sounds good, but it doesn't work like that in the real world."

It's never easy to disagree with Jeffrey Sachs. You might trigger an argument. You might ruffle his feathers. In all likelihood, he'll make you feel small. He might call you "misguided" or "ill-informed" or "ignorant." At Millennium project meetings, where everyone in the room depended on Sachs for his or her paycheck, being a dissenter took courage. And yet in Bamako that summer of 2008, the air was thick with dissension. People in the audience—sincere and earnest employees of a nonprofit organization devoted to ending extreme poverty—were being ordered to transform themselves from social workers into entrepreneurs. Yes, they admired Sachs, and despite occasional doubts, they believed in his mission; however, they disliked and mistrusted Masalawala. Who was he to lecture them about the "real world"?

Another hand in the audience shot up. "In my opinion, we are moving too quickly," someone said. It was Dr. Rebbie Harawa, head of the Millennium village in Malawi. Smart and outspoken, with a Ph.D. in soil science from Cornell University, she is highly respected in her field. In Bamako, she decided to speak her mind, whatever the consequences. The farmers in her village had managed to double or triple yields in the past two growing seasons, and now she was being told that wasn't good enough. "I think what's important is that we are helping people who are hungry," she said. "That is our job."

Sachs insisted that he was not abandoning small-hold farmers, according to Harawa. But what options did he have? At current prices, there was no way the project could keep subsidizing farmers. At the same time, farmers could only afford inputs on their own if they earned a generous profit on their crops. That was precisely why Sachs and Masalawala were pushing for irrigation, high-yield crops, "Millennium Farms" branded products, business proposals, and venture capital. If all went well, Sachs told the audience, there would one day in every village be sizable commercial agriculture enterprises—enterprises in which every villager would own shares. "That's where we are heading," he said enthusiastically. "We are going to be bold!"

In the villages, most people were still trying to rise above the level of subsistence farming. Here and there a lucky few, underwritten by the Millennium project, were managing to diversify their crops, earning some desperately needed cash by selling onions, tomatoes, chili peppers, and cabbage to their neighbors. A handful of people in the villages could be described as small-scale entrepreneurs. And yet here, in a shabby conference room at the Azalai Hotel Salam, Sachs and Masalawala were talking about a speedy transition to commercial agricultural enterprises as though the only barrier to success was a lack of courage and determination.

"I don't think there's anyone who didn't know we would have to make this transition," interrupted Pete Ondeng, another senior member of the Millennium project's staff in Africa. "It's that the transition is coming faster than we expected. The work of nonprofit organizations is radically different than the work of commercial organizations."

"Either you step up to the plate, or you don't," said Masalawala dispassionately.

Chapter 17

A Very Tall Order

Going into the planting season of late 2008, David Siriri had a sense of foreboding. It weighed heavily on him, the pressure to generate income in Ruhiira. He did his best to find links to markets and to locate buyers for surplus crops. He made a few stabs at writing business plans. He nourished one cottage industry after another and encouraged almost any enterprising idea that was presented to him.

Thanks to the Millennium project, a building boom of sorts was under way in Ruhiira—the granary, a new school, repairs to the health clinic. Thus Siriri designed a training program to teach young people to make sun-dried adobe bricks: making bricks was a practical way to put to work the now-unemployed banana boys. As well, inspired by a Colorado-based nonprofit called BeadforLife ("Eradicating Poverty One Bead at a Time"), he established a bead-making enterprise: diligently, a dozen women spent their days fashioning beads from dried banana leaves and glue.

Invariably, visitors to Ruhiira—*mzungu,* mainly—were invited to meet the bead makers and to admire their handiwork. Everywhere you looked there were banana beads: baskets of banana beads, strands of banana beads, banana bead bracelets, banana bead anklets, banana bead necklaces, banana bead earrings. . . . Measured by output, the enterprise was a great success. As a means of eradicating poverty, however, it was less successful. Not even Siriri could ignore the fact that the market for banana-bead jewelry was limited.

Now that Siriri was expected to think like an entrepreneur, he was having second thoughts about his suitability for the job he'd accepted. Honestly, he asked himself, what did he really know about starting a business? He was a soil scientist—a man with a Ph.D. in agroforestry—and it pleased him that, in terms of crop yields and diversity, he was making progress on agriculture in Ruhiira. Augmenting household incomes was another matter altogether. "Frustrating," Siriri described it to me.

The proposed deal with the World Food Program—a sure thing, Siriri had been led to believe—was falling apart. For months there'd been one delay after another. Outside consultants, trained to judge whether Ruhiira's beans conformed to the WFP's rigorous standards and specifications, made round after round of inspections. Not once but three times the food inspectors demanded that Ruhiira's beans be fumigated against weevils, a process that, all in all, cost the farmers 3 million Ugandan shillings. More quality control was required; after all, there were moldy beans, sprouted beans, discolored beans, shriveled beans, and beans damaged by insects, not to mention extraneous matter among the beans (dead weevils, rodent excreta, twigs). All such imperfections had to be identified and the flawed beans discarded. Next, the inspectors insisted that Ruhiira's beans be transported in special bags marked with the World Food Program logo, a requirement that cost the farmers even more money and effort. And still the farmers had not been paid for the beans.

Someone in the know advised Siriri, sotto voce, that he should simply bribe the inspectors and be done with it. Siriri shrugged off the temptation. In the real world, as every Ugandan knows, bribing officials is the way things get done, but there was no point trying to explain that fact of life to his bosses in New York.

Meanwhile, with each passing month, the market price of beans was climbing higher and higher, to the point that the deal brokered with the World Food Program was no longer advantageous. The farmers started to rebel. Calmly, Siriri tried explaining to the people of Ruhiira that a contract is a contract; it's nonnegotiable no matter what happens. It wasn't his fault that the WFP was an incompetent, lumbering, myopic bureaucracy.

Ruhiira's farmers were not a bit interested in the nuances of contract law and demanded to be released from any obligation to the World Food Program. When Siriri stood his ground—"My hands are tied," he told them—a mob of farmers descended on the Millennium project's office, smashed a window, threatened Siriri's staff, and impounded one of the project's trucks.

Angry farmers were only one of Siriri's many problems. Another planting season was about to begin, and he had nowhere near enough money to buy the fertilizer and seeds he'd promised to supply. Worse, he was supposed to be rolling back subsidies on fertilizer and seeds. "We're asking our farmers to pay fifty percent of the inputs we give them," he said. "But one bag of DAP is now one hundred dollars, and there is no way a farmer is going to contribute fifty percent of that."

Meanwhile, Jeffrey Sachs was urging the villages to offer low-interest loans for inputs. Drawing on his budget, Siriri was expected to extend credit to farmers for fertilizer and seeds, with the idea that after the harvest, once they'd sold their crops, they would pay back the cost of the inputs. To Siriri, this was not a realistic plan. "I said to him, 'Jeff, to be honest, we are not ready for input credits. We need to keep subsidizing. These are peasants, living hand to mouth, and you are telling me to extend to them a one-million-dollar line of credit that must be paid back? That's a very tall order indeed!'"

According to Siriri's rough calculations, farmers who borrowed money for inputs would have to more than double their yields *and* sell their entire surplus just to break even. Even if that hopeful outcome came to pass, Siriri was not confident that he would be repaid. "People in the village are still playing in the Minor Leagues, and he wants to take them to the Olympics," he said, referring to Sachs.

In an e-mail to Sachs's deputy, John McArthur, Siriri outlined his concerns. "We have only $60,000 in our budget for fertilizer, but now we need three times as much," he told him urgently. "What should we do?" McArthur was sorry, but there just wasn't enough money to go around. He was working to solicit donations from a large American fertilizer company, but for the time being, he said, Siriri would have to be creative.

The only solution Siriri could see was to keep a high level of subsidies in place, no matter what New York demanded. "I do not have a better solution," he said. "If we don't keep the subsidies, we will unravel everything we have accomplished. If we don't keep the subsidies, I am sure the farmers will decide not to use any fertilizer."

In New York, Sachs too grappled with the problem of how to pay for inputs. His staff was racing to find financial institutions willing to launch an agricultural credit program in the villages. Meanwhile, with time running short, decisive action was needed: the only solution that made sense to him was to forge ahead and quickly put in place an agricultural credit system funded by the project alone. "I don't want to slow down in some misguided attempt to design a perfect system—that's how the World Bank does things," Sachs said. "If that was our approach, nothing would ever happen."

As Sachs must have known, there's a good reason why financial institutions are reluctant to lend money to small-hold African farmers; volumes of literature have been written on the subject, all pointing to the fact that repayment rates are dismal.

Since at least the 1950s, the West has struggled to establish financially viable agricultural credit programs in the developing world. Between the 1950s and the 1980s, when the idea was largely abandoned as unworkable, economically speaking, the World Bank alone spent $16 billion on agricultural credit.

In the best of times, collecting debts from poor people is a challenge; making loans to poor African farmers is especially risky. If drought or disease wipes out a harvest, how does a bank get repaid? As collateral, the typical African farmer has nothing but his small plot of land. Even if all goes well, there's no knowing what a farmer might earn: from one season to the next, the market price of a crop may soar or collapse, depending on all sorts of global macroeconomic variables. "The inadequacies of rural financial markets reflect real risks and real transaction costs that cannot simply be wished, or legislated, away," concluded the World Bank's 2008 Development Report.

Unable to borrow money from banks or microfinance institutions, desperate farmers depend on local moneylenders, who typically charge between 10 and 30 percent interest a month. One farmer in Ruhiira, Frank Kanyankore, borrowed 60,000 shillings, or $30, from a moneylender, with the agreement that he would pay back 96,000 shillings after six months. It was a large amount of money for him, but his wife was sick, with the result that he had unexpected medical expenses, and had to hire a laborer to help him in the field. When the time came to pay back the moneylender, Kanyankore was broke; at that point, he begged the moneylender to extend his loan for another six months.

In the end, Kanyankore's initial 60,000 shilling loan, compounded, ballooned to 153,600 shillings—the equivalent of an annual interest rate of 155 percent. He did his best to pay off the loan; finally he just gave up, and the moneylender, in lieu of cash, took possession of a chunk of Kanyankore's farm.

Sachs approached the conundrum of agricultural credit with his usual impatience and blind faith. In late 2008 and early 2009, in three of his villages, he decided to hand out low-interest loans, on the spot, to every single farmer. No one needed to prove his creditworthiness or put up collateral or offer evidence of financial responsibility. "If we did it a little on the fly, it's because there was a crisis" is how John McArthur would later defend the decision.

Sachs took for granted a kind of mutual accountability and respect; he'd convinced himself that the villagers were as committed to him as he was to them. "We took this proposition that they would repay us," added McArthur, when I pressed him to explain why the project was willing to trust people with no credit history. "They committed to us that they would."

In short, the Millennium Villages Project failed to recover its investment. Repayment rates in Mali weren't bad. But of the ten thousand farmers who received loans in Sauri, the Millennium village in western Kenya, around two-thirds defaulted. In Mbola, Tanzania, default rates were even higher, somewhere in the range of 99 percent. Some farmers were too poor to repay their loan. Others, perhaps, didn't understand the terms of the loan. At the same time, many farmers felt under no particular obligation to pay back the Millennium project. Cleverly, a number of them arbitraged the loans, taking fertilizer on credit, then reselling it elsewhere at market prices. Or else they used the fertilizer themselves, then quietly sold their surplus crops, while assuring the Millennium project's loan officers that their crops had failed. There were stories of men using Millennium's money to pay for funerals and school fees. Some farmers spent the money at local bars.

In its annual reports for 2008 and 2009, the Millennium Villages Project neglected to disclose details of its failed agricultural credit program (just as it neglected to disclose the failure of Dertu's livestock market). One report did in fact acknowledge that in Mbola "a number of factors," including "the variability of the rains and a grasshopper infestation," had led to "lower than expected" repayment rates. Another report mentioned "several challenges," the particulars of which were glossed over, and noted that in Sauri "the task of introducing a universal access credit system . . . proved significant." Precisely what was signified is not spelled out.

For internal purposes, the Millennium Villages Project commissioned two postmortem reports to discover why so few farmers had upheld their side of the "mutual-accountability bargain." When I asked in New York for copies of the reports, my request was dismissed: the reports were not "rigorous," I was informed; they were "impressionistic" and "non quantitative." Millennium had nothing to gain from handing over the reports to an inquisitive journalist, I inferred; the role of the press was to focus on the project's worthy achievements and thus mobilize public support for its goals. The bumps and potholes on the road to ending extreme poverty are no one's idea of good news.

Chapter 18

I Have Been Failed by the Markets

One afternoon, in a classroom at Ruhiira's Nyakitunda Primary School, a "health facilitator" was lecturing an audience of women on the dangers of diarrhea. He held up flash cards illustrating the "four F's" of bacterial transmission: Food, Flies, Fingers, and Feces. He passed around a laminated image of dirty cooking utensils covered with flies and strewn on the ground outside a hut. He then contrasted that example of poor hygiene with an image of three or four freshly washed pots resting on a raised wooden rack. Next, he handed out bars of soap and explained the benefits of a simple hand-washing contraption known as a "tippy tap"—a foot lever pulls a string that tips a jug to start the flow of water. He devoted a great deal of time to discussing the proper construction of pit latrines: three meters deep, thirty meters away from any water source, tightly fitted with a lid.

In this modest way—in small, incremental steps—the lives of people in Ruhiira were getting better. David Siriri could see progress; so much good work had been done since his arrival in Ruhiira. In the area of health, the Millennium Villages Project had invested more than $1.2 million since 2006, three times as much as the Ugandan government had spent in the village, and that $1.2 million was very well spent when you considered how much healthier the people were. A medical staff of just ten (none of whom were doctors) when the project started had grown to fifty-three, including two doctors and thirteen midwives. The number of babies born with the help of a trained birth attendant had increased fivefold, chronic malnutrition was down, and the prevalence of malaria had fallen from 17 percent to less than 1 percent.

The project had invested nearly $600,000 in education, a sum that, combined with growing government resources, represented a sharp increase in funding. True, Ruhiira's primary school had almost no textbooks; classes were severely overcrowded (typically fifty students per teacher); an estimated 40 percent of Ruhiira's students could barely read and write; and a good number of teachers, moonlighting to make ends meet, rarely showed up at school. Nevertheless, Siriri was pleased that new classrooms had been built and that enrollment was up, thanks in part to the school-feeding program he'd put in place. To help Ruhiira's best students continue their education, the Millennium project was underwriting the cost of secondary school for sixteen students.

Investments in infrastructure had been rewarded too: looking out from his house, perched on a hilltop, Siriri observed with satisfaction the many new roads crisscrossing the steep slopes below.

When it came to increasing people's incomes, however, Siriri saw nothing but failure. Pineapple couldn't be exported after all, because the cost of transport was far too high. There was no market for ginger, apparently. And despite some early interest from buyers in Japan, no one wanted banana flour. "I have been failed by the markets," he said soberly.

On one level, the cardamom crops had exceeded Siriri's expectations: the spice thrived in Ruhiira's moist valleys. However, as soon as Siriri tried to sell it, he hit a roadblock. "We proved it could be grown," he said, "but when I took it to the buyers they asked me, 'Is it organic?' and I had to tell them 'No! Of course it is not organic!' In Ruhiira we have run-off fertilizer that comes down from fields in the hills above—so no, I am sorry to say it is not organic."

As for starting a poultry enterprise in Ruhiira, Tyson Foods' feasibility study had exposed "several obstacles" and "hurdles": poor roads; insufficient water; high-priced chicken feed; a dependence on child labor; a lack of export markets; and low local prices for eggs. There was also a risk of bio-insecurity; in fact, concluded Tyson, Ruhiira was a "breeding ground for disease outbreaks." If Siriri could address these obstacles, Tyson Foods would gladly reconsider the matter. "We never heard from them again," Siriri told me.

Ruhiira's "Entrepreneurship Development and Business Skills Training Program" had been a disappointment. A handful of the entrepreneurs had managed to make something of their training—one man started a successful venture selling veterinary drugs, for example—but most of them never even got started. "In big towns, business is easy," Siriri remarked. "But in the village it is hard to get peasants to think like businesspeople."

After eight months in business, Emmy Byamukama's Twimukye Poultry Farm went under. The cost of chicken feed had been higher than he'd projected. Building a chicken coop was more complicated and more expensive than he'd anticipated. His chickens took a long time to begin producing eggs; and when they did start laying, there weren't enough eggs to turn a profit.

To start his business, Byamukama had applied for a loan from Ruhiira's Savings & Credit Co-operative, the small village credit union supported by the Millennium Villages Project. When the loan failed to be approved, he borrowed 800,000 shillings from a moneylender at interest of 20 percent a month. Then his business failed. To pay off the loan, he sold the chickens and the chicken coop, at a steep discount. Then he sold five of his eight goats. After all that, he still owed the moneylender 600,000 shillings—a debt that was consuming his wife's entire schoolteacher's salary. Now Byamukama was back to subsistence farming.

Siriri blamed himself for every failure in Ruhiira. The optimism with which he had initially approached his job had been replaced, not by cynicism exactly, but by frustration and a sense of inadequacy. It occurred to him that, in a way, the donkey fiasco could be viewed as a symbol of his own work. Within months of the animals' arrival in Ruhiira, four of the eight donkeys that were supposed to transport water from the valleys up to the hills had dropped dead of exhaustion; thereafter the entire donkey scheme was written off as a misguided experiment.

As for the PVC pipes, a deal had finally been brokered with JM Eagle to transport ten containers of water pipes to Ruhiira. JM Eagle agreed to pay the cost of shipping the containers to Mombasa, on Kenya's coast. From there the Millennium Villages Project would pay $60,000 to have the containers trucked to Ruhiira—an arduous one-thousand-mile journey all the way across Kenya, past Nairobi and Kisumu, to the eastern border of Uganda, down and around Lake Victoria, through Kampala, and finally, turning southwest toward Rwanda, up the narrow dirt roads to the hills of Ruhiira. But the pipes did not reach the port of Mombasa, because in the Indian Ocean the cargo ship transporting the containers was seized by a gang of Somali pirates. Siriri was reasonably confident that the pipes would one day make their way to Ruhiira; still, he couldn't help but view this latest setback as an ominous sign.

David Siriri is a patient man—long-suffering, he likes to say. His own life was well on course. He now had four children, and on the little plot of land he'd bought all those years ago in a suburb of Kampala, he and his wife were slowly building a house. Every other weekend, when he could afford the time, he traveled by bus to Kampala to visit his family and work on the house. Already the basic structure was in place—three bedrooms, a concrete floor, a tin roof, and windows. Just as soon as he'd saved enough money, he'd install indoor plumbing and replace the outdoor pit latrine with a proper bathroom. Instead of the charcoal fire in the yard, he'd build a real kitchen with a real stove.

But what about Ruhiira? Where would the village be in a few years, once the project had run its course and Siriri had moved on? On the one hand, he could see clear signs of economic activity in Ruhiira. Like Ahmed Mohamed in Dertu, Siriri noticed the growing number of corrugated tin roofs in the village. And as he remarked proudly, many more people owned bicycles, and new shops had opened in the village's commercial center. On the other hand, how much of that economic activity was the result of a real, lasting increase in income? "If you ask me if incomes here have increased, I'm not sure what I would tell you," he said. "I am not sure."

Long ago the Millennium Villages Project had set as its goal sustainability—a goal it defined as the maintenance of "economic progress without a loss of momentum, a drop in living standards, or a decline in social services." Would Ruhiira reach that goal? "I am not sure," Siriri repeated. "I am just not sure."

Part Seven

I didn't plan on this—I didn't plan on everybody descending to flakiness. . . . I mean, God forbid someone should actually *do* something! There's no accountability at all! There's no will to solve problems, that's for sure. The system is so dysfunctional I sometimes feel like I'm shouting in the wind.

—Jeffrey Sachs

Chapter 19

Misinformation and Politics

It was Ramadan, and Dertu was quiet. A dog limped along the town's deserted main street. Half-naked children slept on mats. In the shade beneath a shop's corrugated tin awning, two women were sifting grain. Ahmed was away again, in Garissa or maybe in Nairobi. He was rarely in Dertu these days. More and more of his time was devoted to handling administrative duties, to writing progress reports and grant proposals, and to meeting with various government officials and NGOs. Mainly, he was preoccupied with the urgent business of raising money.

With the Millennium Villages Project approaching its fifth year, Dertu's budget had been cut drastically. All the villages faced budget cuts: phase one of the project was winding down, and Jeffrey Sachs was having a hard time convincing donors or venture capital funds to underwrite phase two. In the West, unemployment was way up, people were losing their homes, and poor Africans were no longer a priority (if they ever had been). No one seriously believed the G8 would follow through on its promise of doubling foreign aid to Africa.

One after another, rich countries were reneging on their pledges to the poor, and Sachs was raging. "The problem is," he said, "one hundred and ten percent of the air is being sucked out of the room by the financial crisis." One after another, he named the culprits: "Japan pledged two hundred million for agriculture—nothing was ever seen of that. Sarkozy pledged a billion euros—not one penny has been seen from that. I was at a dinner when Berlusconi pledged a billion euros—he said, 'Sarkozy's done it, now Italy will do the same.' Naturally there were snickers in the room, and nothing came from that. The United States of course has done nothing."

He went on: "It's a farce. It's all a farce. And it's a little weird for me, I have to tell you, because I didn't plan on this— I didn't plan on everybody descending to flakiness. . . . I mean, God forbid someone should actually *do* something! There's no accountability at all! There's no will to solve problems, that's for sure. The system is so dysfunctional I sometimes feel like I'm shouting in the wind."

By nature, however, Sachs is an optimist. If the G8 wouldn't deliver on its promises, he'd look elsewhere; to China, for example. Suddenly, from Angola to Zambia, the Chinese were all over sub-Saharan Africa. They were "cutting deals at a dizzying pace," Richard Behar wrote in a cover story for *Fast Company*, "securing supplies of oil, copper, timber, natural gas, zinc, cobalt, iron, you name it."

Of course, China's interest in Africa was exploitative. The Chinese were ruthless: they backed Africa's most corrupt strongmen, disregarded human rights, and hoarded African resources. Then again, maybe development was development, no matter the moral and ethical cost. The Chinese weren't only extracting Africa's raw materials; they were also building bridges, dams, pipelines, hospitals, football stadiums, and telephone networks. Trade between China and Africa was now approaching $100 billion a year. China was lending more money to Africa than even the World Bank, it was said.

The Chinese approach to development seemed to work in China—hundreds of millions of Chinese had been lifted out of poverty—so why couldn't it work in Africa? Sachs was willing to give China the benefit of the doubt. "They're not jaundiced, fatigued, or in a mind-set of endless treadmills, but they actually want to do something," he told me. "So when China says that they'll do ten billion dollars in cheap credit to Africa over three years, I'm ready to bet they'll do ten billion over three years. When the G8 says they're going to do twenty billion dollars over three years, I don't know whether that's going to be one billion, two billion, five billion, eight billion, twelve billion, or even by some chance twenty billion."

After all, when it came to making the investments needed to end extreme poverty, what difference did it really make where the money came from? "The amounts required are very small," Sachs continued. "So if it ends up coming through companies, if it ends up coming through China, if it ends up coming through individual contributions, if it ends up coming through social movements, if it ends up coming through consumer activism, if it ends up coming through Millennium Villages' branded products, if it ends up coming through official development assistance—that is not really the main point. The main point is that it happens."

As for his own immediate needs, in the best case Sachs hoped to raise $100 million for phase two of his project. He was willing to make do with less—$50 million or $60 million would be acceptable. So far, however, including $2 million that the fashion designer Tommy Hilfiger had just agreed to donate to Ruhiira, he'd received commitments for approximately $10 million from various foundations and individuals. Perhaps China would help out. Maybe Soros would throw in more money. The Islamic Development Bank was a possible donor. Sachs was working every angle. In the meantime, however, the staff in all the Millennium villages was nervous: What if Sachs couldn't find more money?

In Dertu, there was another problem: Ahmed had overrun his budget. To pay Dertu's mounting bills, he'd requested one advance after another from New York, with the result that his remaining balance was precariously low. In the village, rumors were circulating that Ahmed had been overcharged by unscrupulous contractors. He was naïve or too trusting, some people said. He'd spent 2 million Ksh for a new fence that should have cost just 400,000 Ksh, someone claimed. Others reported that hundreds of thousands of shillings had vanished without a trace. Receipts could not be found. Microfinance loans had not been repaid. Supplies purchased by the project were never delivered. There was talk of questionable bookkeeping—something about low-level staff members being ordered to acknowledge receipt of petty cash they'd never received.

Ahmed dismissed these accusations as "misinformation and politics." He was deeply hurt by the rumors. Why would the community try to undermine him? Why would people speak ill of him? It made no sense. Look at how much he had done for Dertu! For the past four years, he had devoted his life to this village; he'd given everything he could to the Millennium project. With a resigned shrug, he concluded that envy must be fueling the rumors. "Some people are not happy that Ahmed is close to Jeff Sachs," he said, when I reached him by phone. "Because of Ahmed's sincerity, because of Ahmed's hard work, some people are resentful."

He resolved not to be dragged down by pettiness. "We don't succumb to those nonsenses," he said. "We stay above that." He was on his way to Nairobi to deliver a lecture and was busy preparing for an upcoming meeting in Addis Ababa. So much was happening. Had I seen the new brochure he'd made about Dertu? Did I know about the French ambassador's visit to Dertu? A British filmmaker was coming to Dertu to make a documentary about the African drylands. His job was no longer just about Dertu; it was far bigger than that.

Ahmed had taken to heart the Great Professor's goal of expanding the Millennium Villages Project all across Africa. "Jeff Sachs is a great man," he said, solemnly. "Because of him, I am dreaming of having a string of eighteen Millennium villages through North Eastern Kenya," he added, echoing

Sachs's vision of transforming all of North Eastern Province into one huge Millennium district. "If we succeed, the impact can radiate through other parts of Kenya, across the borders to Ethiopia and Somalia, across the whole Sahel. Imagine the contribution to the whole region!"

With Ahmed gone for months at a time, his deputy, Idris, now controlled the flow of information and resources in Dertu. He took easily to his new position of authority. As a member of the same Aulihan subclan as the majority of Dertu's inhabitants, he claimed that he was better able to control the villagers than Ahmed, who belonged to a different subclan. Subtly, he let the rest of the Millennium staff know that as an Aulihan, he alone had the community's trust.

One morning during Ramadan, reclining on a prayer mat in the Millennium project's tented compound, his head propped on a pillow, Idris acknowledged one visitor after another, supplicants begging for his favor and goodwill. Wearing a loose-fitting djellaba and a white kufi, he nodded, calling on the first of his visitors to speak. Two members of the Subcommittee of Hay Distributors stepped forward.

Ahmed had managed to convince the people of Dertu to cut the long grass after all; now that the benefits of hay were understood, however, there wasn't enough of it to last through the long dry season. The Subcommittee of Hay Distributors needed to know: Would only the poorest households receive the hay, or should smaller amounts be given out equally to all households? Quickly, Idris settled the matter.

An old man with a creased face, his beard dyed orange with henna in the style of Somali elders, spoke next. He demanded a job as night watchman for the health clinic. While the old man was speaking, Idris cleaned his fingernails with the blunt end of a matchstick. The old man was begging Idris to take pity on him. Unmoved, Idris shook his head: the job was already taken. Now the chairman of the Millennium Villages Committee stepped forward. The community had accused him of stealing money—10,000 Ksh were missing from the community's bank account, and he was being blamed. He wanted Idris to come to his defense.

Someone else wanted help paying his son's school fees. Someone else wanted Idris to send the project's pickup truck to find his lost camel. Another man pleaded to have water trucked to Bahuri, a settlement just south of Dertu, where the one reservoir of rainwater had been dry for the past twenty-nine days. "You have pack animals," replied Idris. "Why do you not go and fetch water with these pack animals?" A herder whose camel had been attacked by a lion needed help from a veterinary health care worker.

Still more people approached Idris. There had been a dispute between a shopkeeper and a Kenyan soldier, someone explained, and the soldier was threatening to arrest the shopkeeper. To sort things out, Idris was needed immediately in the village center. "I am sorry," he sighed from his mat. "I cannot go. I am too tired and thirsty."

It was just past noon, with the temperature hovering around one hundred degrees Fahrenheit. There would be nothing to eat or drink until sunset, after the fourth prayer of the day. Idris stood up, dusted off his djellaba, and with a wave of his hand, ordered everyone to leave him. He needed to rest. "Come back later," he commanded, "after Iftar."

While Idris was asleep, a man approached Fatuma Shide, the Millennium project's health coordinator for Dertu, imploring her to send the project's truck to fetch his sick wife. Fatuma refused. The man raised his voice. The vehicle is just sitting there, unused, he insisted. Fatuma pointed to a donkey cart. "Use that," she said. The man started to shout, Was Fatuma aware of his cousin's status? He was a member of the Millennium Villages Committee! Fatuma stood her ground, and the man stormed off. "You are misusing the project," Fatuma yelled after him. "We are not here to change your lifestyle! That vehicle will be gone the moment we leave!"

Walking away from the Millennium compound, Fatuma and I headed toward the center of town. "These men are idle," she said bitterly. "And the Millennium project, we are making it worse—we are spoon-feeding them. They were using the donkey carts, but now that we have a vehicle they demand we use it to transport them. We must be strong. We are supposed to be the change agents."

Ever since the launch of the Millennium project, Fatuma had been empathetic and patient with the people of Dertu. She'd visited them in their *aqals,* listened to their concerns, and occasionally brought them small gifts from Garissa. She'd made many close friends. Now, disenchanted with the project, she talked openly about finding another job.

Idris had positioned himself as the village's "rainmaker," she complained; she'd been excluded from all decision making. She was sure that her higher-ups in Nairobi and New York did not know about the problems in Dertu. Ahmed was nowhere to be found these days. Jeffrey Sachs had visited Dertu twice, each time for no longer than two or three hours. His deputy, John McArthur, had not yet made it as far as Dertu.

Fatuma passed a group of men loafing under an acacia tree in the village center. "You see," she cried, pointing to the men. "I ask them, 'What are you doing?' They tell me, 'Fatuma, we are planning.' Planning, they say! But they are doing nothing, only rumor mongering." While the men stood idly under a shade tree, their wives gathered wood, fetched water, milked camels, cooked, swept, cared for children, and tended the sick. "At the age of thirty-five," Fatuma went on, "the women they look the age of sixty."

Gathering the bottom of her long *jibab,* Fatuma marched across the hot sand to the health clinic. "Look here," she said, arriving at the half-built maternity ward where three Bantu Kenyans, members of the Kamba tribe, were laying floor tiles. "Look at this!" The men had been recruited from another province to do the kind of manual labor that Dertu's Somalis wouldn't or couldn't perform for one reason or another. The Millennium project was paying the laborers 500 Ksh, about $6.50, a day. Why would anyone import labor to Dertu? "Because Somali men are lazy!" pronounced Fatuma.

Idris had awakened from his nap. Adjusting the pillow under his head, he swatted some flies circling overhead. The sun came through the straw tent, and everything was streaked with light. "Somali men are not lazy," he protested. "We are very proud people. We are descendents of Abraham, and if you descend from Abraham, you don't do manual labor. We don't cook. We don't make tea. We don't clean or sweep. We don't do construction or garbage collection. Our only business is animal herding."

Perhaps I was witnessing the "formidable pride of the Somali nomad," as described by the British scholar Ioan Lewis in his classic study of 1961, *A Pastoral Democracy.* Lewis wrote about the Somali nomad's "extraordinary sense of superiority" and "his firm conviction that he is sole master of his actions and subject to no authority except that of God."

Idris went on: "Once I met a man who was Irish—he didn't even know his great-grandfather! We look at you Europeans, and we can't imagine how you do not know who your great-grandfather is. Abraham is eighty-five generations removed from me—I can count every one of my fathers up to Abraham. *Every* good Somali can count his ancestors back to Abraham."

Every Somali child is taught to recite not only the Koran

but also the names of every one of his ancestors. A well-trained memory is part of the culture's ancient oral tradition. Somalis who can demonstrate "lineal purity," direct descent from Abraham, are noblemen; the rest are commoners or infidels, though not all commoners are equal. To a Somali, the lowest commoners are Bantu Africans. Brought to Somalia two centuries ago by Arab slave traders, the Bantu are still marginalized in the Horn of Africa. They are known as *jareer,* an ethnic slur whose etymology is the Somali word for "hard," as in the "hard" hair of blacks (as opposed to the softer, finer hair of ethnic Somalis and Arabs). The *jareer* were brought in to do manual labor in Dertu, to lay the floor tiles at the health clinic for 500 Ksh a day, while the local Somali men stood around the acacia tree in the village, chewing khat.

Sundown finally arrived, and with it Iftar. In a flash, the sun dropped off the horizon without a trace. The people of Dertu broke their fast. Idris drank a jug of water and ate handfuls of dates. Then, facing Mecca, he knelt down on a mat to pray. When he was finished, he settled back on his pillow, accepted the plate of *ugali* and boiled goat that was brought to him, and began receiving visitors.

A little after ten p.m., two men came rushing toward the Millennium compound and past the night watchman. Help was urgently needed, they informed Idris. An old man somewhere in the bush, about ten miles away, was convulsing and vomiting blood. He had to be brought to the health clinic right away.

"It will have to wait until tomorrow," Idris replied. "There is no light in the sky, and he is far in the bush. If the vehicle's tire is punctured, what will we do?"

"It is an emergency," one of the men insisted.

Idris shook his head. "All day we were here—why didn't you come earlier to make this request?"

Voices were raised. Back and forth in Somali. The old man had tuberculosis, it was explained. "He will die!" shouted the second man.

Idris didn't move. He was snacking on fried *kac kac* now. "Enough!" he said, dismissing the elders. "I can do nothing tonight. We will collect him early in the morning."

Chapter 20

A Version of Progress

In May 2009 the government of Kenya promoted Dertu from a "location" to a "division," an administrative region one step down from a district. According to a posting on the Millennium Villages blog, Dertu's new administrative status was "marked with jovial celebrations"; it was a testament to the project's success:

> When the project started in 2006, there were less than ten houses with iron sheets yet today there are well over 200 houses. The once poorly equipped clinic . . . is today the most vibrant in the region, treating and immunizing five times as many cases per month as before the project started. In terms of water, Dertu's borehole is the most reliable water source within the region and Dertu Primary school is today housing almost three times more pupils than in 2006. . . . Based on the above and many more development advantages that the Millennium Villages project and partners brought, Dertu clinched the top position and was consequently selected as the newest division within Lagdera District.

Indeed, there were signs of progress in Dertu—more congestion, for one thing. Nomadic pastoralists, immigrants from other parts of North Eastern Province, squatters, and refugees from the war in Somalia continued to settle in Dertu with their families, attracted by the village's relative wealth. In an unending "sea of poverty," every Millennium village represents an island of prosperity.

In the town center, men were dragging wooden carts loaded high with branches; a Bantu Kenyan had set up a shoeshine stand; traveling salesmen hawked bedsheets, Bic pens, machetes, flip-flops, and bags of cornmeal and yellow split peas diverted from the World Food Program. "From the American People: Not to be Sold or Exchanged," read a warning printed on the bags.

Coca-Cola was now available in Dertu. A small pharmacy ("Al-Aqsa Drug-Store") and a hardware store had opened. There was even a "lodge," a dormitory of sorts with six beds, each available for between fifty cents and four dollars a night (depending, it seems, on whether you were a local or a *mzungu*). For breakfast, guests of the lodge were offered freshly fried *mandazi,* a kind of East African doughnut. Whereas it had once been difficult to find anything to eat in Dertu, there were now three restaurants in town.

The grandest restaurant was an open-air hut with a tin roof and cracked plastic lawn chairs. It belonged to the village chief of Dertu, Jelle Dolal Bulle, whose wife and seven daughters served a tasty meal of boiled goat with rice, French-fried pota-toes, and a tomato and red onion salad. Jelle's competitive advantage was having the only refrigerator in the town. He kept it on display in the middle of the restaurant, where it was powered by a very big, very noisy generator. At the same time, he had a side business recharging cell phones. Outside his res-taurant a shortwave radio was playing American pop classics: Kool & the Gang, Peter Frampton, the Backstreet Boys.

For all that, Dertu still had no running water or electric-ity or paved roads. It had no industries or long-term jobs or anything that appeared likely to last once the Millennium project folded its tents and left town. It was startling to see how quickly Dertu's wide-open, pastoral landscape had been turned into something resembling a shantytown. Most people lived in squalor, their *aqals* jammed together, patched with black or green polyurethane bags, and covered in cardboard, burlap bags, and plastic tarps. Slow streams of slops made their way along the narrow footpaths between the *aqals*.

The community latrines paid for by the Millennium Villages Project were clogged or overflowing, or else they had caved in; no one could agree on whose job it was to maintain them. In a ditch piled high with rotting garbage, a frenzied flock of Marabou storks ripped apart the carcass of some beast. Flimsy polyurethane bags, officially banned by the Millennium project, clung to every brake and thornbush. The Garbage Committee had ceased to function, if it ever did function. No one knew what had happened to the 60,000 Ksh that Ahmed had given the committee to buy rakes and wheelbarrows.

It wasn't easy to impose order on Dertu. The government of Kenya had tried to create a town plan of sorts. But as soon as the people of Dertu heard that their haphazard settlements were to be razed, their *aqals* torn down and replaced by the government's version of progress, a fight had broken out: the people weren't about to move. "They say, 'Our village was here before you came,'" reported Ahmed. "They say, 'We will not agree to your plan. This is our village not yours.'" In a matter of months, the land surveyors sent by the government had been chased out of town.

Without a formal government survey, there could be no land titles or property rights, and without land titles or property rights, nothing of permanence could be built in Dertu. "Oh dear, oh dear, I am so frustrated!" cried Ahmed. "How can you implement without a plan? How can you design a town without a map? How can you build a permanent house if someone will come along and say to you, 'My camels used to graze here—this is my land, remove the house'?"

He paused, apparently to reflect on what he had just said. "You cannot," he concluded.

By 2010, over a period of just three and a half years, the Millennium Villages Project and its partners had poured $2.5 million into Dertu. Inevitably, perhaps, there were growing rifts between neighbors, caused by infighting and envy. Clans quarreled for control over the project's largesse. The village's growing resources had thrust the people of Dertu into a new economic order marked by inequality. People were more discontented than usual. And neither Ahmed nor Idris seemed prepared to defuse the situation. On such matters, the *Millennium Villages Handbook* does not offer guidance.

Sahlan understood that to prosper in the new Dertu, you had to know the right people. Even that wasn't enough; to survive, you needed ingenuity and cunning. She had half a dozen competitors now, tea shops started by pastoralist dropouts, many of whom, it occurred to her, were more resourceful than she was. At first, she'd been grateful to the Millennium Villages Project for the taste of material wealth it offered her, but now she craved so much more. She realized she'd been mistaken to believe that her future would be any different from her past.

Squatting over a three-stone fire, still making chapatis and chai for the customers of her tea shop, Sahlan cataloged the Millennium project's sins of omission; it hadn't delivered what it promised. "They have not built permanent houses," she told me sullenly, "they have not brought us more water, they have not put up a secondary school, they have not supported people with money to start businesses, and in the rainy season the road is still not passable."

Madame Sofia, Dertu's school principal, was just as unhappy.

For one thing, she had given up her television set; it used more fuel than she could afford. The Millennium Villages Project had given her hope, when in fact there was no hope, or so it seemed to her. The new classrooms she had been promised were never built, a partially constructed storeroom was left unfinished, and the laptop computers donated by Sony had not been connected to the Internet. (Apparently, the computers themselves had vanished.)

We walked across the school's dusty playing field. "According to expectations," Madame Sofia went on, "the Millennium has not been good to us." Yes, she admitted, two new dormitories had been built, but already they had fallen into disrepair. SUPPORTED BY THE MILLENNIUM VILLAGES PROJECT, read a hand-painted sign outside the boys' dormitory, OFFICIALLY OPENED 23RD MARCH 2009. She pointed to the broken windows and the flaking walls covered in graffiti. Showers had been installed, but there was no running water. A metal utility sink had been ripped from the wall. The overhead light didn't work. Behind the top bunk of a rusting bed, someone had scrawled: "Millenion [*sic*] have done nothing in this school."

One of Dertu's more prominent citizens, Ali Abdi Mohamed, owner of the Al-Aqsa Drug-Store, filed a written complaint against the Millennium Villages Project. With the help of a computer-literate friend in Garissa, he outlined the community's grievances in a three-page (typed) letter, which he then delivered to Farah Maalim, member of parliament for the district that encompasses Dertu:

COMPLAIN AGAINST MVP
1. The project was supposed to be community driven, but MVP staff driven project hence this created dependence syndrome;
2. The project is supposed to be bottom top approached but it is visa versa;

3. No sense of ownership of the project;

4. No transparency and accountability;

5. Offices operate from Garissa which is 100 kilometers [away]. Most of the project funds is used to hire vehicles;

6. No planning of project and implementation i.e. sitting together with the community for planning;

7. Some of the goals were neglected i.e. empowerment of women;

8. Field office not operational and building is semi-permanent;

9. Maternity wing no light and women are delivering in the dark;

10. Dormitory constructed by MVP but no beds, mattresses, bed sheets and pillows and also no light i.e. children are lying on the floor;

11. Incompetent staffs are working on the project i.e. nutritionist as a community facilitator;

12. Whenever a visitor comes to Dertu they don't allow community and the visitors to exchange ideas and views;

13. They use divide and rule system of colonials to carry out their interest;

14. Four computers donated to the school through MVP and no where to be seen.

In a nutshell, those fourteen complaints summed up the dissatisfaction felt in all the villages. Hardly perceptible at first, a profound pessimism had settled over the entire Millennium Villages Project.

At the Millennium Villages' head office in New York, so many staff members had quit or been replaced that I finally lost track. Peter Kaye, the chief marketing officer ("a strategist with a passion for making a difference"), was gone within a year of joining the project. His position was eliminated, the idea of mining "channels of consumer giving" having been dropped, apparently. Geoff Gottlieb, a young economist whom Sachs had hired with fanfare to develop the Millennium project's agricultural credit program, also left after a year. Even Rustom Masalawala had been let go. He never did manage to convince a social investment fund to underwrite business ventures in the Millennium villages.

"In hindsight it's like we were set up to fail," said a member of Sachs's inner circle in New York. "It's not that Jeff's ideas are wrong—he's a big, inspiring thinker. It's that the project's ambition moved more quickly than the capacity. It makes me feel like a chump. It makes me feel totally hollow."

In Nairobi, the Millennium team for East Africa started to bad-mouth the executives in New York. Sachs and his deputy, John McArthur, were "imperial" and "arrogant." "They ask no questions, they solicit no information," said one frustrated manager when I passed through Nairobi. "It's just one long monologue from New York—orders given to be executed by us. They are utterly out of touch with what is actually going on."

The term *rural development tourism* was coined by the scholar Robert Chambers in *Rural Development,* his influential 1983 book about why outsiders remain ignorant about rural poverty. His thesis, in short, is this: with their "hectic excursions from the urban centre," development experts don't see behind the facade. The more distinguished a visitor happens to be, the greater his ignorance and self-deception. "They come, and they sign the book, and they go. They only talk with the buildings," writes Chambers, quoting destitute Africans. "*Ils ne savent pas qu'il y a ici des gens vivant*"—"They don't realize there are living people here."

Jeffrey Sachs's observations on the ground were necessarily limited—by the pressures of time, by language, culture, education, background, preconceptions, and ingrained models of thought. Wherever he went in Africa, he was greeted by a spectacle: villagers danced for him, dignitaries put on their Sunday suits and praised him, dozens of photos were snapped, and just before his arrival, schools and clinics were scrubbed clean. His view of what was happening in the villages wasn't wrong; it was incomplete. Real progress had been made, by all means; nevertheless, the villages had serious, deep-rooted problems, problems that for one reason or another Sachs refused to acknowledge.

Ali Abdi Mohamed had suggested in his written complaint that Sachs and his team were guilty of neocolonialism. Anthropologists might phrase it differently: in their view, economists like Sachs tend to approach development with a set of assumptions that are "breathtakingly ethnocentric and empirically incorrect," to quote Katy Gardner and David Lewis's *Anthropology, Development and the Post-Modern Challenge.* Blinded by an "inherently optimistic" Western view of modernization, they begin with the premise that there is one path to economic growth—their own.

"This is not meant to be a command-and-control project," Sachs told me, "so I'm glad to hear I don't know everything happening in the field." Sometimes, however, I suspected that Sachs didn't really want to know what was going on in his villages. His theories were trumping reality. By 2010 the Millennium Villages Project had become a cumbersome bureaucracy with hundreds of dependent employees. One hundred twenty million dollars and Sachs's reputation were riding on the outcome of this social experiment in Africa. Was anyone prepared to smash the glass and pull the emergency cord?

Chapter 21

What Mistake Has Ahmed Done?

Exactly four years after he joined the Millennium Villages Project, in the spring of 2010, Ahmed Mohamed was fired. He never saw it coming, and months after the fact he was still in disbelief. The slope of his shoulders, the long, deep lines on his face, the listless gait—he looked defeated. "They sent auditors," he said when we met one evening for dinner in Garissa. "They spread misinformation. Money is missing, but God forbid I have not taken the money or even a small baby cow in Dertu! I have my morals!"

Again and again Ahmed replayed the chain of events that had led to his dismissal. "For me being a very straight and honest person, I went to Nairobi to discuss the problem," he explained, justifying himself. "But I am not aware that already a decision has been reached by the Millennium system. I am too sincere. In the middle of the meeting, I am told, 'Ahmed, a decision has been made—you will not be in Dertu anymore.'"

That night, unable to sleep, he wrote an e-mail to Jeffrey Sachs. "I wanted to know what he felt about it," he told me. "I was trying to cool myself at this trying moment of my life." The following day he received in response a brief e-mail. "It is an internal matter," wrote Sachs. "I can do nothing about it."

"That was the last communication we had," said Ahmed. "I am feeling betrayed. I am feeling I was abandoned. I had worked with this project very, very sincerely, even putting in my own money, and all my own time. For the community of

Dertu and the future generations of Dertu, I know I did a lot. I changed many people's lives. I am proud of that. It is always good to be sincere, and one day we will know the truth. If you are a sincere person, truth will always prevail. In myself I know I have contributed—I have contributed immensely, I have contributed sincerely, I have contributed tremendously. So in me I feel I am a giant, and I know one day I will get my likeness. The rest, God knows. I have no regrets. I will forgive, but to forget is difficult."

He poked at his uneaten plate of rice and chicken. "Please," he said, "I am asking Jeff one question: What mistake has Ahmed done to deserve this?"

What mistake *had* Ahmed made? According to his immediate boss, Belay Begashaw, an Ethiopian responsible for the Millennium Villages Project in East Africa, "The reason Ahmed left us is because he finished his contract with us. You know how many people's contracts we terminate each week? It's a totally normal process. If your contract is finished, it is finished. Ahmed finished his contract with us."

Sitting in his office in Nairobi, Begashaw crossed his arms defiantly. A short, solidly built man with a small mustache, he was wearing a gray suit and an open-collared purple shirt stretched tightly over his broad stomach. When I asked for a copy of the auditor's report on Dertu, he scowled. "Which report?" he replied with a straight face. "Honestly I do not know of this report. There are many reports. Every month we are sending people to the villages to review work. People are coming with all kinds of reports."

He looked at his watch. It was big and very shiny. He went on: "We send people every day to write reports. This is a very normal process. This is absolutely normal actually. Like other villages there are some issues to be corrected. It's just a normal course."

Back in New York, I was given the same story, more or less.

"Look, these are internal HR issues, not public information. I'm trying to be as helpful as I can," John McArthur said unhelpfully. "If there was a management change with my staff, I'm not going to talk to a—well, frankly, I'm not going to give a journalist the exact details on that."

And what about the auditor's report? "It was an internal audit, not an external audit. KPMG was brought in to do an internal report, which is different from calling it an external audit for formal public review," McArthur said, unraveling the semantics of forensic accounting.

"In these management systems, you have a process," he continued. "You know—program planning, budgeting, resource tracking, checking of outcomes. And we had—well, there were concerns that were raised that this wasn't tight enough. You know, 'How does A link to B link to C?' And we had questions as to how A was linked to B was linking to C. In a very difficult environment, obviously, you need to have a systematic check on that stuff. And there's no bank in the middle of Dertu with transactions slips and everything, so there's just a lot of complex systems to check. And so that's what they did— they went in and said, 'How are these systems working? How are plans being linked to resources being linked to tracking on these resources and linked to outcomes?' And we learned that the systems needed to be strengthened considerably."

He paused, composed himself, and then went on, slowly now: "Look, I can only say the same thing in so many ways. We decided they needed to be strengthened, all these pieces. It's a systems issue. There was no finding of mass misbehavior, but you still have to submit receipts so that you can cross-reference—you know, is the thing there in the end, is everything being tracked appropriately, and is there an accountant sitting there managing every entry and cross-referencing, and are the appropriate dual signatures going on every check and all that stuff. That doesn't mean the money's gone missing. It means that your systems aren't tracking everything. That's an accounting function. So that's the type of thing we decided needed to be strengthened—how all this stuff is tracked."

Was he trying to say that money had not been stolen in Dertu? "You know, I can't say that with certainty—and frankly I don't really want to get into it," McArthur replied. "I can't say that no money was stolen because I'm not there and I don't have the report in front of me. . . . One of the problems was that there wasn't proper accounting staff in place. And so in that environment certain people can take advantage and they can do marginal misbehavior or they can do significant misbehavior. Might people have done marginal misbehavior? It's possible. I do know that the reporting systems weren't what they needed to be to track, you know, every expenditure in a way that we felt was adequate."

Would it be possible to get a copy of the KPMG report? "I don't think so," he answered. "No, I don't think it's possible."

One afternoon in late spring, a few weeks after Ahmed was fired, I sat down with Jeffrey Sachs in the garden of his town house on Manhattan's Upper West Side. How much did he know and care about the loss of his top man in Dertu? "Basically, I don't really know in detail the story of what happened in Dertu," he began casually. "I liked Ahmed and was, you know, impressed by him, but apparently the community was not."

Columbia University had paid $8 million for Sachs's town house in 2002, part of a package of benefits designed to lure him from Harvard. Apart from its six bedrooms and working fireplaces, what makes the house particularly appealing is its south-facing garden. The day we met, with the tulips in full bloom, he was grateful for that garden. He'd been up most of the night working to meet the deadline on his new book, *The Price of Civilization,* a critical diagnosis of America's economic and political ills. Of course, Africa and the Millennium Villages Project were of foremost importance to him. Increasingly, however, Sachs found himself preoccupied with catastrophes in his own country. Paralysis in Washington, the budget deficit, a president beholden to lobbyists, the decline of civic virtue—"a first-rate mess," he called it.

Sachs returned to the subject of Ahmed: "I think he was, or they felt he was, forming cliques and not doing the right things, and we heard also—you know, we heard from the community, we heard from the local parliamentarian, and I heard internally that they were not impressed by him. I wasn't part of the review, but apparently there was a lot of community unhappiness. The parliamentarian felt Ahmed wasn't doing a good job, that he was losing a lot of opportunities, that things should be moving faster, and that the community was not happy, you know, in terms of openness, participation, transparency, and all the rest."

Sachs went on: "For me it was hard to judge, but anyway I don't follow these things site by site, so I'm not going to get into the details. You know, we've changed lots of staff in this project. It's a big project. There are hundreds of people, and I believe, I mean, there are just so many things going on, this is not a major stumbling block. There's lots of staff changing over time.

"From my point of view, that place is like Job," he said, alluding to Dertu and the biblical book of Job. "Just one disaster after another: droughts, floods, Rift Valley fever, rinderpest—you name it. It's part of this general phenomenon, which is that water is the most powerful gradient across the villages. Where water control is extremely low and rainfall is extremely low, we see the worst crises. And that's why we're launching a pastoralist-only project starting in July, using Dertu as a model. Do you know about it? It's important. The Drylands Initiative, we're calling it. My view is that this is the hot spot of the entire world, and that it's not a coincidence that Afghanistan, Yemen, Somalia and so forth are in the situation that they're in. . . ."

Part Eight

This isn't an intellectual exercise or a spectator sport. I'm trying to get something done. That's what I do for a living.

—Jeffrey Sachs

Chapter 22

An Island of Success

In the beginning, it was easy to ignore or discredit critics of the Millennium Villages Project: they were ignorant, according to Sachs, or misinformed or misguided. He wrote off hostile journalists and bloggers as irresponsible thinkers, impediments to the greater good. "Either you decide to leave people to die or you decide to do something about it," he'd say.

Between his extraordinary command of historical facts and his combativeness, Sachs can flatten almost any opponent. Sometimes his tactics get ugly. In 2009, when the economist Dambisa Moyo published *Dead Aid: Why Aid Is Not Working and How There Is a Better Way for Africa*, Sachs devoted more than two thousand words in *The Huffington Post* to Moyo's book: her ideas about foreign aid were "farcical," "simplistic," and "mistaken." With characteristic condescension, he took a mean-spirited swipe at her personally, describing her as "an African-born economist who reportedly received scholarships so that she could go to Harvard and Oxford but sees nothing wrong with denying $10 in aid to an African child for an anti-malaria bed net."

Sachs had launched the Millennium Villages Project in 2006 for two reasons: to test his theories about ending poverty, and to demonstrate that his proposed series of interventions could be used on a grand scale to eradicate extreme poverty across Africa. Five years later, in 2011, he was bragging about his success. As distributed by the Millennium project, reams of press releases, progress reports, blog posts, Twitter feeds, in-house videos, and pamphlets confirmed the happy results of Sachs's experiment. According to the Millennium project's annual report, it had led to "a stunning transformation of 500,000 lives." The report goes on to praise the project's "tremendous success," "tremendous strides," "remarkable progress," and "major breakthroughs." Sachs's prescription for ending poverty was endorsed by his boss, UN secretary-general Ban Ki-moon, who called it "a case study in what is possible, even in the poorest of places in the world."

"The thrilling news is that the communities in the Millennium Villages are on track," announced Sachs in 2011, as phase one of his project was about to end. "We are seeing dramatic gains in the fight against poverty, hunger, and disease. Incomes are rising, hunger is falling, and health is improving." That was true in part, but it wasn't the whole truth. By 2011, not even Sachs could ignore the wide and growing skepticism about the wisdom of his project.

Progress had been made, certainly; the data, uneven and inconclusive though they were, confirmed as much. Then again, what did the data really demonstrate? Was this history in the making, as Sachs had claimed? Had he really discovered the solution to extreme poverty? "Sachs is essentially trying to create an island of success in a sea of failure," remarked the economist William Easterly, "and maybe he's done that, but it doesn't address the sea of failure."

Some development experts dismissed the project outright. Yes, in Sachs's villages, the prevalence of malaria had dropped, more women were giving birth with the help of trained birth attendants, child mortality was down, and generally speaking, people were better nourished. At the same time, those and similar improvements were happening all across sub-Saharan Africa, not only in the Millennium villages. One after another, reports from UNICEF, the World Bank, and the IMF confirmed that the lives of Africans were slowly improving. Between 2000 and 2010, for example, deaths from malaria fell by a third in Africa. Infant mortality rates dropped sharply. More African children than ever attended primary school. More Africans had access to safe drinking water. And in the midst of a global economic crisis affecting Europe and the United States, a number of sub-Saharan African economies were doing surprisingly well. "Africa could be on the brink of an economic takeoff," predicted a 2011 World Bank report, "much like China was 30 years ago, and India 20 years ago."

A decade ago *The Economist* had written off Africa as "The Hopeless Continent." Now even a cautious interpretation of statistics showed that the poorest of the African poor were slightly better off than they once were. For the first time since the World Bank began tracking such figures in 1981, the proportion of sub-Saharan Africans living in extreme poverty (defined as living on less than $1.25 a day) had fallen below 50 percent. The numbers were still shocking. And besides, the $1.25-a-day yardstick was arbitrary—more than half a billion people in sub-Saharan Africa continued to live on less than $2 a day. Still, the numbers pointed to a promising upward trend. "People used to worry, 'Is Africa going to be poor forever?'" said Charles Kenny, a senior fellow at the Center for Global Development. "Well, it doesn't really look like it, does it?"

Was there a direct correlation between Sachs's carefully planned interventions and progress in his villages? If so, would some or all of that progress have happened one way or another, with or without the Millennium project? Is foreign aid the decisive factor in reducing extreme poverty, or should other key factors—increased trade and better government, for example—be taken into account? "The design of the project makes it impossible to carry out a truly rigorous assessment of the project's effects," concluded a damning critique of the Millennium Villages Project written by Michael Clemens and

Gabriel Demombynes, development experts with the Center for Global Development and the World Bank, respectively. There was no reliable way to evaluate the Millennium project, they insisted, because the data used to measure outcomes in the villages were radically flawed.

For one thing, there was no control group. "This has the advantage of simplicity but the major disadvantage of leaving unknown what might have happened in the villages if the project had not occurred," wrote Clemens and Demombynes. "It attributes any observed changes to the interventions, when in fact some or all of those changes might have occurred in the absence of the Millennium Villages Project." Looking closely at regional statistics and trends, and adjusting the Millennium project's reported results accordingly, they concluded that the actual impact of the project was only half of what Sachs had claimed.

According to a *New Yorker* profile of the economist Esther Duflo, written by Ian Parker, Sachs had at one time asked for Duflo's advice about the best way to measure the results of the Millennium Villages Project. Duflo runs the Abdul Latif Jameel Poverty Action Lab at MIT. She's famous for subjecting social policy interventions to randomized control trials, using the same rigor to establish cause and effect that pharmaceutical companies use to test drugs. She has won a MacArthur "genius" fellowship and in 2010 was awarded the John Bates Clark Medal for the most promising economist under the age of forty. Duflo explained to Sachs in an e-mail that while it was too late to use her methods to evaluate the first phase of his project, she could suggest better ways to measure outcomes going forward. He never replied.

A few months later, as quoted in *The New York Times,* Sachs dismissed Duflo's scientific approach to development. "Millennium villages don't advance the way that one tests a new pill," he argued.

Duflo was outraged. "He adopts this completely anti-scientific attitude," she said. "I am not really asking for a crazy standard of proof, just comparing."

"I don't think they're on target, I don't think they're good science, and I don't think they're apropos," Sachs told me, referring to published critiques of the Millennium Villages Project. To focus on metrics—on "sustainability" and "scalability" and "randomized control trials"—is, in Sachs's opinion, to reduce the lives of human beings to crude economic terms, to abstractions. "We are not waiting fifteen years for results—we are trying to move as fast as possible to help people who are suffering." In effect, he wanted us to trust him, to accept without question his approach to ending poverty, to participate in a kind of collective magical thinking.

Meanwhile, a growing number of journalists, economists, and development experts were uncovering inconsistencies and errors in the Millennium project's published results. Clemens and Demombynes, for example, wouldn't let up. "The project has claimed large impacts on school enrollment, vaccination rates, mobile phone ownership, malaria prevalence, HIV testing, access to improved water and sanitation, use of insecticide-treated bednets, and several others, and asserted that it is a 'solution to extreme poverty,'" they wrote on *The Guardian*'s *Poverty Matters Blog*. "None of these claims is supported by published peer-reviewed research. The claims are also impossible to independently verify."

A Kenyan economist, Bernadette Wanjala, and her colleague Roldan Muradian concluded in a report that increased agricultural yields in the Millennium village of Sauri had not translated into higher household incomes. On a similar note, *The Economist* stated that the Millennium Villages Project had failed to prove that a "big push" in foreign aid was the way out of extreme poverty. On his blog, Lawrence Haddad, director of the UK's Institute of Development Studies, asked the obvious question: "Who on earth will pay for this once the donors leave?"

In each case, Sachs responded angrily: *The Economist* was "mistaken," he wrote; Wanjala and Muradian's conclusions were "outlandish"; Haddad's critiques "reflect[ed] a real misunderstanding"; a negative article in the *Daily Mail* was "filled with falsehoods and distortions."

In the view of Sachs's loyal inner circle, any attack on the project revealed a deep-rooted cynicism about foreign aid and development. Yes, Sachs may have a colossal ego, and he may be flawed; but what his followers see above all is a selfless genius driven to improve the world. As they'll tell you with affection, Sachs is a "shit disturber," willing to use bare-knuckled tactics to advance his agenda on behalf of the poor and disenfranchised. "This is Nobel Prize–winning stuff that Jeff is working on," said his deputy, John McArthur. "Of course, he'll never get the Nobel—but he should."

It was easy to sit back and criticize, to engage in "armchair criticism," as Sachs called it. How many more studies were needed before the rich world agreed to alleviate the suffering of poverty-stricken Africans by providing them with mosquito nets, high-yield seeds and fertilizers, microfinance, emergency obstetrical care, antiretroviral medication, and other life-saving interventions? Sachs wasn't seeking the approval of academics: ever since his work in Bolivia back in 1985, he'd been in the business of actually making things happen.

"It's a different kind of activity," he said, distancing himself from his armchair critics. "This isn't an intellectual exercise or a spectator sport. I'm trying to get something done. That's what I do for a living. It's not about being right and wrong—although being right is important in terms of the ultimate effect. But it's about whether a large number of people operating in various organizations and in various positions and with various motives and incentives coalesce around an idea."

To those who said he'd failed to take his Millennium project to scale, Sachs replied: baloney. "If you're asking, 'Was the model a franchise, where every country would have the golden arches of the Millennium Villages [Project] in its villages?' the answer is no, absolutely no."

He measured success more broadly, more subtly. "If three hundred million bed nets are distributed, that's what I call scaling up," he said defiantly. "If a dozen countries adopt agricultural programs to help their small-hold farmers, that's what I call scaling up. If the concept of integrated, rural development becomes second nature across a lot of the development community, that's what I call scaling up. If you mean that Jeff Sachs, personally, is the one doing each of those things; well, I don't have time and it's not my goal to have under my mandate a hundred thousand villages or five hundred thousand villages or whatever it is. My goal is to help propagate methods, tools, and ideas—and to show how things can be done. That's what I'm trying to do. And that's what we're doing."

Chapter 23

I Cry for Ahmed

A drought was gripping the Horn of Africa—not just another drought, but the worst one in modern history. It was the summer of 2011, the land was parched, Dertu's water hole had run dry, and people's emaciated livestock were being eaten alive by hyenas and lions. Everywhere you went, roads were littered with animal carcasses. Starving Somalis, more dead than alive, were streaming across the border into Kenya. At the already overcrowded Dadaab refugee camps near Dertu, aid workers struggled to handle the influx. "A vision of hell," the BBC called it.

North Eastern Province was more dangerous than ever. The radical Islamist group Al Shabab was rumored to be moving from Somalia into Kenya. The insurgents were hungry, violent, and armed with Kalashnikovs. For the first time since I'd started reporting in Africa, I hired armed escorts to accompany me from Garissa upcountry. At every checkpoint, jumpy policemen demanded to see documents, inspected our vehicle, then waved their rifles to let us through. We were warned to stay off the roads after nightfall.

Arriving in Dertu, I found the people despondent. Nearly a year and a half had passed since Ahmed was fired, and over time the memory of all that Ahmed had done for Dertu had grown. By this time, everything that was wrong with Dertu— the irreversible poverty, the dysfunction, the violence, the endless cycle of devastating droughts—was blamed on Ahmed's absence. "When Dr. Ahmed left, everything left," said Mohamed Ahmed Abdi, a village elder.

"He was a man of development," said the village chief, Jelle Dolal Bulle. "He treated us like his children, and now the community of Dertu we are very much missing Ahmed."

In the shade of a tree, the people of Dertu gathered to eulogize Ahmed. "When Ahmed was here, so many *mzungu* came to Dertu—from New York, from Sweden," recalled Madame Sofia. "Ahmed brought the name of Dertu to the world. Now in a whole year we are having no more visitors."

Sahlan nodded. "*Waan ooyeey Ahmed in uu soonokhdo,*" she said—"I cry for Ahmed to come back." From her perspective, life in Dertu was worse than ever. "It is God who has brought us this drought," she despaired. A hum of agreement ran through the crowd. God was punishing the people of Dertu.

"Since Ahmed has left us, there is only demoralization," someone else said. "We appeal for the Millennium project to come back the way it was, *Insha'Allah.* But they are telling us there is no budget, no funds, no money for Dertu."

Leaning against the tree, the itinerant schoolteacher Abdullahi Bari Barow smiled. Since my last visit to Dertu, Abdullahi had lost his job: so many people had fled town in search of water that the Millennium project had disbanded its mobile school. "In Somali we have a phrase," he remarked knowingly. "*Ruux markuu kula jooga ma jeclid, markuuse tako baa tebi.* It means when somebody is with you, you hate him—but when he leaves, you miss him so much."

A new boss was in charge of the Millennium Villages Project in Dertu. Born in North Eastern Province, Dr. Dabar Abdi Maalim was an ethnic Somali and a devout Muslim. He was a "good man" and a "religious man," the people in Dertu said, but he was not Ahmed. He held a Ph.D. in community health from Britain's University of Reading, where his doctoral thesis was devoted to the influence of culture on rates of immunization among nomadic Somalis. Before coming to Dertu, he had worked for the World Health Organization, helping to coordinate emergency medical relief in North Eastern Province.

Dabar's job in Dertu was to continue the Millennium project's development work, to build on the foundation that Ahmed had spent four years putting in place. When he arrived, however, he found "a village asunder," as he put it to me. The foundation of the village had cracked wide open, and now, instead of running a development project, he was running a one-man emergency relief operation, racing to stave off famine.

"When I accepted this job, it was suggested that I should put together a proposal for bringing irrigation to Dertu—but we don't even have water for drinking," he said. "It is not so simple to bring about the end of poverty when every few years comes a drought and you go back to where you started."

A few days later I was in the Nairobi airport, drinking a cold Tusker, waiting to board my flight home. The day I landed in New York, Al Shabab made its presence known in North Eastern Province: on a road I know well, a gang of Somali militants held up at gunpoint and took hostage a Kenyan driver for CARE, the humanitarian aid organization. That was just the beginning. A few weeks later, on Kiwayu, a Kenyan island just south of Somalia, gunmen burst into a British couple's beachfront bungalow at three a.m., shot the man dead, dragged his wife to a speedboat, and took off for Ras Kamboni, a Somali fishing town and well-known base camp for Islamic militants. In Manda, another Kenyan island, Al Shabab took a French woman hostage. Two medical doctors working in the Dadaab refugee camps were kidnapped.

In October, in retaliation, Kenyan forces stormed into Somalia—a futile exercise that gave Al Shabab even more reason to terrorize Kenya. The official response from an Al Shabab spokesman: "Mujahideen fighters will force them to taste the pain of the bullets."

In Garissa, Al Shabab goons in black balaclavas hurled hand grenades into two churches and fired assault weapons into the crowd of worshippers. North Eastern Province went into lockdown: every Westerner I knew was fleeing; humanitarian agencies were pulling out as fast as they could. Dertu was more isolated than ever. My reporting was done, and my family wanted me home for good. I didn't have to put my life at risk. But what about the people of Dertu? What choices did they have? To quote Sachs once more: either you decide to leave people to die or you decide to do something about it.

The drought and violence in North Eastern Province were examples of what the Millennium Villages Project referred to as "artifacts"—unexpected or unintentional disturbances that, through no fault of the project, shatter the bell jar that protects Sachs's vulnerable experiment. But why in the world were drought and violence and hostage taking unexpected in sub-Saharan Africa?

Uganda too was in a state of crisis. Everywhere in the country people were being squeezed, the prices of food and gasoline were soaring, and the Ugandan shilling was worth less every day.

All through 2011 demonstrations, initially small and restricted to Kampala, became larger and more numerous. Protesters were beaten, fired at with rubber bullets and water cannons and tear-gas grenades. The opposition leader Kizza Besigye was arrested, dragged into the back of a pickup truck by heavily armed police officers, and charged with inciting violence and disobedience. In the town of Masaka, halfway between Ruhiira and Kampala, a two-year-old child was killed when military police fired live ammunition at a crowd of unarmed protesters.

David Siriri prayed that the country was not sliding back to the Uganda of his impoverished youth. He tended to steer clear of politics, but to him it was obvious that the government of Uganda had other priorities: acquiring fighter jets, for example. In the spring of 2011, shortly before he was sworn in for his fourth term in office, it was confirmed that President Museveni had spent $750 million on six brand-new, long-range Su-30MK Russian fighter jets for Uganda's military. "How can they buy fighter jets while people have nothing to eat, no basic health care, [and] the infrastructure is in tatters?" cried Kizza Besigye. "The money that could be spent to improve our affairs is being stolen or opulently spent on other things."

Other unexpected "artifacts" were destabilizing the Millennium Villages' experiment. In Mali, from one day to another, the democratically elected president, Amadou Toumani Touré, was ousted in a military coup d'état, with the result that one of the most stable countries in Africa was in utter chaos. In the northern city of Timbuktu, Tuareg rebels overran the Millennium project's offices, stealing everything they could get their hands on, including the project's computers and its Toyota pickup truck. The staff managed to escape, barely. The project's team leader, Bakary Yacouba Diabate, paid a member of the Arab militia 500,000 West African CFA francs (about $1,000) to lead himself and his family to safety. They left Timbuktu in the middle of the night, traveling down the Niger River for four days on a *pinasse,* a long wooden canoe with a small motor. A few days later two other staff members made it out by *pinasse,* part of an evacuation organized by the World Food Program.

Before long all of northern Mali, a vast desert region larger than France, had fallen into the hands of radical Islamists linked to Al Qaeda. There were reports of violent repression. Innocent people were being whipped and beaten. A couple accused of having a child outside marriage was stoned to death. A man caught stealing sheep had his hand sawed off.

There was almost no way to communicate with Toya, the Millennium project's model village outside Timbuktu; according to people who had escaped by the skin of their teeth, the situation in the village was dire. Tuareg rebels stole the community health workers' Ericsson cell phones. They stole one hundred tons of fertilizer that had been donated to the Millennium village by the Minnesota-based Mosaic Company. They stole Toya's entire supply of diesel fuel, with the result that the village's water pumps were idle and the rice crops could not be irrigated.

Because of the ongoing catastrophe, the Millennium project was forced to abandon Toya. "What can we do?" said Amadou Niang, director of the Millennium Villages Project for West Africa. "All our gains are lost. All is gone. Five years and four or five million dollars of interventions and everything is lost."

Chapter 24

It Is What It Is

On October 3, 2011, at the UN Headquarters in New York, Jeffrey Sachs officially launched phase two of the Millennium Villages Project with the stunning announcement that $72 million had been pledged. "Millennium Villages, on Track to Reach 2015 Goals, Launch Final Phase" was the headline of the press release handed out that day. Everything was proceeding according to plan: the project was "an inspiring example" of how to achieve the UN's Millennium Development goals, a "brighter future" was assured, the end of extreme poverty was in reach.

Once again George Soros was the project's lead donor: his foundations were putting up $47 million, nearly two-thirds of the total amount pledged. Standing under the bright lights, Sachs gripped Soros's hand tightly and smiled.

The announcement came as a relief to David Siriri. It meant that Ruhiira wouldn't have to be abandoned after all; he'd been granted a few more years to complete the project. He was determined to solve the daunting problem of the village's water supply. He would make sure that Ruhiira was at last connected to the national electric grid. He would find cash crops to generate income for the villagers—coffee, for example. Using simple manual pulping machines, local farmers could not only cultivate coffee but process it as well. The idea was promising.

Sometimes, when he was feeling especially optimistic, Siriri believed he would accomplish all those things and more. Other times, he was not at all sure. The Millennium Villages Project was winding down. Behind the scenes, Sachs was negotiating to raise another $20 million or $30 million from the Islamic Development Bank. Even if that money came through, however, funding for phase two was roughly half of what it had been for phase one: on a per capita basis, Ruhiira's annual budget would fall to $25 per person. Besides, there were strings attached to the $72 million pledge announced for phase two. For one thing, $20 million of that sum was not guaranteed; it would be made available for loans, contingent on the villages coming up with "investment-worthy business projects" that met with Soros's approval. For another thing, the $72 million included the value of donated goods and services: mosquito nets from Sumitomo Chemical, antimalaria drugs donated by Novartis, and technical support provided by Ericsson. All through phase one, Siriri had been seriously short of money, and now he was being asked to do with far less. How would he manage?

According to his bosses in New York, Siriri would have no problem adjusting to this new period of austerity; as soon as funding from the Millennium project dried up, other donors (local governments, NGOs, foreign aid donors) would be stepping in to cover the shortfall. To quote the plan drafted by the Millennium project:

> The Project will work with each host government, both nationally and locally, to ensure a smooth handover of functions over the next five years, so that 2015 does not mark a jarring "discontinuity" when the Project ends. During this time, more of the public services, such as schools and clinics, will rely on the government itself, as funding from the MVP is gradually withdrawn. Timetables will be established with host governments to ensure a smooth handover of leadership positions. Budgetary allocations

will be discussed with the host governments as well, so that as MVP support is tapered down, local government and NGO support can sustain or even expand the respective public sector activities.

To put all that in plain language, interventions that had previously been funded by the Millennium Villages Project—health care, education, agricultural inputs, and infrastructure—would continue to be funded, but only if local governments or foreign aid donors stepped in. How likely was that to happen?

Siriri doubted that the Ugandan government would make up the shortfall. "The government has even failed to cover its basic budget, so where will they find additional money for Ruhiira?" he told me. "I have talked with them and I can see their sincerity. But they don't have any money to give. It is not happening."

The Millennium villages were well provided for. Relatively speaking, they were "islands of prosperity," a fact that made it unlikely that they'd be given the government resources that the Millennium project expected and had planned for. Why funnel money to a Millennium village when so many other African villages were in far greater need of support?

As for depending on international donor agencies, it was wishful thinking. In the first place, the G8 had fallen far short of its promise to double foreign aid to Africa. Moreover, in 2011, for the first time in over a decade, the G8 had actually *reduced* spending on foreign aid. The United States had cut back its foreign aid budget—not counting "war-related" aid going to Afghanistan and Iraq—and Congress was calling for still more cuts.

Where on earth would the money come from to complete the work in the Millennium villages? I asked Sachs. "It is what it is," he replied. "And that's not meant to be callous."

It was 2012. He was fifty-seven and his hair was grayer than I'd remembered. He looked tired—"battle-scarred" was the phrase later used by one member of his staff. In a long, rambling interview in his office at Columbia University's Low Memorial Library, he answered my questions slowly, with less energy and more caution than usual.

Back in 2005, Sachs had set out to end extreme poverty once and for all, definitively: the title of his book, *The End of Poverty,* made clear the huge scope of his ambition. "This is a village that's going to make history," he had proclaimed in 2005, while visiting his first Millennium village with Angelina Jolie. "It's a village that's going to end extreme poverty."

Now, seven years later, he insisted that I'd misunderstood him. "My goal was to help end extreme poverty," he demurred. "And that remains my goal." His quest was more modest, more realistic than I had assumed: the Millennium Villages Project was not the definitive answer to poverty, he hedged, but a "working model." He was "optimistic that he could reach his targets in most places." He "hoped" (but was no longer certain, I inferred) that the project would continue and that it would be "as self-sustaining as possible."

"Am I trying to help governments see why this model is feasible and useful? Yes," he said. "Do they believe that? Yes. Do they want help doing that? Yes. Is that happening? In many ways, yes. Is it happening as well as it should happen? Not yet. One has to keep pushing."

Officially, the Millennium Villages Project wasn't scheduled to end until 2015, yet it seemed to me that Sachs had distanced himself from his ongoing African experiment. His impassioned articles and speeches and interviews and tweets now centered on income inequality in the United States, climate change, the collapse of Greece, tax reforms, greed on Wall Street, the decline of moral standards, chaos in the euro zone, gun control, and the political vacuum in Washington. He was all over the place.

Along with other left-leaning economists, he lobbied for a "Robin Hood tax" on Wall Street (take from the rich, give to the poor) and for raising America's minimum wage from $7.25 an hour to $9.80. Shouting from a soapbox at Zuccotti Park, he joined the Occupy Wall Street protesters, decrying the immorality of the rich and powerful and accusing "reckless billionaires" of destroying the nation. "That's why we're here!" he roared, in the midst of the crowd. "It's not because we're envious! It's not because we think wealth is bad! It's because we think you cheat! It's because you don't follow the law! It's because you don't pay your taxes!"

He'd had a realization: the world's problems were so deeply interconnected that it was no longer possible to focus solely on poverty, hunger, and disease in Africa. "For a long time," he said, "I wanted to simplify the problems by putting aside the rich world's issues and so forth and focusing on extreme poverty. But it's all interconnected." A huge storm ("this very, very dark cloud," in his words) was moving in: humanity was facing an overwhelming number of urgent and overlapping economic, environmental, and social threats. The title of one of his many jeremiads is "A World Adrift."

In one of his op-eds published in *The New York Times* ("The New Progressive Movement"), Sachs outlined a manifesto for radical change in society: "To put it simply: tax the rich, end the wars and restore honest and effective government for all." In the *Financial Times,* he accused both Democrats and Republicans of being "accomplices to the premeditated asphyxiation of the state." Using his Twitter account (@JeffDSachs), he fired off hundreds of 140-character screeds: "The ancient Greeks called it kakistocracy: government by the most unprincipled"; "The people who 'won't' help themselves are the Wall Street bankers getting $$$$ taxpayer bailouts"; "Incompetent German leadership is killing the Eurozone"; "The 'debate' on energy shows the deceit & shortsightedness of our politics.

Not a word about climate change. Gutless"; "America's a corporatocracy now"; "Memo to the next president: Need a plan to reduce carbon emissions and help save this planet"; "News Corp is neck deep in corruption. Fox, WSJ: lies & more lies"; "Washington caters to the rich, ignores the rest."

Sachs was like a sawed-off shotgun, scattering ammunition in all directions, and the result was a watering down of his message, whatever the message happened to be. The media no longer portrayed him as a "virtuoso" or a "wunderkind." The "Jeff Sachs for President" committee, established at the height of his celebrity in 2005, had been disbanded, its sachsforpresident.org website a blank. His most recent book, *The Price of Civilization: Reawakening American Virtue and Prosperity,* published in late 2011, had not been particularly well received: *The New York Times* hadn't bothered to review it.

For a brief time in the spring of 2012, Sachs put himself in the running to become president of the World Bank, though he had no hope of being elected. "Mr. Sachs's chances of getting the job are slim," to quote *The Economist.* "Mr. Sachs has . . . ridden the wave of celebrity, teaming up often with such stars as the U2 singer, Bono. But those days of poverty porn at rock concerts (slo-mo famine on giant screens to accompany the music) have also drawn to a close."

Sachs's office window was streaked with rain. He had spent nearly two hours answering my questions, and they were starting to irritate him. It had been a long day. For a few moments, we sat in silence. Then he said: "I believe in the contingency of life." There are no certainties. Nothing can be predicted. "When I say I have conviction, it's the conviction that this is the best we can do. I'm not betting the planet on anything. This isn't one grand roll of the dice. The world is complicated, hard, and messy."

In the beginning, Jeffrey Sachs had set out on a quest to validate his scientific approach to ending poverty. He'd used the

Millennium Villages Project as a laboratory to test his theories and to prove that his series of "interventions" could transform the lives of the world's poorest people. He'd spent more than $120 million on his experiment. For all that, however, he had misjudged the complex, shifting reality in the villages. Africa is not a laboratory: Africa is chaotic and messy and unpredictable.

"You can have a firm conviction even in an uncertain world—it's the best you can do, actually—and that is the nature of my conviction," Sachs concluded. "I don't feel it's worth asking if this is the best of the best—it's the best we can do with what we have."

For many years I reported on big corporations and on people we now refer to as "the one percent," first for *Forbes, Fortune,* and *The New York Times Magazine,* then for *Vanity Fair.* I interviewed billionaires on their Gulfstreams, on their yachts, in Greenwich, Connecticut, on the island of Mustique, and one time on a chairlift in Sun Valley, Idaho. I wrote about a hedge fund manager who was building a house for himself that was bigger than the Taj Mahal. I published a book about the failed $163 billion merger of AOL and Time Warner.

By 2006, I'd had enough. That year somebody spent $140 million for a Jackson Pollock—the highest price ever paid for a painting, apparently. For the first time in history, the Dow Jones Industrial Average closed above 12,000. That was also the year that housing prices hit their peak. Something was out of whack, off-kilter. And suddenly it struck me: the one story that really mattered was the story of poverty.

Beginning in the fall of 2006, on assignment from *Vanity Fair,* I spent six months reporting on Jeffrey Sachs's campaign to end extreme poverty. I traveled with him to three sub-Saharan African countries, sat in on meetings with heads of state, heard him give countless speeches, and threw myself into the task of understanding the history, or failed history, of international development. Eventually, the six months I spent following Sachs stretched out to six years and resulted in this book.

I wanted to write about Africans who live in extreme poverty. I wanted their stories to be heard. "Above all," I wrote in my initial proposal for this book, "I would like to write a story of hope." It was a sobering task, illuminating, and far more difficult than I imagined.

Tracing the flow of foreign aid to Africa, and sitting in on backroom negotiations in New York, Washington, London, and in the presidential palaces of some of Africa's capital cities, I started to grasp the complex politics of poverty. I recorded hundreds of hours of interviews and filled so many notebooks that, stacked up, they looked like model skyscrapers on my desk.

Every few months, as circumstances allowed, I headed to Africa. I visited Mali and Ghana in West Africa. I traveled north to Ethiopia and Djibouti. For the most part, however, my time was spent in East Africa: Kenya, Tanzania, Malawi, and Uganda. Sometimes I accompanied Sachs on his official trips to Africa; more often I opted to journey on my own, to accept the hospitality of camel herders and small-hold farmers, and to share meals with people in their huts. I immersed myself in the lives of people in two remote villages: Ruhiira, in southwestern Uganda; and Dertu, in the arid borderland between Kenya and Somalia. I can't begin to express my gratitude for their generosity. They opened their lives to me. They allowed me to see the world differently, more clearly.

On one of my first trips to Uganda, I had a beer with a young African doctor. He'd never been to the United States (in fact, he'd never been outside Uganda), but from what he'd seen on television, and from all he'd read and heard from travelers, it seemed unimaginably beautiful. "In America," he said wistfully, "you are living in heaven on earth."

Acknowledgments

I am indebted to Jeffrey Sachs for giving me the access I needed to write this book and for allowing me to shadow him in his work. We didn't always see eye to eye, yet he never asked to see my manuscript; nor did he try to censor me. I am grateful to him and to members of his staff. In New York, Erin Trowbridge deserves particular mention, as does Glenn Denning. In Africa, Ahmed Mohamed and David Siriri were extraordinarily generous and forthcoming, responding to my questions with humor and patience. I was inspired by their resilience and their faith.

Without Graydon Carter, this book would not exist: in 2006 he gave me the go-ahead to write an article for *Vanity Fair* that became the cornerstone of *The Idealist*. From the outset, Elyse Cheney championed my project, trusting that it would come to fruition. With each draft, Bill Thomas offered invaluable suggestions and advice. My father, Peter Munk, offered crucial support. My brother Marc-David Munk, a physician, joined me twice during my travels in Africa, and offered vital medical insight. Lara Santoro gave the final manuscript an exacting read. Nadia Zonis double- and triple-checked dates, names, quotations, citations, and other relevant facts and figures. Janet Biehl was a meticulous copy editor. Mickey McConnell and Maureen Spratt transcribed every one of my recorded interviews. And, of course, I could not have traveled through Africa without the help of guides, translators, drivers, and bush pilots:

thank you Joseph Mugo, Christopher Nsubuga, Shakilah Bint-Shiekh, Asia Abdi, and Ronald Purcell.

My deepest gratitude goes to my brilliant mother, Linda Munk, who died on April 16, 2013, as this book was going to press. I've lost count of how many drafts she edited and re-edited. Sometimes, for one reason and another (faulty logic, redundancy, dead metaphors, awkward syntax, lazy thinking), she'd strike out entire passages, and I'd start again. She taught me all I know about good writing and critical thinking. She forced me to do my best.

My children, Lucas and Sofia, have grown up with this book. Wise beyond their years, they put everything into perspective for me, and have promised to bake a cake as soon as the book is published.

Finally: I could not possibly have finished this book without Peter Soriano. I can't thank you enough. You came into my life at just the right moment.

Notes

Introduction

1   **"My name is Bono"**: Jeffrey D. Sachs, *The End of Poverty: Economic Possibilities for Our Time* (New York: Penguin, 2005), xv.

2   **"one of the smartest people in the world"**: MTV Networks, *The Diary of Angelina Jolie and Dr. Jeffrey Sachs in Africa*, 14 September 2005.

2   **"end the suffering of those still trapped by poverty"**: Sachs, *End of Poverty*, 3.

2   **the problem can be solved by 2025**: Ibid., 1.

3   **After all, two billion people on the planet are scraping by**: The most current data report that, as of 2008, 805.9 million people live on a dollar or less a day and that 2.47 billion people live on two dollars or less a day. Shaohua Chen and Martin Ravallion, "An Update to the World Bank's Estimates of Consumption Poverty in the Developing World," briefing note, World Bank, 3 January 2012.

3   **their life expectancy hovers around fifty**: Paul Collier, *The Bottom Billion: Why the Poorest Countries Are Failing and What Can Be Done About It* (New York: Oxford University Press, 2007), 7. For current data on life expectancy of Africans in general (as opposed to the "bottom billion"), by country and sex, see Haidong Wang et al., "Age-Specific and Sex-Specific Mortality in 187 Countries, 1970–2010: A Systematic Analysis for the Global Burden of Disease Study 2010," *Lancet* 380, no. 9859 (15 December 2012).

3   **per capita income**: All references to per capita income are "Gross National Income per capita, PPP" for 2011, defined by the World Bank as "GNI converted to international dollars using purchasing power parity." (An "international dollar" has the same purchasing power in the cited country as does a U.S. dollar in the United States.) Complete data, by country, are available at http://data.worldbank.org/indicator/NY.GNP.PCAP.PP.CD, accessed 11 February 2013.

3   **"The countries at the bottom"**: Collier, *Bottom Billion*, 3.

4   "**Have you seen the children dying?**": Jeffrey Sachs, speech delivered at the Millennium Promise Conference, Montreal, 9 November 2006.

Chapter 1. Shock Therapy

9   "**He never had a rebellious day in his life**": Andrea Sachs, interview by author, 13 December 2006.

9   "**His father was extremely bright**": Joan Sachs, interview by author, 15 December 2006.

10   "**Sachs not only fought against precedent**": Will Muller, "Perseverance of Young Lawyer Reopened Apportionment Battle," *Detroit News,* 20 May 1962.

10   "**I was teaching the graduate macroeconomics course**": Martin Feldstein, interview by author, 18 December 2006.

11   "**In the beginning, Jeff would say**": Sonia Ehrlich Sachs quoted in John Donnelly, "The New Crusade," *Boston Globe,* 3 June 2001.

11   "**I was twenty-five years older**": Gonzalo Sánchez de Lozada, interview by author, 1 February 2007.

13   "**Kuroń sat at a crowded desk**": Sachs, *End of Poverty,* 115.

14   "**This strategy can be called a 'shock' approach**": Jeffrey Sachs and David Lipton, "Summary of the Proposed Economic Program of Solidarity," paper presented to Jacek Kuroń, August 1989, personal files of Jeffrey Sachs.

14   "**One of the most spectacular**": Lawrence Weschler, "A Grand Experiment," *New Yorker,* 13 November 1989.

14   "**Polish shock therapy has been described**": Susan Benkelman and Ken Fireman, "The Economy Doctor: Can Jeffrey Sachs' Prescriptions Save Russia Before Political Unrest Kills the Patient?," *Newsday,* 2 February 1992.

14   "**shock program will cause disruptions**": Sachs and Lipton, "Summary of the Proposed Economic Program."

15   "**pure, unmitigated disaster**": Weschler, "Grand Experiment."

15   "**In any event**": Sachs and Lipton, "Summary of the Proposed Economic Program."

15   "**Look, when a guy comes into the emergency room**": Sachs quoted in Weschler, "Grand Experiment."

15   "**virtuoso**": Sylvia Nasar, "Three Whiz Kid Economists of the 90's, Pragmatists All," *New York Times,* 27 October 1991.

15   "**probably the most important economist**": Peter Passell, "Dr. Jeffrey Sachs, Shock Therapist," *New York Times Magazine,* 27 June 1993.

15 "He was clearly capable": Nasar, "Three Whiz Kid Economists."

16 "I mean, Jeff had some good articles": Robert Barro, interview by author, 16 December 2006.

16 "I said, 'Gee, you know'": Naomi Klein, *The Shock Doctrine: The Rise of Disaster Capitalism* (New York: Metropolitan Books, 2008), 279.

16 "If Poland can do it": Sachs quoted in Passell, "Shock Therapist."

16 "As a broad measure": Jeffrey Sachs, speech presented on receiving the Frank E. Seidman Distinguished Award in Political Economy, Memphis, Tenn., 26 September 1991.

17 In one decade, between 1989 and 1999: Joseph E. Stiglitz, "Whither Reform? Ten Years of the Transition," paper presented at the Annual Conference on Development Economics, World Bank, Washington, D.C., 28–30 April 1999.

17 "a misunderstanding of the very foundations": Ibid.

18 "I took a ridiculous amount of criticism": Jeffrey Sachs, e-mail to the author, 23 April 2007.

19 Since the industrial revolution: Angus Maddison, *Growth and Interaction in the World Economy: The Roots of Modernity* (Washington, D.C.: AEI Press, 2005), 7. While the industrial revolution began officially in the late eighteenth century, historians generally agree that its full force was not felt until the early nineteenth century. Maddison uses 1820 as the starting date.

19 "Economists say": Sachs quoted in Douglas Birch, "Ailing People, Ailing Economies," *Baltimore Sun,* 12 November 2000.

Chapter 2. Ahmed Maalim Mohamed

20 when the colonial powers carved up Africa: Of the many histories of modern Africa, I relied above all on Martin Meredith's authoritative *The Fate of Africa: A History of 50 Years of Independence* (New York: Public Affairs, 2005). Surveying the haphazard way in which the colonial powers carved up Africa in the late nineteenth and early twentieth centuries, Meredith quotes Britain's then prime minister, Lord Salisbury, as saying, "We have been giving away mountains and rivers and lakes to each other, only hindered by the small impediment that we never knew exactly where they were."

21 "To the people who live in the Northeastern region": Quoted in Nene Mburu, *Bandits on the Border: The Last Frontier in the Search for Somali Unity* (Trenton, N.J.: Red Sea Press, 2005), 131.

21 "O you who make such a sound of beauty": B. W. Andrzejew-

ski with Sheila Andrzejewski, trans., *An Anthology of Somali Poetry* (Bloomington: Indiana University Press, 1993), 7.

23 "a military onslaught": Alex de Waal, *Famine Crimes: Politics and the Disaster Relief Industry in Africa* (Bloomington: Indiana University Press, 1997), 40.

24 "The hyenas now don't even eat": Charles Mohr, "Drought in Kenya Results in Famine," *New York Times,* 7 April 1971.

25 Eventually, however, the Kenyan government revised: BBC World Service, "Kenya Admits Mistakes Over 'Massacre,'" 18 October 2000.

25 the actual number of people: Alex de Waal, "Genocidal Warfare in North-East Africa," in *The Oxford Handbook of Genocide Studies,* ed. Donald Bloxham and A. Dirk Moses (New York: Oxford University Press, 2010), 542.

Chapter 3. The End of Poverty

29 "I remember when [Sachs] came to Haiti": Dr. Paul Farmer, interview by author, 10 December 2006.

30 With an annual investment of $66 billion: Hope Steele, ed., *Macroeconomics and Health: Investing in Health for Economic Development,* report of the Commission on Macroeconomics and Health, chaired by Jeffrey Sachs (Geneva: World Health Organization, 20 December 2001), 103.

30 "He's not embarrassed": Richard Feachem, interview by author, 19 December 2006.

30 "Jeff really changed the way we think": Dr. Paul Farmer, interview by author, 10 December 2006.

31 "It is often said that past aid to Africa": Jeffrey Sachs et al., "Ending Africa's Poverty Trap," *Brookings Papers on Economic Activity* 1 (Washington, D.C.: Brookings Institution Press, 2004), 117–216.

31 Since the end of the colonial era: William Easterly, "Can the West Save Africa?," National Bureau of Economic Research, Working Paper no. 14363, September 2008.

32 "Millions of people die every year": Jeffrey Sachs, speech delivered at the 61st session of the UN General Assembly, New York, 27 November 2006.

32 "I'm a happily married single parent": Sonia Ehrlich Sachs quoted in John Donnelly, "The New Crusade," *Boston Globe,* 3 June 2001.

33 "He's an irritant": Bono (Paul David Hewson), interview by author, 6 February 2007.

33   "**this magnificent battering ram**": Mark Malloch Brown, interview by author, 19 December 2006.

34   "**clinical economist**": Jeffrey Sachs, *The Price of Civilization: Reawakening American Virtue and Prosperity* (New York: Random House, 2011), 6.

34   "**you had stood on a London street corner**": Adam Hochschild, *Bury the Chains: Prophets and Rebels in the Fight to Free an Empire's Slaves* (New York: Houghton Mifflin Harcourt, 2005), 7.

34   "**Slavery had existed before money**": Ibid., 2.

34   "**bend history**": Robert F. Kennedy, "Day of Affirmation Address," speech presented at the University of Capetown, Capetown, South Africa, 6 June 1966.

35   *Time* **magazine added him to its list**: "The Time 100," *Time,* 18 April 2005.

36   "**How do you know what would have happened**": Esther Duflo, "Social Experiments to Fight Poverty," speech presented at TED Conference, Long Beach, Calif., 10 February 2010.

37   **for $6 billion in 2000**: Comcast Corp. acquired Lenfest Communications in January 2000 for 121.4 million shares of Comcast common stock, then valued at $6.077 billion, plus $1.777 billion of debt. (See Comcast's 1999 Form 10-K Annual Report, filed with the Securities and Exchange Commission on 1 March 2000.) The Lenfest family, which at the time owned half of Lenfest Communications (AT&T owned the other half), received 60.7 million shares—of which 56 percent, or 33.992 million shares, went to Gerry and Marguerite Lenfest, and the balance to their children.

38   "**the first rung on the ladder of development**": Sachs, *End of Poverty,* 14. (This is one among many uses of the phrase by Sachs.)

38   "**Millennium Villages Project**": "United Nations Millennium Declaration," resolution adopted by the 55th session of the UN General Assembly, New York, 8 September 2000.

38   **Less than a year into the project**: Sachs, *End of Poverty,* 236.

39   "**This is a village that's going to make history**": MTV Networks, *The Diary of Angelina Jolie and Dr. Jeffrey Sachs in Africa,* 14 September 2005.

39   "**to help to build a country**": Michael Lewis, "The Speculator: A Trip with George Soros," *New Republic,* 10 January 1994.

40   "**Almost unanimously,**" **Soros told me**: George Soros, interview by author, 22 November 2006.

40   "**There's a certain messianic quality about him**": Ibid.

40   **Soros proceeded to override his board of directors**: "Soros Invests

$50 Million in Poverty Ending Projects in Africa," Millennium Promise press release, 13 September 2006.

41   **"I don't know whether I want to describe it**": George Soros, interview by author, 22 November 2006.

Chapter 4. It Doesn't Get Harder Than This

46   **"highway banditry and hijacking**": Taya Weiss, *Guns in the Borderlands: Reducing the Demand for Small Arms,* Monograph no. 95 (Pretoria, South Africa: Institute for Security Studies, 2004).

46   **a permanent state of catastrophe**: For a thorough background report on the long-standing instability of North Eastern Province, see Ken Menkhaus, "Kenya-Somalia Border Conflict Analysis," prepared for USAID and Development Alternatives Inc. (Nairobi: USAID, 2005).

47   **the camps housed an estimated 300,000 refugees**: Josh Kron, "Somalia's Wars Swell a Refugee Camp in Kenya," *New York Times,* 11 November 2010.

48   **"change agents**": Bronwen Konecky and Cheryl Palm, eds., *Millennium Villages Handbook: A Practitioner's Guide to the Millennium Villages Approach* (New York: Earth Institute at Columbia University, 2008). Note: There were a number of earlier drafts and iterations for internal use only.

50   **But twenty liters was not nearly enough**: According to the respected *Sphere Handbook 2011: Humanitarian Charter and Minimum Standards in Humanitarian Response* (Geneva: The Sphere Project, 2011), the minimum quantity of water needed for drinking, cooking, and personal hygiene is between 7.5 and 15 liters per person per day.

51   **Kenya's parliament rewarded themselves**: For more on the outsize compensation of Kenya's parliamentarians, see Kathrin Behnke et al., *The Dynamics of Legislative Rewards: An Empirical Analysis of Commonwealth Countries for the World Bank Institute* (London: London School of Economics, 2008). As noted on p. 83, "Kenyan MPs [are] among the highest paid legislators not only in Africa but in the world."

51   **"Create opportunities for critical mutual and collective reflection**": Konecky and Palm, eds., *Millennium Villages Handbook.*

Chapter 5. Every Problem Has a Solution

62   **Joseph Kony**: For an outstanding (if now somewhat dated) profile of Kony and the L.R.A., see Elizabeth Rubin, "Our Children Are Killing Us," *New Yorker,* 23 March 1998.

62 **An estimated twenty-four thousand children had been abducted**: This is the low end of the "24,000 to 38,000 children" estimated to have been abducted by the L.R.A. as of April 2006, according to Phuong Pham, Patrick Vinck, and Eric Stover's "Abducted: The Lord's Resistance Army and Forced Conscription in Northern Uganda," report prepared for Berkeley-Tulane Initiative on Vulnerable Populations, June 2007.

63 **"The Honorable Excellency who is going to the United Nations"**: Yoweri K. Museveni, "Ours Is a Fundamental Change," swearing-in address, 29 January 1986, reprinted in Museveni, *What Is Africa's Problem?* (Minneapolis: University of Minnesota Press, 2000), 8.

63 **a $30 million Gulfstream IV:** More recently, in 2011, Museveni replaced his GIV with a new $50 million GV.

63 **"influence peddling, vote buying, nepotism"**: Center for Basic Research, "The Impact of Political Corruption on Resource Allocation and Service Delivery in Local Governments in Uganda," report prepared for Transparency International Uganda, March 2005.

63 **Year after year, as much as half**: Marie Chêne, "Overview of Corruption in Uganda," U4 Anti-Corruption Resource Center, Transparency International, 4 March 2009.

Chapter 6. Everything Is Written

69 **fertility rates drop**: Sachs, *End of Poverty,* 323–26.
76 **"One of my strongest memories"**: Carl-Henric Svanberg, Ericsson AB, "Letter from the CEO," *2009 Annual Report,* 6.

Chapter 7. It Will Be Sweet Like Honey

80 **"At the most basic level"**: Sachs, *End of Poverty,* 244.
81 **"settle the landless, create employment"**: World Bank (Agriculture Operations Division, Eastern Africa Department, Africa Regional Office), *Project Completion Report. Kenya. Bura Irrigation Settlement Project (Credit 722-KE/LOAN 1449-KE),* report no. 8493 (Washington, D.C.: World Bank, 30 March 1990).
82 **"doomed"**: Ibid.
83 **the average *dilal* in Garissa made between 15,000 and 20,000 Ksh**: Yacob Aklilu and Andy Catley, *Livestock Exports from the Horn of Africa: An Analysis of Benefits by Pastoralist Wealth Group and Policy Implications* (Somerville, Mass.: Feinstein International Center, Tufts University, 2010).

87 **He hoped to have as many as one thousand Millennium villages**:
[Jonathan Ledger], "The Magnificent Seven: How a Few Simple
Reforms Can Lift African Villages Out of Poverty," *Economist*,
27 April 2006.

Chapter 8. A Pipe Dream

93 **"The Economic Burden of Malaria"**: John Luke Gallup and
Jeffrey D. Sachs, "The Economic Burden of Malaria," *The American
Journal of Tropical Medicine and Hygiene* 64, no. 1, supp. (January–
February 2001).

93 **"Fever destroys the capacity to work"**: Italian government quoted
in Frank Snowden, *The Conquest of Malaria: Italy, 1900–1962*
(New Haven, Conn.: Yale University Press, 2006), 93.

94 **In India, for example, where malaria had killed 800,000 people**:
Malcolm Gladwell, "The Mosquito Killer," *New Yorker*, 2 July 2001.

94 **in self-defense, it mutated**: Sonia Shah, *The Fever: How Malaria
Has Ruled Humankind for 500,000 Years* (New York: Farrar, Straus
and Giroux, 2010), 217.

94 **Sri Lanka, for example**: Andrew Spielman and Michael D'Antonio,
Mosquito: The Story of Man's Deadliest Foe (New York: Hyperion,
2001), 172–78.

95 **"All you have to do is fly over"**: C. P. Gilmore, "Malaria Wins
Round 2," *New York Times Magazine*, 25 September 1966.

95 **"It just blows my mind how little money"**: Bill Gates quoted in
Michael Specter, "What Money Can Buy," *New Yorker*, 24 October
2005.

95 **global funding for malaria control soared**: N. Ravishankar et al.,
"Financing of Global Health: Tracking Development Assistance for
Health from 1990 to 2007," *Lancet* 373, no. 9681 (20 June 2009).

96 **aimed to cut deaths from malaria in half by 2010**: Roll Back
Malaria, *The Global Malaria Action Plan for a Malaria-Free World*
(Geneva: Roll Back Malaria Partnership, WHO, 2008), 125. The
stated target was "to reduce malaria mortality and morbidity by
50%" in sub-Saharan Africa by 2010 and to reach "near zero
mortality" by 2015.

96 **the distinguished Swiss parasitologist Christian Lengeler**: Christian Lengeler, "Insecticide-Treated Bed Nets and Curtains for Preventing Malaria," *Cochrane Database of Systematic Reviews*, no. 2,
art. no. CD000363 (2004).

96 **Lengeler reckons that the task of moving one million bed nets**:
Urs Heierli and Christian Lengeler, *Should Bednets Be Sold, or*

Given Free? The Role of the Private Sector in Malaria Control (Berne: SDC Swiss Agency for Development and Cooperation, 2008).

97 **"unethical"**: Jeffrey Sachs, Awash Teklehaimanot, and Christopher Curtis, "Towards Sustainable Malaria Control—Authors' Reply," *Lancet* 370, no. 9600 (17 November 2007).

97 **"one of the shocking crimes"**: Sachs quoted in Leslie Roberts, "Battling Over Bed Nets," *Science* 318, no. 5850 (26 October 2007).

97 **"one Starbucks coffee a year"**: Jeffrey Sachs, "The $10 Solution," *Time,* 4 January 2007.

97 **"One day's Pentagon spending"**: Jeffrey Sachs, "Bursting at the Seams," Reith Lectures, BBC Radio 4, 11 April 2007.

97 **Every year epidemiologists count 250 million cases of malaria worldwide**: World Health Organization, *World Malaria Report 2008* (Geneva: World Health Organization, 2008).

98 **The big foreign aid donors had spent years**: Heierli and Lengeler, *Should Bednets be Sold, or Given Free?.*

98 **an inconvenient but inevitable part of everyday life**: Shah, *Fever,* 125.

99 **And yet by 2007, despite the donors' best efforts**: Kara Hanson et al., "Household Ownership and Use of Insecticide Treated Nets Among Target Groups After Implementation of a National Voucher Programme in the United Republic of Tanzania," *British Medical Journal* 339:b2434 (2 July 2009).

99 **Even fewer people were actually using them**: The percentage of Tanzanians who slept under an insecticide-treated net in 2007 was 20.5, according to Sabine Renggli et al., "Design, Implementation and Evaluation of a National Campaign to Deliver 18 Million Free Long-Lasting Insecticidal Nets to Uncovered Sleeping Spaces in Tanzania," *Malaria Journal,* in press.

99 **The reason Tanzanians weren't using bed nets**: Sachs is not alone in arguing that demand for bed nets is price sensitive. One recent study concludes that, compared to the demand for free bed nets, demand drops by 60 percent if the price is increased to just 60 cents: see Jessica Cohen and Pascaline Dupas, "Free Distribution or Cost-Sharing? Evidence From a Randomized Malaria Prevention Experiment," *Quarterly Journal of Economics* 125, no. 1 (February 2010).

99 **"Giving away free bed nets is not development"**: Julie McLaughlin, interview by author, 10 March 2008.

100 **"With due respect to his renown[ed] reputation"**: Private letter from Bergis Schmidt-Ehry, program manager of GTZ's Tanzanian German Program to Support Health, to Vincent Mrisho, coordinator of the Global Fund in the office of Tanzania's prime minister,

2 July 2007. Note: In 2011, GTZ was folded into GIZ, a new umbrella organization for Germany's development agencies.

101   **"A mass net distribution on its own"**: Christian Lengeler e-mail to Jeffrey Sachs et al., "Re: Tanzania is on track," 13 July 2007.

101   **"Frankly," Sachs informed Lengeler**: Jeffrey Sachs e-mail to Christian Lengeler et al., "Re: Tanzania is on track," 13 July 2007.

101   **"One day's Pentagon spending"**: Ibid.

Chapter 9. Complacency and Fear

103   **Kilimanjaro Hotel Kempinski**: In 2011, after a change in management, the hotel was renamed Hyatt Regency Dar es Salaam, The Kilimanjaro.

104   **more than $2 billion in foreign aid:** Elena Rotarou and Kazuhiro Ueta, "Foreign Aid and Economic Development: Tanzania's Experience with ODA," *The Kyoto Economic Review* 78, no. 2 (December 2009).

104   **"neocolonial"**: Mwalimu Julius Nyerere, "Leadership and the Management of Change," speech delivered at the Quinquennial General Conference of the Association of Commonwealth Universities, Ottawa, Canada, 17 August 1998.

104   **"The English have a proverb which says"**: Mwalimu Julius Nyerere, "Arusha Declaration," policy statement presented on 5 February 1967, reprinted in Nyerere, *Freedom and Socialism: A Selection from Writings and Speeches, 1965–1967* (Oxford: Oxford University Press, 1969).

108   **less corrupt than Russia, for example**: As measured by Transparency International's 2011 Corruption Perceptions Index, on a scale of 0 to 10 (where 0 is "highly corrupt" and 10 is "very clean"), Tanzania scores 3, Russia scores 2.4, and Kenya scores 2.2.

110   **"free or highly subsidized"**: "WHO Releases New Guidance on Insecticide-Treated Mosquito Nets," World Health Organization press release, 16 August 2007.

110   **"bold but achievable"**: "Secretary-General Announces 'Roll Back Malaria Partnership' on World Malaria Day to Halt Malaria Deaths by Ensuring Universal Coverage by End of 2010," United Nations press release, 25 April 2008.

110   **"On behalf of the people, leaders and governments"**: Jakaya Mrisho Kikwete, "Statement by H. E. Jakaya Mrisho Kikwete, President of the United Republic of Tanzania, and Chairman of the African Union, in Response to the UN-SG Call to Action on Malaria," PR Newswire, 25 April 2008.

111 **Not long afterwards a $200 million grant came through**: More than half of this money, $112.3 million, was funded in Round 8 of the Global Fund, approved in 2008. An additional $14.6 million for insecticide-treated nets (out of a total $35 million for all malaria-related interventions) was approved in 2008 by the President's Malaria Initiative (see PMI's "FY09 Malaria Operational Plan: Tanzania," 16 November 2008). Other major partners included the World Bank's Booster Program for Malaria Control in Africa.

111 **"None of us could have imagined"**: Christian Lengeler, interview by author, 10 September 2010. For a detailed report on recent efforts to control malaria in Tanzania, see Roll Back Malaria, *Focus on Mainland Tanzania,* Progress & Impact Series no. 3 (Geneva: Roll Back Malaria Partnership, WHO, January 2012).

111 **300 million bed nets across sub-Saharan Africa**: To reach the 2010 target of universal coverage for populations at risk, Roll Back Malaria estimated that 350 million long-lasting insecticidal nets were needed in all. Assuming that 50 million to 100 million nets were already in circulation, Roll Back Malaria concluded that 250 million to 300 million additional nets were needed. See Roll Back Malaria, *The Global Malaria Action Plan for a Malaria-Free World* (Geneva: Roll Back Malaria Partnership, WHO, 2008), 125.

111 **Let's say that universal coverage of bed nets *is* achieved**: In December 2012, the World Health Organization announced that great progress had been made toward the goal of universal coverage, and as a result 1.1 million lives were saved around the world. However, WHO also noted that after a rapid expansion between 2004 and 2009, global funding for malaria prevention and control had leveled off between 2010 and 2012, and the number of nets delivered in sub-Saharan Africa had dropped from a peak of 145 million in 2010 to 66 million in 2012: "This means that many households will be unable to replace existing bed nets when required, exposing more people to the potentially deadly disease." WHO, "New Report Signals Slowdown in the Fight Against Malaria," news release, 17 December 2012.

Chapter 10. David Siriri

115 **"Uganda is from end to end one beautiful garden"**: Winston Churchill, *My African Journey* (London: Hodder & Stoughton, 1908; New York: W. W. Norton, 1990), 56–57.

116 **"habits of obedience, self-control, purity, and truth"**: Mrs. Sumner,

"The Responsibilities of Mothers," printed in Angela Burdett-Coutts, ed., *Woman's Mission: A Series of Congress Papers on the Philanthropic Work of Women by Eminent Writers* (New York: Charles Scribner's Sons, 1893), 68.

117　**"I am not an ambitious man"**: Idi Amin quoted in Leslie Alan Horvitz and Christopher Catherwood, *Encyclopedia of War Crimes and Genocide* (New York: Facts on File, 2006), 15.

117　**"Even Amin does not know"**: Russell Miller, "Amin's Murders: Minister Defects with Full Story—Word Exclusive," *Sunday Times* [London], 5 June 1977.

118　**exports of coffee, tea, and cotton dropped**: Mark Baird et al., *Uganda: Country Economic Memorandum* (Washington, D.C.: World Bank, 1982), 5.

120　**World Agroforestry Center**: At the time Siriri worked there, it was called the International Center for Research in Agroforestry.

Chapter 11. A Green Revolution

122　**Sadati and his fellow banana boys**: For a thorough look at the *matoke* market chain in Uganda, see K. Nowakunda, D. Ngambeki, and W. Tushemereirwe, "Increasing Small-Scale Farmers' Competitiveness in Banana (*Musa* spp.) Production and Marketing," *Acta Horticulturae* 879 (2010): 759–66.

123　**"A typical, inefficient exploitive market chain"**: Erastus Kibugu, interview by author, 14 January 2007.

124　**No one used chemical fertilizers or high-yield seeds**: Even when compared to those of such other Eastern African countries as Kenya, Malawi, and Ethiopia, Uganda's farming practices are outdated. For an explanation, see Stephen Bayite-Kasule, "Inorganic Fertilizer in Uganda—Knowledge Gaps, Profitability, Subsidy, and Implications of a National Policy," briefing paper, International Food Policy Research Institute, 2009.

125　**rural poverty fell from 64 percent to 50 percent**: World Bank, *World Development Report 2008: Agriculture for Development* (Washington, D.C.: World Bank, 2007), 46.

125　**"one of the most important triumphs of targeted science"**: Sachs, *End of Poverty*, 259.

125　**"The good news to me is that there's absolutely nothing wrong"**: Jeffrey Sachs, "What Will It Take to Meet the Millennium Development Goals?," speech presented at the Royal Society for the Encouragement of Arts, Manufactures and Commerce (RSA), London, 13 September 2007.

125   "It's like hitting the sixty-four-billion-dollar jackpot": Ibid.

126   **farmers receive $15 billion a year**: According to the Environmental Working Group's Farm Subsidy Database, from 2006 to 2010, the U.S. Department of Agriculture spent an average of $16 billion a year on farm subsidies.

126   **In Europe, the figure is around $70 billion**: According to farmsubsidy.org, the European Union spends around €55 billion a year on farm subsidies.

126   **Why, even the average European cow**: The source for the oft-quoted figure of 4,000 Swiss francs ($4,300) is Silvio Borner, professor emeritus at University of Basel; in a 13 April 2012 e-mail to the author, he referred to it as a "rough guesstimate."

126   **"present-biased preferences"**: Esther Duflo, Michael Kremer, and Jonathan Robinson, "Nudging Farmers to Use Fertilizer: Theory and Experimental Evidence from Kenya," *American Economic Review* 101, no. 6 (October 2011).

127   **"The Enlightenment commitment to reason"**: Sachs, *End of Poverty*, 353.

128   **The entire cost of the inputs**: Millennium Promise, *Uganda: Millennium Villages Cluster Report: Quarters 1–2, 2007* (New York: Millennium Promise, August 2007).

128   **At harvest time in February 2007**: Millennium Villages Project, *Annual Report for Ruhiira, Uganda, Year 2: February 2007–February 2008* (New York: Millennium Villages Project/UNDP, 2008).

128   **"Maize is everywhere!"**: Tumushabe Boneconcila, quoted in Millennium Villages Project, *The Ruhiira Millennium Village Round Up: Testimonies of Success*, no. 1 (January 2011).

Chapter 12. *Awaire, Awaire*

131   **where the Millennium Villages Project had so far invested $3.5 million**: Internal figures provided to the author by the Millennium Villages Project show that in 2006 and 2007 the project spent a total of $3,491,738 in Ruhiira.

135   **"I know that if you spend enough money"**: Simon Bland, interview by author, 17 January 2007.

136   **"Sustainability within the Millennium Villages Project"**: Millennium Villages Project, "Millennium Villages: Concepts, Sustainability, and Scalability," draft report, 2007.

136   **"Rick and I went to see Jeffrey Sachs"**: Tom Ryan, interview by author, 7 October 2008.

138   **The brand book included a list of adjectives**: "Ending Extreme

Poverty Begins with a Focused Brand," brand book prepared by Consumer Capital Partners for Millennium Villages Project, 2008.

138 **"Extreme poverty ends here. It has to"**: Nitro Group (now Sapient-Nitro), brochure prepared for Millennium Promise, September 2008.

139 "**a strategist with a passion**": Personal profile on "Peter Kaye's Page," posted to Brand Farm social network, http://thebrandfarm.com/profile/PeterKaye, accessed 3 February 2013.

139 **"Getting money from USAID and DFID"**: Jeffrey Walker, interview by author, 8 September 2009.

140 "**Today we must proclaim a bold objective**": Henry Kissinger quoted in William Robbins, "U.S. Proposes 3 New Groups on Hunger," *New York Times,* 6 November 1974.

140 **the G8 leaders promised to double aid to Africa**: "Highlights of the G8 Communiqué on Africa," Gleneagles Summit, 8 July 2005.

141 "**Professor Sachs advises us that we shall get more money**": Ezra Suruma, interview with author, 16 January 2007.

141 "**Finance Minister of the Year**": "Finance Minister of the Year/Africa: Dr Ezra Suruma, Finance Minister, Uganda," *Banker,* 5 January 2009.

Chapter 13. Capitalist Philanthropy

143 "**We are capitalists and opportunists**": Roben Farzad, "Can Greed Save Africa?," *Business Week,* 10 December 2007 (posted online 29 November 2007).

143 "**The idea is to create real, rising income**": Rustom Masalawala, interview by author, 13 February 2008.

148 "**in the hundreds of thousands of dollars**": "Business Plans in the Ruhiira Cluster, Uganda: Ginger Production Business Plan," draft for Millennium Promise, November 2008.

148 **Already the WFP was purchasing around $50 million a year**: Henri Leturque and Jonathan Mitchell, "WFP's Agriculture and Market Support (AMS) in Uganda 2009–2014: Mid-Term Evaluation," strategic evaluation report no. OE/2011/019 prepared for the World Food Program, October 2011.

149 **In Toya**: Note that there are (at least) two places in Mali named Toya. One is the small Millennium village of Toya in the *cercle,* or subdivision, of Timbuktu. The other (which appears on Google Maps) is not a village but a larger "commune" in the *cercle* of Yélimané near Senegal.

151 "**Rather than sit around waiting for piped water**": Rustom Masalawala, interview by author, 2 November 2008.

Chapter 14. Setbacks

155 "**Business Plan for Small-Scale Milk Processing**": Ahmed M. Mohamed and Idris S. Kolon, "Business Plan for Small-Scale Milk Processing and Marketing in Dertu," revised draft, 16 July 2008.

156 "**This is the fourth email**": Rustom Masalawala e-mail to Ahmed M. Mohamed, "Re: Farewell," 15 July 2008.

157 "**Horn of Africa: Exceptional Food Security Crisis**": International Federation of Red Cross and Red Crescent Societies, "Horn of Africa: Exceptional Food Security Crisis," Emergency Appeal MDR64003, 11 December 2008.

157 "**the perfect storm**": Sachs quoted in Jeffrey Gettleman, "Famine Looms as Wars Rend Horn of Africa," *New York Times,* 17 May 2008.

157 "**This is to inform you that the two boreholes in Dertu**": Ahmed M. Mohamed e-mail to Glenn Denning et al., "Break Down of Dertu Borehole," 7 February 2008.

157 "**I usually liken boreholes to babies**": Maimbo M. Malesu e-mail to Ahmed M. Mohamed, "Re: Break Down of Dertu Borehole," 7 February 2008.

157 **multiple water sources**: Alex R. Oduor, Global Water Partnership Associated Programme, "Enhancing Percapita Water Storage at the Dertu Millennium Village, Garissa-Kenya," report prepared for RELMA-in-ICRAF World Agroforestry Center, Nairobi, 28 February 2006.

157 "**empower the local community**": Maimbo M. Malesu e-mail to Ahmed M. Mohamed, 7 February 2008.

159 **$14,000 a month in "profit"**: Millennium Villages Project, *Annual Report: January 1–December 31, 2008* (New York: Earth Institute, Columbia University, 2009).

161 "**an end in themselves**": M. H. Doran, A. R. C. Low, and R. L. Kemp, "Cattle as a Store of Wealth in Swaziland: Implications for Livestock Development and Overgrazing in Eastern and Southern Africa," *American Journal of Agricultural Economics* 61, no. 1 (February 1979).

161 "**It is the old story of the vicious circle**": Colonial administrator quoted in N. W. Sobania, *Background History of the Mt. Kulal Region of Kenya: IPAL Technical Report Number A-2* (Nairobi: UNESCO/UNEP Integrated Project in Arid Lands, December 1979), 179.

Chapter 15. *Insha'Allah*

162   "**Virtually every society that was once poor**": Sachs, *End of Poverty*,
      315–17.
163   **When a girl is six or seven years old**: For a thorough study on
      female genital cutting in North Eastern Province, see Guyo W.
      Jaldesa et al., "Female Genital Cutting Among the Somali of
      Kenya and Management of Its Complications," *FRONTIERS
      Final Report* (Washington, D.C.: Population Council, February
      2005).

Chapter 16. I Am Thinking We Are Not Ready for This

169   "**By the end of the conference**": Steven Wisman, "Millennium Vil-
      lages Conference, Bamako, June 23–27th, 2008: Goal, Objectives
      and Expected Results," internal document, 14 May 2008.
170   "**value-cost ratios**": [Geoff Gottlieb], "Value-Cost Ratios," presen-
      tation for the Millennium Villages Project, June 2008. For more on
      fertilizer use in Africa, including an explanation of why value-cost
      ratios are often too low to be profitable, see Global Development
      Network's Policy Research Paper 3, "Improving the Effectiveness,
      Efficiency and Sustainability of Fertilizer Use in Sub-Saharan
      Africa," June 2012.

Chapter 17. A Very Tall Order

174   **the deal brokered with the World Food Program**: Despite the
      problems in 2008 and 2009, Ruhiira's farmers signed one final,
      smaller contract to sell fifty-seven tons of beans to the World Food
      Program in 2010. Since then, the WFP has made no further pur-
      chases of Ruhiira's produce. In Uganda as a whole, the WFP has
      struggled to meet its goal: in 2010, purchases from small-hold
      farmers totaled $33 million, well below the target of $100 million.
      See Henri Leturque and Jonathan Mitchell, "WFP's Agriculture
      and Market Support (AMS) in Uganda 2009–2014: Mid-Term
      Evaluation," strategic evaluation report no. OE/2011/019 prepared
      for the World Food Program, October 2011, x–xi.
177   **the World Bank alone spent $16 billion on agricultural credit**:
      Elizabeth Coffey, *Agricultural Finance: Getting the Policies Right*
      (UN Food and Agricultural Organization and Deutsche Gesell-
      schaft für Technische Zusammenarbeit, 1998), 1.

177 "**The inadequacies of rural financial markets reflect real risks**": World Bank, *World Development Report 2008: Agriculture for Development* (Washington, D.C.: World Bank, 2007), 144.

178 "**If we did it a little on the fly**": John McArthur, interview by author, 14 July 2009.

179 "**a number of factors**": Millennium Villages Project, *The Millennium Villages 2009 Annual Report* (New York: Earth Institute, Columbia University, 2010).

179 "**several challenges**": Millennium Villages Project, *Annual Report: January 1–December 31, 2008* (New York: Earth Institute, Columbia University, 2009).

179 **two postmortem reports**: After a year of requests, one of the reports—Mary Nyasimi, "Qualitative Assessment of Sauri Input Credit Scheme: Anthropological Perspectives. Preliminary Results," Millennium Villages Project, March 2009—was given to me "for background" only. I still await the other report, authored by Ousmane Diouf, about the credit scheme in Mbola, Tanzania.

Chapter 18. I Have Been Failed by the Markets

180 **In the area of health**: Millennium Villages Project, "Ruhiira: Master Expenditure Chart, 2006–2009," internal budget report, March 2010.

180 **A medical staff of just ten**: Millennium Villages Project, *Harvests of Development in Rural Africa: The Millennium Villages After Three Years* (New York: Earth Institute, Columbia University, June 2010), 66.

180 **The number of babies born with the help of a trained birth attendant**: Ibid., 66–67.

181 **The project had invested nearly $600,000 in education**: Millennium Villages Project, "Ruhiira: Master Expenditure Chart, 2006–2009," internal budget report, March 2010.

181 **To help Ruhiira's best students continue their education**: Millennium Villages Project, *The Millennium Villages 2009 Annual Report* (New York: Earth Institute, Columbia University, 2010).

182 "**breeding ground for disease outbreaks**": Jenise Huffman, director of sustainability at Tyson Foods, Inc., e-mail to Theresa Wolters, operations manager of Millennium Villages Project for East and Southern Africa, "Uganda—Hurdles to Overcome Before Getting a Poultry Project," 4 November 2008.

183   **the pipes would one day make their way to Ruhiira**: In November 2010, the pipes finally arrived in Ruhiira and eight months later, in July 2011, the first phase of the system went live with forty public and twenty-seven private water points. Jeffrey Sachs and JM Eagle CEO Walter Wang attended the ribbon cutting.

184   **"economic progress without a loss of momentum"**: Millennium Villages Project, "Millennium Villages: Concepts, Sustainability, and Scalability," draft report, 2007.

Chapter 19. Misinformation and Politics

188   **"cutting deals at a dizzying pace"**: Richard Behar, "Special Report: China Storms Africa," *Fast Company,* June 2008.

188   **Trade between China and Africa**: According to the World Trade Organization, trade between China and Africa totaled $84.21 billion in 2009. Two years later, in 2011, it totaled $132.69 billion.

189   **Tommy Hilfiger**: "Tommy Hilfiger Named Millennium Promise's First MDG Global Leader," Millennium Villages press release, 23 June 2010.

190   **A British filmmaker was coming to Dertu**: Zoe Flood, "Thriving in the Drylands," documentary film produced for the Millennium Villages Project, 2010.

194   **"formidable pride of the Somali nomad"**: Ioan M. Lewis, *A Pastoral Democracy: A Study of Pastoralism and Politics Among the Northern Somali of the Horn of Africa* (Oxford: Oxford University Press, 1961), 1.

195   *jareer,* **an ethnic slur**: Catherine Lowe Besteman, *Unraveling Somalia: Race, Violence, and the Legacy of Slavery* (Philadelphia: University of Pennsylvania Press, 1999), 116.

Chapter 20. A Version of Progress

197   **"marked with jovial celebrations"**: Ahmed Mohamed, "Dertu Promoted to the Administrative Status of Regional Division," *Millennium Villages Blog,* 18 November 2009.

200   **$2.5 million into Dertu**: Internal figures provided to the author by the Millennium Villages Project show that from the second half of 2006 to the end of 2009, the project contributed $1,230,288, while other donors (NGOs and corporate partners) contributed $1,278,568. (In addition, $502,108 came from the government of Kenya.)

201 **"Complain Against MVP"**: Ali Abdi Mohamed, "Complain Against MVP," 2009, personal files of Ali A. Mohamed. Note: The original document lists seventeen bulleted complaints, plus two pages of more-detailed comments.

203 **"hectic excursions from the urban centre"**: Robert Chambers, *Rural Development: Putting the Last First* (Essex, U.K.: Pearson Education, 1983), 8.

203 **"They come, and they sign the book"**: Ibid., 12.

203 **"*Ils ne savent pas*"**: Adrian Adams, "An Open Letter to a Young Researcher," *African Affairs* 78, no. 313 (October 1979), quoted ibid.

204 **"breathtakingly ethnocentric"**: Katy Gardner and David Lewis, *Anthropology, Development and the Post-Modern Challenge* (London: Pluto Press, 1996), 14.

Chapter 21. What Mistake Has Ahmed Done?

206 **"The reason Ahmed left us"**: Belay Begashaw, interview by author, 17 June 2010.

207 **"Look, these are internal HR issues"**: John McArthur, interview by author, 25 June 2010.

208 **paid $8 million for Sachs's town house**: Blair Golson, "The Sachs Appeal: Columbia Buys $8 M. Townhouse for New Econ Star," *New York Observer,* 11 November 2002.

Chapter 22. An Island of Success

213 **"an African-born economist who reportedly received scholarships"**: Jeffrey Sachs, "Aid Ironies," *Huffington Post,* 24 May 2009.

214 **"a stunning transformation of 500,000 lives"**: Millennium Villages Project, *Millennium Promise 2010 Annual Report* (New York: Millennium Promise, 2011), 46.

214 **"a case study in what is possible"**: Ban Ki-moon quoted in Millennium Villages Project, *Harvests of Development in Rural Africa,* 7.

214 **"The thrilling news is that the communities"**: Sachs quoted in *The Millennium Villages Project: The Next Five Years: 2011–2015* (New York: Millennium Villages, October 2011), 3.

214 **"Sachs is essentially trying to create an island of success"**: William Easterley quoted in Jeffrey Gettleman, "Shower of Aid Brings Flood of Progress," *New York Times,* 8 March 2010.

215 **deaths from malaria fell by a third in Africa**: World Health Orga-

nization, *World Malaria Report 2011* (Geneva: World Health Organization, December 2011).

215   **Infant mortality rates dropped sharply**: Gabriel Demombynes et al., "Africa's Success Story: Infant Mortality Down," *Africa Can . . . End Poverty Blog*, World Bank, 7 May 2012.

215   **"Africa could be on the brink"**: World Bank, *Africa's Future and the World Bank's Role in It* (Washington, D.C.: World Bank, March 2011), 4.

215   **"The Hopeless Continent"**: "The Hopeless Continent," *Economist*, 13 May 2000.

215   **the proportion of sub-Saharan Africans living in extreme poverty**: From a high of 56.5 percent in 1990, the figure declined to 47.5 percent in 2008. "World Bank Sees Progress Against Extreme Poverty, But Flags Vulnerabilities," World Bank press release, 29 February 2012.

215   **continued to live on less than $2 a day**: The current data report that 562.3 million people in sub-Saharan Africa live on $2 or less a day. See Chen and Ravallion, "An Update to the World Bank's Estimates of Consumption Poverty in the Developing World," 3 January 2012.

215   **"People used to worry"**: Charles Kenny quoted in Annie Lowrey, "Dire Poverty Falls Despite Global Slump, Report Finds," *New York Times*, 6 March 2012.

215   **"The design of the project makes it impossible"**: Michael A. Clemens and Gabriel Demombynes, "When Does Rigorous Impact Evaluation Make a Difference? The Case of the Millennium Villages," Center for Global Development, Working Paper no. 225, October 2010.

216   **According to a *New Yorker* profile of the economist Esther Duflo**: Ian Parker, "The Poverty Lab," *New Yorker*, 17 May 2010.

216   **"Millennium villages don't advance"**: Sachs quoted in Jeffrey Gettleman, "Shower of Aid Brings Flood of Progress," *New York Times*, 8 March 2010.

216   **"He adopts this completely anti-scientific attitude"**: Duflo quoted in Parker, "The Poverty Lab."

217   **"The project has claimed large impacts"**: Michael A. Clemens and Gabriel Demombynes, "Millennium Villages Project Needs Proper Evaluation," *Poverty Matters Blog*, 19 October 2011.

217   **Bernadette Wanjala, and her colleague Roldan Muradian**: Bernadette M. Wanjala and Roldan Muradian, "Can Big Push Interventions Take Small-Scale Farmers Out of Poverty? Insights from

the Sauri Millennium Village in Kenya," Center for International Development Issues Nijmegen, working paper, 2011.

217   **"big push"**: "The Big Push Back," *Economist,* 3 December 2011.

217   **"Who on earth will pay for this"**: Lawrence Haddad, "Jeff Sachs: LVP of the MVP?" *Development Horizons Blog,* 14 October 2011.

218   **"mistaken"**: Jeffrey Sachs, "Challenges at the Cutting Edge of Fighting Global Poverty," *Huffington Post,* 4 December 2011.

218   **"outlandish"**: Ibid.

218   **"reflect[ed] a real misunderstanding"**: Jeffrey Sachs and Prabhjot Singh, "Learning in and from the Millennium Villages: A Response to Lawrence Haddad," *Millennium Villages Blog,* 16 October 2011. As of February 2013, this post was no longer accessible on the *Millennium Villages Blog;* however, excerpts (including this quotation) could be found elsewhere on the Internet.

218   **"filled with falsehoods and distortions"**: Jeffrey Sachs, "How the *Daily Mail* Twisted the Facts to Fight Help for the Poor," *Millennium Villages Blog,* 7 July 2012.

218   **"This is Nobel Prize–winning stuff"**: John McArthur, interview by author, 6 March 2009.

219   **He measured success more broadly**: As this book was going to press, the Millennium Villages Project's director of global communications stated in an e-mail to me that five African countries have announced plans to "scale up the Millennium Villages across the nation," a development that she described as "one of the biggest successes and 'proofs of concept' of the project" and "essential evidence that [the project] is, indeed, hitting its marks." In fact, while several countries, including Nigeria, Rwanda, and Senegal, have adopted certain technologies and methods used by the Millennium Villages Project, no country has yet rolled out Millennium villages "across the nation."

Chapter 23. I Cry for Ahmed

220   **"A vision of hell"**: "Horn of Africa Drought: 'A Vision of Hell,'" *BBC News,* 8 July 2011.

221   **He held a Ph.D. in community health**: Dabar Abdi Maalim, "The Cultural and Behavioural Determinants of Immunisation Among the Nomadic Somali Community of Garissa District, North Eastern Province," Ph.D. diss., University of Reading, 1999.

222   **"Mujahideen fighters will force them"**: Will Ross, "Kenya's Incursion into Somalia Raises the Stakes," *BBC News,* 17 October 2011.

223   "**artifacts**": John McArthur and Jeffrey Sachs, "Updated Concept Note on the Millennium Villages Project: Scalability, Sustainability, and Early Lessons," Millennium Promise, draft paper, 2009.

223   **Everywhere in the country people were being squeezed**: Fred Ojambo, "Uganda's Shilling Declines to 18-Year Low on Corporate Demand for Dollars," *Bloomberg*, 9 August 2011.

224   "**How can they buy fighter jets**": Kizza Besigye quoted in Katrina Manson, "Uganda's Museveni Sworn in for Fourth Term," *Financial Times,* 13 May 2011.

225   "**What can we do?**": Amadou Niang, interview by author, 10 July 2012.

Chapter 24. It Is What It Is

226   "**Millennium Villages, on Track to Reach 2015 Goals**": "Millennium Villages, on Track to Reach 2015 Goals, Launch Final Phase," Millennium Villages Project press release, 3 October 2011.

226   "**an inspiring example**": Ibid.

226   "**brighter future**": Ibid.

227   "**investment-worthy business projects**": Ibid.

227   "**The Project will work with each host government**": *The Millennium Villages Project: The Next Five Years: 2011–2015* (New York: Millennium Villages, October 2011), 23.

228   **In the first place, the G8 had fallen far short**: According to *The DATA Report 2011* (ONE, 4 May 2011), 7: "The G7 increased their annual development assistance to sub-Saharan Africa by $11.197 billion between 2004 and 2010, delivering 61% of the $18.227 billion increases they promised in 2005. The increases delivered were largely a result of the US, Japan and Canada surpassing their targets and the UK nearly meeting its very ambitious commitment. Three countries—Italy, Germany, and, to a lesser extent, France—were responsible for most of the G7's shortfall." Note that DATA refers here to the G7 (as opposed to the G8) because one G8 member (Russia) had made no commitment in 2005.

228   **Moreover, in 2011, for the first time**: *The DATA Report 2012: Europe's African Promise* (Washington, D.C.: ONE, 11 April 2012). For details on 2011 foreign aid spending by country, see "Development: Aid to Developing Countries Falls Because of Global Recession," OECD press release, 4 April 2012.

228   **Congress was calling for still more cuts**: Making sense of U.S. foreign aid budgets is difficult because total figures include expen-

ditures unrelated to humanitarian or development aid. "Foreign aid not related to war spending was cut by $2.2 billion from 2011," according to Susan Cornwell, "U.S. Foreign Aid Escapes Slashing Cuts in Fiscal 2012," Reuters, 19 December 2011. However, according to the OECD, the cut in the nation's Official Development Assistance (narrowly defined as disbursements that promote the "economic development and welfare of developing countries as its main objective") was around $659 million in 2011. Meanwhile, according to AidFlows.org (a partnership among the OECD, the World Bank, and the Asian Development Bank), the United States slightly increased ODA in 2011.

229   **"This is a village that's going to make history"**: MTV Networks, *The Diary of Angelina Jolie and Dr. Jeffrey Sachs in Africa*, 14 September 2005.

230   **"Robin Hood tax"**: See robinhoodtax.org.

230   **raising America's minimum wage**: Jeffrey Sachs et al., "Time to Raise the Minimum Wage," letter to U.S. congressional leaders, 23 July 2012, http://www.epi.org/publication/raise-minimum-wage/, accessed 3 February 2013.

230   **"That's why we're here!"**: Jeffrey Sachs, speech delivered at Occupy Wall Street, Zuccotti Park, New York City, 15 October 2011, video recording at http://www.youtube.com/watch?v=mB_eoUqbKDw, accessed 3 February 2013.

230   **"A World Adrift"**: Jeffrey Sachs, "A World Adrift," *Project Syndicate,* 22 April 2012.

230   **"To put it simply: tax the rich, end the wars"**: Jeffrey Sachs, "The New Progressive Movement," *New York Times,* 12 November 2011.

230   **"accomplices to the premeditated asphyxiation"**: Jeffrey Sachs, "America Has Lost the Battle Over Government," *Financial Times,* 15 August 2012.

230   **"The ancient Greeks called it kakistocracy"**: Jeffrey Sachs, Twitter post, 22 January 2012.

230   **"The people who 'won't' help themselves"**: Jeffrey Sachs, Twitter post, 30 December 2011.

230   **"Incompetent German leadership is killing the Eurozone"**: Jeffrey Sachs, Twitter post, 14 December 2011.

230   **"The 'debate' on energy shows the deceit"**: Jeffrey Sachs, Twitter post, 17 October 2012.

231   **"America's a corporatocracy now"**: Jeffrey Sachs, Twitter post, 17 January 2012.

231   **"Memo to the next president"**: Jeffrey Sachs, Twitter re-post from

Columbia University's Earth Institute (@earthinstitute), 5 November 2012.

231   **"News Corp is neck deep in corruption"**: Jeffrey Sachs, Twitter post, 2 May 2012.

231   **"Washington caters to the rich"**: Jeffrey Sachs, Twitter post, 28 December 2011.

231   **"Mr. Sachs's chances of getting the job are slim"**: [Jonathan Ledger], "The End of Live Aid," *Baobab Africa Blog, Economist,* 8 March 2012.

Author's Note

233   **on the island of Mustique**: Nina Munk, "Dennis the Menace," *Vanity Fair,* May 2001.

233   **on a chairlift in Sun Valley**: Nina Munk, "Steve Wynn's Biggest Gamble," *Vanity Fair,* June 2005.

233   **bigger than the Taj Mahal**: Nina Munk, "Greenwich's Outrageous Fortunes," *Vanity Fair,* July 2006.

233   **the failed $163 billion merger**: Nina Munk, *Fools Rush In: Steve Case, Jerry Levin, and the Unmaking of AOL Time Warner* (New York: HarperCollins, 2004).

233   **$140 million for a Jackson Pollock**: Carol Vogel, "A Pollock Is Sold, Possibly for a Record Price," *New York Times,* 2 November 2006.

233   **on assignment from *Vanity Fair:*** Nina Munk, "Jeffrey Sachs's $200 Billion Dream," *Vanity Fair,* July 2007.

Printed in the United States
by Baker & Taylor Publisher Services